For Catherine

STUART HALL

WITH BILL SCHWARZ

Familiar Stranger
A Life Between Two Islands

PENGUIN BOOKS

PENGUIN BOOKS

UK | USA | Canada | Ireland | Australia
India | New Zealand | South Africa

Penguin Books is part of the Penguin Random House group of companies
whose addresses can be found at global.penguinrandomhouse.com.

First published by Allen Lane 2017
Published in Penguin Books 2018
001

Set in 10.44/12.9 pt Dante MT Std
Typeset by Jouve (UK), Milton Keynes
Printed in Great Britain by Clays Ltd, St Ives plc

A CIP catalogue record for this book is available from the British Library

ISBN: 978-0-141-98475-9

What do you call one's self? Where does it begin? Where does it end?

Madame Merle, in Henry James,
The Portrait of a Lady (1881)

. . . one simply cannot and will never be able to fully recuperate one's own processes of thought or creativity self-reflexively . . . I cannot become identical with myself.

Stuart Hall, 'Through the Prism of an Intellectual Life',
in Brian Meeks (ed.), *Culture, Politics, Race and Diaspora: The Thought of Stuart Hall* (2007)

Contents

Contents

List of Illustrations

Preface

Bill Schwarz

This is Stuart Hall's book, comprising his story. Those familiar with his writings will know, however, that through his lifetime he was committed to working and writing collaboratively, often with people much younger than he was. No book exists which is authored solely by him. And this book, too, carries traces of other hands.

There was never a single moment when Hall decided that he was going to embark either on a memoir or on a project of this kind, at least not on the scale on which it turned out. Some twenty years ago he and I were contracted to submit a short manuscript in the form of a conversation seeking to illuminate the major contours of his intellectual life. He was won both by the brevity and by the dialogic potential of the venture. We signed the contract and, after some predictable delays, a series of recorded interviews took place. I spent a summer transcribing them, and with that done we'd more or less hit the word limit. The transcription I passed to him contained lengthy annotations, queries and suggestions, as well as a handful of additional questions which needed to be addressed. We were, we imagined, close to completion.

As things turned out we weren't close at all. Hall set about revising and adding to the text, a practice he could never resist as new ideas kept on taking shape in his mind and, on the horizon, he spotted emergent intellectual and political controversies summoning him. Other things – major, urgent preoccupations – intervened for him. We talked regularly and when time allowed he would make sorties on the manuscript. But time passed and progress was slow.

In his last years illness took its toll. Big projects could no longer be undertaken. His mobility lessened and increasingly he found himself housebound. He missed being active in the world. Yet as his body faltered his intellectual restlessness did not. On many matters of the day he felt impelled to have his say. When health allowed he returned to the manuscript and worked on it like a demon. It assumed a renewed significance, representing a lifeline. *Optimism of the will.*

During this period we talked endlessly about the project. He quizzed me, along with countless others, about whatever happened to be on his mind, depending where in the manuscript he'd arrived. He'd jot down notes and return to the computer, maintaining the dialogic structure as he worked. His intellectual lucidity remained true to the end. When he died in February 2014 the manuscript had grown to over 300,000 words.

While his lucidity had not diminished, his capacity to organize a huge, complex manuscript, ranging far and wide over a lifetime's intellectual evolution, was intermittent. In his mind's eye he held a clear idea of the co-ordinates of the final outcome, which he always imagined as a single volume. These comprised the portion which is published here; further chapters on culture, reviewing the range of attendant theoretical debates; a long section on the properties of 'the political' and on the onset of neo-liberalism; and finally chapters devoted to black subjectivity, aesthetics and politics. Some of these were drafted or half drafted; some were in note form; and others existed only as a mental vision.

Owing to deteriorating eyesight, much was composed from memory alone. Seldom could he consult the necessary sources. Readers will find, for example, that there are stories related here which appear elsewhere. In a number of cases the versions don't tally. I decided that on such occasions I shouldn't intervene. This can be a task, if it is ever deemed necessary, for scholars of the future. As Hall says at one point, he was at the end 'fated to mix history with memory and desire – a combination which future historians will treat with due suspicion'.

It's been my job to extract from the overall manuscript what appears here, on his early life, and a sequel which explores the relations between culture and politics. As readers will appreciate, in these circumstances the book can't represent a pure or innocent rendition of Hall's words. The prose presented here is based on the original transcribed interviews; on his subsequent written revisions and the many enlargements, in various states of completion; and on scores of discussions and conversations spanning nearly two decades. Some parts are verbatim, while many others have been constructed from fragments. Organizing the manuscript has involved much labour.

To begin with we retained the original dialogic structure, as Hall was keen that we should, dividing the text between two identifiable voices: the questioner, 'Bill'; and the respondent, 'Stuart'. Even so, the actual interplay between the two voices was inevitably a deal less transparent than this suggested. The book had evolved as a shared manuscript, which changed hands between Stuart and myself over many years for revision and emendation. Over time the authorial provenance of many passages slipped from view. It was as a conversation that the book had been conceived and how it progressed through its early incarnations. At a late stage, however, in discussion with our publishers, the decision was made to recast the manuscript as a first-person narrative. Initially we had misgivings. But we quickly came to be persuaded by the virtue of this solution. Hall's voice is the clearer for it. And while the formal dialogue has disappeared, the dialogic inspiration accounts for the interior organization of the existing narrative. We endeavoured, also, to maintain the conversational tone.

Paul Thompson kindly allowed us to borrow an important segment from his own interview with Hall that covered a significant lacuna. This formed part of the 'Pioneers of Social Research' project under the auspices of the British Library, and we thank the Library for permission to draw from it here. Stuart was conscious of the debt he owed his many friends. He was particularly grateful to Sally Alexander and Jacqueline Rose who, when things got tough, would read to him material which otherwise would have been unavailable to him; and to Beatrix Campbell for the tea and conversations. Nick Beech proved a significant support to Stuart in the final phase and has contributed to the completion of this volume by supplying a cache of articles, papers and references when I needed them, even when he had a million more pressing matters to attend to. Michael Rustin, one of Stuart's family and a comrade in arms of old, provided crucial additional information on the vicissitudes of the New Left.

From the beginning Hall looked to Duke University Press in the US as the ideal home for his work. Duke have been serious in bringing to publication the works of Marcus Garvey and of C. L. R. James and he was delighted by the prospect that his writings would appear alongside them. Ken Wissoker of the Press made the commitment to publish as complete a list of Hall's writings as we believed desirable. This was an extraordinarily spirited, generous offer from a publisher in these days when the trade becomes ever more cut-throat. Plans are afoot for a series of volumes, for the most part organized thematically. We could not have asked for more from Ken and his team. Nor could Stuart. They have given us all that we could have wished. Our thanks to him and to Elizabeth Ault are profound.

On the advice of Neil Belton, in the UK, we approached Tom Penn at Penguin whose enthusiasm for, and commitment to, the project were instant. Tom's investment in the book has remained unfailing, and his sympathies for Hall's work run deep. We are most grateful to him and to Chloe Currens. Thanks to their intervention we are sure this is a better book. We owe much, also, to Linden Lawson whose work as the copy-editor has been supreme.

In assembling and completing this manuscript I thank the Rockefeller Foundation for awarding me a Fellowship at the National Humanities Center in North Carolina. Not only did this provide me with the time and space to complete the manuscripts. The Center is also, in these hard times, magnificent testament to the virtues of the sovereignty of the imagination. I shall always remember everyone there with deep, deep warmth.

Great thanks are due to Caroline Knowles who lived closely, and calmly, with this project as it drew to its completion while I, commensurately, grew ever more frenzied. I'll always treasure her support.

None of this would have happened without the generosity, thoughtfulness and constant goodwill of Stuart's family. Seeing through to publication this most personal of his writings has not always been easy. His children, Becky and Jess, have acted with both enthusiasm and care. His wife, Catherine, has kept a close eye on my welfare, even when she has had so much else to pre-occupy her. She has been involved at every stage in the preparation of the manuscript. I owe her more than I can say.

For me the outstanding difficulty is that Stuart himself was unable to adjudicate on the finished draft. I can imagine his many reservations. He could never return to his writing without being tempted to take it apart and to drive the argument on, or to take it in new directions. This certainly would have been no exception. It pains me greatly that he wasn't able to read what has finally been submitted in his name.

PART I

Jamaica

1. *Colonial Landscapes, Colonial Subjects*

Sometimes I feel I was the last colonial. I was born in 1932 into a coloured middle-class family in Jamaica, still then a British colony. My first sense of the world derived from my location as a colonized subject and much of my life can be understood as unlearning the norms in which I had been born and brought up. This long, continuing process of disidentification has shaped my life. I lived in Kingston, Jamaica, as a child and youth for the first nineteen years of my life. I left for England in 1951 to study at Oxford on a Rhodes Scholarship; and, having decided not to go home, I have lived and worked in Britain ever since.

The story I tell focuses on how I lived the last days of colonialism, in both Kingston and London. I have chosen to close the narrative in the early 1960s, when I was entering my thirties. By then I had stepped outside the immediate impress of colonial subjugation, discovering the means to become a different sort of person. I had met and married Catherine.[1] My life of political activism in London was coming to an end. We moved to Birmingham, where a new future opened up for me at the Centre for Contemporary Cultural Studies. These changes didn't magically resolve the unease which had been incubated as I grew up in a racially subordinate position in colonial Jamaica. It was not an ending like the fabled closures of a Victorian novel. They marked the moment when I came to understand that my life was my own to make, and that obeisance to either colonial Jamaica or to metropolitan Britain, or

---

[1] In the following pages Catherine makes many appearances. This is Catherine Hall, Stuart's wife and partner of some fifty years. In part she appears as the distinguished historian of the relations which in the past bound together Britain and Jamaica. On other occasions she does so as a participant in her own right in the story Stuart Hall tells. She played a significant role in Hall's intellectual life, as she did in the making of this book.

England, was not the only choice before me. Other spaces opened up. These were, I saw, spaces to be made.

In 2011 I celebrated – if that is the right word – sixty years of life in the black British diaspora. Indeed, I am the product of *two* diasporas. This may surprise readers who are more likely to regard the African diaspora as my primordial place of origin. But Jamaica too, as well as being a part of Africa in the New World, is a diaspora of sorts in its own right, a site of the scattering of traditions and people, of diffusion. None of the major groups which constitute Jamaican society originally belonged there. Every Jamaican is the product of a migration, forced or free. Everyone is originally from somewhere else.

My father, Herman, an amiable, stockily built brown man of lower-middle-class background, with kind eyes and a little paunch in his tropical light-brown suit, worked as an accountant. He was lucky enough, given his early prospects, to have landed a job in Port Antonio with the United Fruit Company, one of the US multinationals based in Boston which has dominated the banana trade in Central America and the Caribbean. United Fruit was known throughout the twentieth century for its expertise in summoning the dark arts in Central American politics. My father, who I imagine would have been oblivious to all this, worked his way up the ladder to be the first local – that is, 'coloured man' – appointed chief accountant of the Jamaican branch of the company.

My mother, the formidable 'Miss Jessie', was a handsome, well-tailored brown woman of imposing bearing. Born to light-skinned but not well-off parents – a teacher in the Agricultural School and a postmistress – she was in effect adopted by her prosperous uncle, a prominent lawyer who owned a small estate on the edge of Port Antonio. She was taken to live there in a rather grand house called 'Norwich', which stood on a hill at the end of a palm-lined driveway looking out to the sea. In the final episode of the series *Redemption Song*, which I made for the BBC in 1991, I revisited the ruins of that house, which had been bought but left untouched by the singer Eartha Kitt. It was looked after by a gay man who had worked in the theatre and fashion. He lived in a single room with cupboards stuffed full of show costumes in an otherwise empty house. Like the way of life it represented, 'Norwich' was falling into decay.

My mother's uncles were local professionals – lawyers and doctors – and all their children were educated in England. If my mother hadn't been a woman, she would probably have been sent to England to complete her education too. I think she felt cheated that she hadn't been. The family had originally been slave-owners. An antecedent by marriage, John Rock Grosset, embarrassingly turns out to have been a prominent pro-slavery, anti-abolitionist pamphleteer. Plantation life constituted the aspirational model of her hopes and fears, which she recast for her own family to adopt. This branch of the family tutored her in their ways and refashioned her into one of their own. She enjoyed her capacity to dominate, to take the leading role, to play the *grande dame*. She carried her fearless determination – indeed, her willed stubbornness – in the very set of her body and face. Her tragedy was that, although obviously a highly competent person, after her marriage she never worked outside the family home. The domestic scene and the family became her occupation, which she dominated and governed – unlike many other Jamaican middle-class families where, at that time, the men ruled. But I think the lack of a more fulfilling public role was one of the many sources of her abiding sense of dissatisfaction.

Both my siblings – my brother, George and my sister, Patricia – were some years older than me. Pat's working life as a personal secretary was interrupted by a serious breakdown. She spent much of the rest of her later life caring for George and for my parents. She is still alive, living in residential care in Jamaica, looked after by my cousin, Sister Maureen Clare.

Kingston, where we lived, was a typical, large, bustling, over-crowded, often ramshackle colonial city. It looked out on a circular harbour, one of the safest and most magnificent of its kind in the world, which was almost fully enclosed by a narrow snake of land, the Palisadoes, at the end of which stood what was left of the old town, Port Royal. This had been the main base of the British pirate fleet which, in the Elizabethan period, harried the galleons from the Spanish Main on their way from South America back to Europe with loot from the silver mines. In fact piracy, though a freelance illegal venture, had an ambiguous relationship to the Crown. One of the most notorious pirates, Sir Henry Morgan, actually became for a time a governor of the island. Most of Port Royal had been destroyed or submerged by an earthquake in 1692, which everyone believed was a just and fitting judgement on its wicked, licentious way of life, on its vice and illicit wealth. People said that if you listened hard you could still hear the bells of the cathedral tolling beneath the waves – pleading for forgiveness, perhaps?

Jamaica itself, the tropical island, still resides deep in my being. Much of the south and parts of the north are relatively flat, ideal for planting sugar cane. Elsewhere the land is steeper, suited to bananas, citrus fruits and a range of local delicacies. The estates and cattle farms are on the flatter terrain. Coffee is a high mountain crop. A lot of the interior is thickly wooded, subtropical and promiscuously fertile. Behind Kingston rise the high peaks of the Blue Mountains, which form part of a longer mountainous spine running almost the full length of the island. Everywhere, the narrow roads climb their perilous way up the hillsides and plummet down again into the valleys.

Deeper in the interior was the terrain of the 'country people', especially the subsistence peasant families on half-acre smallholdings or scratching a livelihood in the hillside villages, as well as the day-rate labourers, cane-cutters and banana-growers and those who serviced village life. On their tiny family plots they grew anything that could be consumed, or taken down to the weekly market and sold alongside the flotsam and jetsam of local rural life: re-tread tires, clapped-out motor parts and multiply renovated electrical goods. The dwellings of the poor subsistence farmers often consisted of tin-roofed huts and rough, lean-to wooden houses perched precariously on the terraced hillsides, every inch of which was used productively.

Except in the most remote areas, a multitude of small villages emerged at road intersections, often consisting of nothing more than a few shacks clustered around an improvised bar or an all-purpose store. Sometimes, as in the more remote Cockpit country, the terrain breaks up into jagged, serrated peaks and troughs. At regular intervals the main roads pass through crowded, sweltering, small country towns. The roads hugged the sea wherever possible, or ran just inland from long, sandy beaches fringed by coconut palms. The undergrowth offered shortcuts to the glaring-white sand and the majestic blue-green rolling waves of the Caribbean lying beyond. All along the coast were small fishing villages. The finest of these became much touted by the travel industry as centres of the tourist holiday 'paradise'.

The seat of government had been established by the early *conquistadors* in Spanish Town, with its imposing examples of early architecture still intact in the main square. The British transferred the capital to Kingston. Today, half the population lives in and around Kingston. It is by far the most important urban centre, and dominates social, political and cultural life. When I was growing up its streets ran down to the harbour and the docks. The smaller side streets sported a multitude of tiny, improvised businesses – tailors, hairdressers, shoemakers, freelance mechanics, day-labourers, domestic servants, gardeners, washerwomen, hairdressers, self-employed odd-job people mending clothes and shoes, dressmakers in an economy not yet addicted to the ready-made, untrained mechanics and a legion of ingenious repairers. These improvised ventures coexisted alongside the large, swanky department stores selling upmarket or foreign branded goods. This was the commercial and administrative centre of Jamaican life. It still contained the House of Assembly, the law courts, lawyers' chambers, the cathedral, the headquarters of many established companies, the old Ward Theatre, some of the government ministries, the stadium, the Institute of Jamaica, the art gallery and, at its rim, the craft market, whose sellers competed raucously to win the favour of passing tourists. One road out of town passed the asylum – the old Rockfort, with prisoners digging at the chalk face – the hot baths, the seaplane wharf and the road out to the airport.

However, in more recent times the balance of the metropolis has shifted remarkably. As one drives up the foothills towards

St Andrew's, the residential part of Kingston, the manicured lawns of 'uptown' Kingstonians indulgently spread themselves across the landscape. The gardens are well tended (everyone up here has a gardener) and the houses grand (everyone has servants, now called 'helpers'), although the grandest are often in showy bad taste. The more prosperous Kingstonians have moved higher up still, taking refuge in the surrounding hills which look down on the city. The Hope Road leads to the edge of the city and takes you up to the University of the West Indies Mona Campus, the Hope Botanical Gardens, the Reservoir and my old school, Jamaica College. Then, suddenly, it ends at Papine Corner and begins the vertiginous climb up to Mavis Bank and into the Blue Mountain mist.

Downtown Kingston used to be the main shopping centre, reached by bus and tram; but these shops have since become dispersed across the city uptown into US-style malls. The narrow roads to the harbour led into the heart of lower Kingston's massively poor, casual-labour or unemployed ghetto areas where living conditions were poverty-stricken, dwellings often no more than corrugated-tin shacks clustered around shared tenement yards, with the only available running water from a common standpipe. Some of these became notorious ghettos, like Trench Town and Tivoli Gardens, the no-go, garrisoned centres of rival political factions and of petty and organized criminal activities – the topic of Bob Marley lyrics.

These landscapes represent my sharpest memories of Jamaica, more so – perhaps surprisingly – than the people who inhabited them. Time has overtaken the latter. But I often relive the forbidding climb along precipice-sided potholed roads up into the mountains; then beginning the descent on the other side down towards the north coast, with the aquamarine ocean glimmering seductively ahead through the trees. The wind has a balmy softness in the early morning before the sun sets fire to everything. The body unfolds from inside as the day warms up. (I have never really stopped being cold in Britain.) The sea has a powerful, enticing presence in my memory: swimming before breakfast, the water still as glass; or at midday, sliding through the ever-changing green depths at Discovery Bay; or in the afternoon, riding the surging, spume-tipped – and scary – ocean waves at Boston Beach, followed by jerk-pork and festival barbeques. Festival, I should explain, is a cross between bread and dumpling.

I recall looking up the ravine at Bog Walk Bridge (then with room for only one car at a time) at the immense bamboo fronds swaying in the wind, and the orange and yellow blossom of the poinciana and poui trees; the lush, subtropical mountain vegetation that runs alongside the twisting Junction Road to my favourite part of the coast, Port Antonio; or clambering over the rocky waterfalls when we stopped at Castleton Gardens to drink fresh coconut water straight from the nut. I have discovered since how much memory of 'the old country' is carried by migrants in food and cuisine. I am still addicted to Jamaican cooking: the creole blend of spices and seasonings – garlic, thyme, pimento, spring onions, Scotch Bonnet hot peppers. I still crave the favourite national dishes, simple and plebeian though they are: fricassee chicken, rice and peas, plantain, salt-fish and ackee, curry goat, fish fritters, pig-tail and stewed peas, escovitched fish, callaloo, shrimp, conch soup, 'run down' patties – usually made from salted mackerel and coconut milk -- and so on. These smells and tastes bring back an entire life which, for me in London, is no longer mine.

One potent memory is the spread of foods you can still find at the Saturday morning markets. I recall how the higglers brought their produce down from the hills in straw baskets carried on their heads. Setting up the market, they created an atmosphere of bustle and hilarity as they greeted one another, reviewed the week in stories and anecdotes, recycling gossip and scandalous tales or rehearsing grievances. This was a very Jamaican scene with its high drama, loud contention, joshing and jostling, taste for exaggeration and caricature, its (often manufactured) sense of outrage – performances which Jamaicans manage to stage on even the most chance encounter. In fact nothing escaped these ladies' eagle eyes. However relaxed they seemed, they were always proprietorially on guard behind their improvised stalls, keeping a sharp lookout for pilferers too inclined to use their casual familiarity to help themselves in passing.

These memories represent now, for me, not so much specific re-collections as a sense of generalized absence – a loss, especially acute since I will probably never be well enough to see them again. They guarantee that I shall be Jamaican all my life, no matter where I am living. Though what that *actually* meant for me, in terms both of the practicalities of my life and of where my sense of belonging was to be located, was much more problematic.

I'm conscious of this feeling of ambivalence as I sit and write. It shadows the words as they form in my mind. I didn't set out to write this book in order to recover my memories of the past. Of course, the question of memory is – tantalizingly, inescapably – an issue. But I don't think I had a clear memorializing project in mind for the book. I certainly don't think of what I write as a memoir in any formal sense, or even as a rehearsal for a memoir. I'm more concerned here, as I have been in much of my more professional academic writing, with the connections between 'a life' and 'ideas'. I've never wanted to write a memoir. I've kept very little of the sort of correspondence on which such accounts extensively depend. Now in my eighties, my memory is at best fitful, episodic, unrelia-ble and no doubt fanciful. In addition, as a result of recent sight impairment, I haven't been able to consult documents which would validate its judgements, although I have had many rich and inform-ing conversations with friends who figure in the story or know parts of it better than I do. But I have not checked its accuracy and I'm responsible for its errors of chronology, fact or judgement.

I have never thought that the detail of my life, of the kind which fills memoirs, was of much intrinsic interest or significance. I have however – as the Chinese saying goes – 'lived in interesting times'. I thought it would be engaging for others to read my reflections on those experiences, ideas, events and memories from the vantage point of someone who lived them, as it were, from the margins.

I was born and formed in the closing days of the old colonial world. They are my conditions of existence. This is, as I see it, the starting point for narrating my life, the source of a curious, unreach-able and abiding unease. I have spent my adult life in the declining imperial metropole. As the great Trinidadian C. L. R. James once said of Caribbean migrants to the UK, we are 'in, but not of, Europe'. 'Europe' was not just another different space and time, but precisely *the reverse* of those conditions of existence into which I had been inserted and called into place by birth and by my early formation. In Jamaica, I wasn't of course an exile. But there is a sense in which, although I belong to it, Jamaica worked to 'other' me. As a consequence, I experience my life as sharply divided into two unequal but entangled, disproportionate halves. You could say I have lived, metaphorically speaking, on the hinge between the colonial and post-colonial worlds; because of radically changing locations, I have belonged, in different ways, to both at different times of my life, without ever being fully of either.

The idea that, because I moved – irrevocably as it turned out – from one world to the other, from colony to metropole, there were no connections between them has always seemed inconceivable to me. But others have tended to see these worlds as much more compartmentalized. And to someone who doesn't know the interior life and spaces of the colonial formation, and how its antinomies were forged, the connections may not appear to be evident, or as evident to them as to me. To me, their interdependence is what defines their respective specificities; in everything they reverberate through each other. Precisely how this occurs isn't easy to explain, so I can't blame anyone – as I see it – for getting it wrong.

This misunderstanding is common. Catherine recently pointed out to me that, although close friends and political colleagues in the New Left during the 1950s and 1960s were committed anti-imperialists, well tutored in anti-colonial thinking, they never perceived me as a raced, colonial subject. Similarly, friends who knew me in the Jamaican context can't really imagine me now, or see how the Jamaican became the other. Jamaican graduate students studying in North America in the 1980s discovered Cultural Studies, with which I had become identified, as a product of an English university, the University of Birmingham – only to find, when I turned up to lecture, that a black Jamaican had somehow been involved in the enterprise from the beginning! Cultural Studies was unknown in the University of the West Indies until pioneers like Carolyn Cooper and Rex Nettleford got hold of it. Some Caribbean people in media studies who refer to my essay on 'Encoding/ Decoding' still don't know I am black.

This isn't simply a matter which is peculiar to me. It turns on an entire history: that of the late colonial migration from the Caribbean to the metropole. More than fifty years ago, in 1960, the essentials of the story were told by the Barbadian George Lamming in his *The Pleasures of Exile*. The various terms we now use to describe the dynamics of the encounter between colonized and colonizer, between black and white, on the terrain of the metropole itself – forgetfulness, disavowal, misrecognition, amnesia – not only indicate the complexity of the phenomenon; they also alert us to the strange imperatives by which the full force of the history of colonialism keeps slipping out of the collective memory of the metropole.

In the 1950s, when I first lived in England, it was as if the West Indian migrant had landed on these shores by some incomprehensible sleight of hand or ruse. Written out of the story – forgotten, disavowed, misrecognized – were the prolonged historical entanglements between the Caribbean and Britain. Britons needed to be reminded of this inconvenient fact. Once the post-colonial amnesia enveloped Britain after the war, very few people, including those on the Left, had – indeed, still have – much clue about the colonial history of their nation or, speaking more personally, can fathom what possible connection there is between the life I lived then and now. They certainly didn't learn much about it at school, until a few brave teachers forced the issue and Black History Month attempted to address the situation.

I remember reacting with disproportionate rage to one of my earliest reviewers, an intelligent and broadly sympathetic English sociologist, who said he didn't understand why I kept banging on about being coloured (or having a chip on my shoulder, as it appears in *The Pleasures of Exile*), since I was from a well-to-do middle-class family, had been educated at a good, English-type school and studied abroad at Oxford. As if to say, what had *he* to complain about? Since the reviewer had – inadvertently, no doubt – identified the central contradiction of my life, I felt, perhaps unfairly, that someone who didn't understand that wasn't likely to get much else about me right.

It's *this* history which lay behind my decision to set about writing this book. I realized that I should try to use this time to track how I see the organic connections and dissonances between the two worlds: the colonial and the post-colonial. That is, how they constantly displaced one another, repeated themselves but always with a difference, simultaneously resonated off, jarred against, mirrored and disrupted one another. Another way of putting it is that I hoped the book might constitute an insight into the contradictory transition points in that old story – the long, tortuous, tortured and never-concluded route out of colonial subalternhood.

There were for me, naturally, many false starts. When I was a boy I thought I was a poet, but the illusion didn't last long. I lacked original talent. My poetry was too derivative. Then I wanted very much to be a novelist, and this persisted until my university days when I had to acknowledge that I wasn't very gifted in that department either. A story by a Jamaican about a displaced Polish-Jewish intellectual, influenced thematically by Isaac Babel and stylistically by Henry James, really wasn't on! People now routinely call me an academic, but that is how I earned my living, not a vocation. I think of myself as a teacher, but this doesn't seem exalted enough for most people. I wanted to be a black intellectual, but it took something of a journey – certainly no flash of insight – to reach this conclusion. The word 'intellectual', though properly recognized in France, is still something of a joke in the more philistine sections of the British intelligentsia and more generally in the public culture. The idea of an intellectual suggests too much posturing, and isn't empirical and home-grown enough for native sensibilities. Politics is a passion, but I have never been formally 'in politics'. Nowadays people say cultural theorist, but although I believe in theory as an indispensable critical tool, I have never been interested in 'producing theory' and, in any case, I am not a theorist of any rank in this age of theory, so I regard the designation of cultural theorist more as a polite, convenient postponement, a holding operation, than a well-understood resolution. However, it's close enough to stand.

There was never a single moment in this trajectory which wasn't impelled by my racial positioning. The details and contours were invariably unpredictable, but the overriding gravity of the fact was constant. Unlike most Afro-Caribbeans now living in the black British diaspora, I arrived in England bearing my navy-blue British passport, the document which proved definitively that, although not properly a citizen, I was a 'subject' of – and so subject to – the British Empire and the Crown. My passport, in this sense, proved a mysteriously ambiguous document to possess, as it did for the Nigerian Chinua Achebe, as he describes in his memoir *The Education of a British-Protected Child*. It was only later, when migration to Britain had increased, that 'black' became politicized. That was when, for Caribbean people, our sense of belonging to the extended British family was brought sharply into question. It evolved into a transcendent political issue when we – the Caribbean migrants in the metropole – came increasingly to be perceived as potential bearers of disloyalty.

In this bid to free myself from living the life of the colonized, I never had any aspiration to be English, nor have I ever become English. Being English, it seemed to me, was not a repository of potential identification – rather, it was just an unwelcome twist of historical fate. It had no traction on my actual life. British might have been more acceptable as an ascribed identity because of the imperial connection, but only because I was indeed one of its subordinate subjects. The Colonial Office in London was indeed our governor. But it felt as if the British were a quite different, and foreign, race.

Skin colour was, absolutely, an issue. But although everyone perfectly well understood what 'black' meant, the very word was taboo, unsayable, especially for the middle classes in Jamaica in the 1930s and 1940s. It betrayed the prevailing prejudices too openly. Race depended on a more euphemistic, coded discourse. Indeed, black wasn't yet universally used even by people who were, in all the obvious senses, 'black'. By choice, the Halls and their circle were coloured. Literally, we were brown; mixed-race would have been more accurate. After all, both branches of my family were of mixed-race background. But even that term was rarely used. Mixed-race would have meant bringing into consciousness the fact that there must also have been – as indeed there were – white traces alongside the manifestly African ones in the family bloodline. But for decades, in both the slave states of the US and in the Anglophone Caribbean, the enslaved people were known as a separate race: as Negroes.

In my case the European element was almost certainly Scottish. From where else would my forefathers have dreamed up both Stuart and the even more ridiculous McPhail as family names? I find this reminiscent of Edward Said having been named Edward, and of his fraught relationship with this unknowable, awkward persona: Edward, the other inside him who caused him much grief. Which side of the family these historic traces derived from is uncertain. Contrary to the contemporary national self-image, the Scots were massively involved in the imperial enterprise, as plantation overseers, attorneys, book-keepers, merchants, medical men and soldiers. Neal Ascherson calls them, with his usual precision, 'the non-commissioned officers of empire'.

I had the melanin coursing through my veins and the skin colour to prove my African origins, although my family found this hard to acknowledge. But I wouldn't have understood myself as African in any meaningful, contemporary sense of the word. Enslavement, violent transplantation, a physically abusive and exploitative labour regime, social dislocation, cultural abjection and a sort of willed forgetting of a humiliating past had, in sum, ruptured our historical connections. This sense of abandonment was already hardwired into the popular Jamaican imaginary and placed identifications with Africa beyond reach for many. The term 'Afro-Caribbean', first adopted in the early years of post-war Caribbean migration to the UK, was followed by a series of more refined, hyphenated voter-registration categories like 'Black Caribbean'. In my case (although it surprises people when I say it), black as a personal identity had to wait for decolonization, the Alabama bus boycott, the

Notting Hill riots, US Civil Rights, Martin Luther King's 'I Have A Dream', Sharpeville, Malcolm X, Stokely Carmichael, Angela Davis, and then later, in the 1970s, black resistance politics in Britain, Rock Against Racism, roots music, reggae, Bob Marley . . .

Contrary to common-sense understanding, the transformations of self-identity are not just a personal matter. Historical shifts *out there* provide the social conditions of existence of personal and psychic change *in here*. What mattered was how I positioned myself on the other side – or positioned myself to catch the other side: how I was, involuntarily, hailed by and interpellated into a broader social discourse. Only by discovering this did I begin to understand that what black identity involved was a social, political, historical and symbolic event, not just a personal, and certainly not simply a genetic, one.

From this I came to understand that identity is not a set of fixed attributes, the unchanging essence of the inner self, but a constantly shifting process of *positioning*. We tend to think of identity as taking us back to our roots, the part of us which remains essentially the same across time. In fact identity is always a never-completed *process* of becoming – a process of shifting *identifications*, rather than a singular, complete, finished state of being.

As a child I may not yet have been black in my head, but, as it happened, I was one of the blackest in my family. Wide colour variations are a common feature within families across Jamaica's uncertain colour spectrum. My grandmother on my mother's side, the notably fair-skinned part of the family, was an expert in racial classification, as that master of structural anthropology, Claude Lévi-Strauss, would have appreciated. She claimed always to be able to detect the complex racial genealogy in the 'fairest' of Jamaicans, especially those trying to 'pass'.

There was reputed to be a 'touch' of East Indian somewhere in our family. But if that was true, I have no idea how it had come about. In fact, typically, no one actually knew. I remember the distinguished black North American intellectual Henry Louis 'Skip' Gates telling me that, in his genealogical research, African-American celebrities who were immensely proud of their 'authentic' African tribal lineage quite often turned out to have mixed-race or white connections somewhere 'back there'. His own, I believe, happened to be Dutch, on the face of it an unexpected connection. When asked about it, however, some of those whom he questioned fantasized about connections with native indigenous princesses which were patently preferable to white associations!

I have no hard evidence either way about our East Indian origins, although my beloved grandmother on my father's side, brown as a nut, looked as if there might be something to it. But this East Indian story could equally well have been another variant of the native American princess fantasy, except that there was not much status in Jamaica in such a claim, since poor Indians were, if anything, more despised than poor blacks. Yet significant numbers of East Indians and Hong Kong Chinese had indeed been brought in as indentured labour when slavery was abolished, although in Jamaica in much smaller numbers than in Trinidad or in British Guiana (Guyana), where their descendants are now the largest ethnic part of the population. But the campaign against indenture – against, in other words, a form of slavery by another name – was relatively successful in Jamaica and the majority of Jamaican East Indians became indigenized, poor but 'free', itinerant market gardeners selling their produce from baskets on the backs of their bicycles. I can't imagine my family claiming to have any close relationship to them. But who knows who had 'close relationships' with whom in plantation societies?

Family folklore had it that there were other ethnic twists in our descent story, including Portuguese-Jewish. But at the time this did indeed seem far-fetched, at least to this brown middle class. However, the Portuguese had at some point taken refuge in Jamaica and some of Jamaica's most distinguished families are, even today, their descendants. I didn't begin to understand this story until recently when our friend Julian Henriques, son of Fernando Henriques, the distinguished anthropologist and author of several landmark texts including *Family and Colour in Jamaica*, helped me to unravel the backstory. The history of Jewish settlement is a riveting narrative.

The number of Jewish migrants of the sixteenth century, escaping from the Inquisition, was later swollen by refugees from other colonies – some from the Haitian Revolution, which expelled the French slaveholders, or, in Spanish America, those fleeing the revolutions against colonial rule in the 1820s and 1830s. Their descendants remain a small minority in the Jamaican population. Even so, their relatively small numbers notwithstanding, they are reputed to be responsible for introducing into the cuisine one of Jamaica's most treasured, popular indigenous delicacies: patties. Many Jamaicans choose patties for lunchtime, without having a clue about their history.

At any rate, neither the idea of my East Indian or Portuguese-Jewish family heritage was as fantastical as my mother's firm, but of course fictitious, conviction that her maiden name, Hopwood, was an Anglicization of Hapsburg, and thus a sure sign of our family's royal – Austrian – heritage. That is the genuine stuff of a Freudian family romance!

In retrospect, perhaps, my confusions about my racial location may seem difficult to understand. I was looking for certainty in an already worryingly undecidable world. Ethnic diversity was not something I aspired to or would have known what to do with. At the time all the complexity seemed irrelevant to the question of who I was. The colonial relationship was just too overpowering. It dominated everything.

These questions of race and ethnicity were never far removed from ones of social class. In my earliest years, like everyone else, I was innocent of the concept of class. But as soon as I became aware of the world 'outside', I always knew my family occupied an intermediary social position between the wealthy white elite and the mass of poor and unemployed Jamaicans. My father held a professional job and earned a respectable salary, although my mother constantly complained that it was not enough. We had a well-appointed house and employed servants. Our family friends were of the same upper-middling sort.

Literally, I was formed as a creole, the product of mixed origins, and born, and thoroughly indigenized into, local society. However, creole was always an ambiguous term, more commonly used in the French- and Spanish-settled islands than in Jamaica. In his *Development of Creole Society in Jamaica, 1770–1820*, the Barbadian poet-historian Edward (Kamau) Brathwaite argues that the word creole is a hybrid Spanish term constructed by combining two words – *crear* (to create, to found) and *colono* (a colonist) – into *criollo*, meaning to be a committed settler, or one native to a country's ways, even if not actually indigenous. Creole society was in fact non-specific as to race and colour. In the New World resident white settlers, born on the islands, were often described as creole; but the category also included enslaved African people, provided they were born in the country of captivity, as opposed to those recent arrivals directly transported into servitude from Africa.

Creole is thus a shifting, elastic concept, perhaps describing who I – and a multitude of other Jamaicans – was. But, given these historical accretions, it calls for a degree of specification.

Similar ambiguities underwrote the very idea of the colonial too. When I was young we tended to think of white Crown subjects from Australia, Canada, New Zealand, South Africa, Rhodesia and Kenya as the 'real' colonials. In Jamaica blacks greatly outnumbered whites. The relative paucity of white women meant there were fewer opportunities for white men to make an acceptable marriage. In fact the white Jamaican population experienced a serious crisis about reproducing itself, and indeed failed really to do so.

Politically, the settler colonies in the early days were governed directly from the Colonial Office and could claim few local political rights. In Jamaica, on the other hand, representative political institutions, such as the Assembly – with a very limited franchise – had existed since the 1660s. Jamaican whites had fought for and vociferously defended their rights as 'free-born Englishmen' until the Morant Bay rebellion two centuries later, when – faced with the terror of black claims – they abolished their own House of Assembly. At that point Britain made Jamaica a Crown colony, governed directly from Whitehall. Tensions between London and the planters in Jamaica continued to be a permanent feature of the colonial relationship. The Legislative Council, when it was formed, had a mixed local and expatriate membership. So it is not difficult to understand, in these circumstances, what an ambivalent identification the term 'colonial' represented across the imperial world.

I'll say something about how this was lived in due course. But here I can note that we drew a crude, although not misinformed, distinction between us, the governed colonial subjects, and them. We knew social hierarchization when we saw it.

Privately, it must be said, the English in Jamaica aroused ambivalent feelings. They were deferred to because of their power, colour, wealth and exalted social position, and due to their leadership of every aspect of our lives. At the same time they constituted for us 'natives' a sort of running joke, a constant source of casual humour, even ridicule, which made us feel superior. They appeared to us so foreign in their dress, manners and behaviour, so uptight, so profoundly in the wrong place!

Finding one's place, socially and subjectively, in the complex social world of the colony was a perilous exercise. But today the picture of the colonial past has settled into a simplistic, polarized black/white binary, especially in the UK. The contradictory juxtapositions of class, racial, colour and cultural divisions in the old colonial world have slipped from collective consciousness.

Some revisionist historians have even contrived to see the imperializing process, once more, as beneficial in its overall effects. The arch-revisionist historian Niall Ferguson suggests that, without the spread of British rule, colonized people would not possess what are now their most valuable ideas and institutions. Pankaj Mishra has produced a serious riposte to such colonial recidivism, seeking to dismantle this specious special pleading, demonstrating the ways in which such archaic ways of thought continue to inform the present.

Colonialism condensed the diversity of global complexities and temporalities into a single narrative, in effect colonizing the multiplicity of everyday stories, such that the one overarching narrative ('the rise and rise of the West') took command. Much of human history was forced into this discursive schema, which worked to justify the colonial order. This was a narrative rooted in an unshakeable conviction of the colonizers' natural, God-given superiority over the degraded lives to which the colonized were consigned.

In fact, though its legacies were not simple, colonialism was founded on, and continues to work, not through its gifts but through the conquest of land and resources, the violent exploitation of labour, the imposition of foreign rule, the subjugation of peoples and the destruction and marginalization of those cultural traditions which are perceived as inimical to colonial authority. Its intervention broke up historic old civilizations. It represents one of the most far-reaching, brutal ruptures in modern history, equivalent in depth to the Holocaust, although – surprisingly? – this is a comparison which is not often made. It irreversibly reshaped societies and individuals. It bequeathed that most soul-destroying of legacies: the contradictory and distorted state of alienation which Frantz Fanon described as 'black skin, white masks'. It went to great lengths to refashion us, the subjugated colonials, as simulacra of itself. It 'othered' us to ourselves. I hope there is space for these in Ferguson's list of 'benefits' too. As such, in this post-colonial moment, the sensibilities of colonialism are still potent. We – all of us – are still its inheritors, still living in its terrifying aftermath.

Thus recognizing myself as a colonized subject meant accepting my insertion into History (capital 'H'), all right – only backwards, upside-down, by negation. For us, 'colonial' carried with it the indelible mark of secondariness which, although only too accurate at one level, was intolerable. This made it impossible for empire to be a repository of positive identification.

So for my generation of Jamaicans, 'colonial' was not something you chose to be. It was an attribute of being, formative because it framed your very existence. As Michel Foucault suggested, it positioned you as a subject-'author' as well as subjecting you to its discourse. But it was also productive because it bred a troubled refusal of, and resistance to, all the values it harboured in its bloodstream: servitude, poverty, patriarchalism, class inequality and racialized difference, of course, but also cultural colonization, all the petty humiliations of daily life. And, perhaps most damaging of all, these psychic imperatives generated the silences, unconscious evasions and disavowals, the self-deceiving double-talk of colonial discourse itself, which so often masks its hidden presences with absences, gaps and silences, making them simultaneously both knowable *and* unspeakable for those living them.

Even today I do not understand the full meaning of the feelings of displacement which gradually came to shadow and transform my life. What I can say is that, through a long and harsh process of disenchantment, I came to feel, even as a youth, at odds with the given circumstances of my birth. So in effect my identity was formed more by resistance to those circumstances I had inherited than by adaptation to what they had tried to make me. You could more accurately say, then, that I was framed by and against 'the colonial'.

To put it another way, my identity was formed as much by what my circumstances had made me as by the often unrecognized or unconscious struggle against my conditions of formation. This is a contradiction which I have come to believe the identification process always involves: identification always generates this paradox. It is one of the cruellest of ironies that, in trying to position oneself as different from what one has been made to be, one is condemned unconsciously to repeat elements of the old self one is trying to surpass. In that sense – one way or another, coming or going, positively or negatively – colonialism 'got' me, made me, unacceptably, who I came to think I was.

What followed, however, was not the success story of grasping freedom. It was rather the less heroic one of finding, and coming to terms with, an alternative route to what could not be transcended. There is something dialectical about this process: the imperatives of identification are perpetually paradoxical. I think that there is an inevitability about the workings of this dialectical circle.

Parents form us, both by cultivating us and at the same time by representing – in the form of compelling internalized psychic symbols of desire, authority and prohibition – those very things we must resist, rebel against, repress, forget or even learn to 'speak' if we are to become subjects in our own right.

In this context, I always think of the work of one of the finest of the black diaspora photographic practitioners of the 1980s whom I greatly admire: the gay, Yoruba-born, artist-photographer Rotimi Fani-Kayode. Rotimi lived and practised most of his adult life outside Africa. He became one of the most significant figures in the explosion of black artistic creativity in the UK in the 1980s, and one of the first to break the silence by bringing male sexuality into the discourses of black representation. He always acknowledged his profound sense of sexual, geographical and familial displacement. His work is a way of both remembering and mourning the losses this represented: mourning his ancestors and their traditions, not by omitting them but by 'masking' them, thus giving them a new sensuous but perverse erotic charge. This was his way of honouring their symbolic power in his life and, at the same time, recognizing his own distance from them. In one of his constructed, masked works, as in Yoruba ritual, he sought to exorcize his ancestors by summoning them up but in another register. He always insisted that he was what he was *because of*, not in spite of, his lost selves. 'My identity', he said, 'has been constructed from my own sense of otherness.' Identity is never singular but is multiply constructed across intersecting and antagonistic discourses, practices and positions.

This touches on the very meanings of post-colonial, that other, entangled, disproportionate phase of my life. Post-colonial is a term of recent coinage. When I was living in Jamaica it was not available or appropriate as a potential identity among middle-class Jamaicans. Indeed, during my time in colonial Jamaica there was nothing 'post-' about it. We were still in the middle of wrestling with colonialism's only-too-present impress, even though the end of empire was coming into view in an inexorable way.

One reason why I could not have aspired to be post-colonial was because my family never thought of themselves, at that time, as part of an emerging anti-colonial struggle, or as belonging to something which could represent itself as 'after colonialism'.

However, post-colonial may be what I have become. I certainly am 'post-' that particular phase of direct colonial rule which prevailed when I was growing up. It is over now. Other forms of neo-imperial power have taken its place. The Union Jack has been lowered, the 'winds of change' have blown, and decolonization, independence and the nationalist revolutions have followed – although, in Jamaica's case, not with the transformative results that many of us at the time had hoped for.

'Post-' is not just a matter of the passage of time. It refers to the way one configuration of power, institutions and discourses, which once defined the social field, has been replaced by another. The old has indeed radically changed its form. However, the old has not been transcended. We continue to stand in its shadow. In the case of the colonial and the post-colonial, what we are dealing with is not two successive regimes but the simultaneous presence of a *regime and its after-effects*. Colonialism persists, despite the cluster of illusory appearances to the contrary.

Jacques Derrida points out that in his use of *erasure* as a deconstructionist strategy by which to undermine metaphysics in philosophy, one can still read the metaphysical concept through which a cancelling line has been drawn. Derrida asks: if existing metaphysical concepts may no longer be serviceable, what options are there *except* to go on thinking with those old contaminated concepts *in their deconstructed state*? That is because there is, as he says, no 'beyond' of philosophy. We are what comes 'after', because the after-effects of what was in place 'before' have not been superseded, overcome or (as the Hegelians have it) sublated. The present still carries the spectres of the past hiding inside it. In the same way, without modernism's break with older forms of mimetic representation, postmodernism could not have existed. The one stands on the shoulders of the other – while, of course, vigorously declaring its independence at every turn!

Though time has been called on colonialism's earlier forms, you have only to read a daily newspaper or turn on the TV news to appreciate that the so-called colonial world is still unfolding – more accurately, unravelling – inside the post-colonial, in the wake, in the devastating aftermath, of an untranscended colonialism: a disaster-littered, protracted, bloody and unfinished terrain which, in its globally transformed state, still occupies our world.

2.   The Two Jamaicas

What Jamaica did I belong to? This puzzle preoccupied me as I was growing up. In part, it was a function of the colonial relation, of being 'othered' to myself. But it was also due to my own social location in the brown middle class, which as a class was acutely conscious of its role as an intermediary formation and lay outside the world of the white planter elite; it certainly existed in an alternative cosmos to that inhabited by the poorer, darker multitude. These constituted what I call here 'the two Jamaicas'. Where was I in this polarized world?

The raison d'être of the coloured middle class was its intermediary position between the European-oriented governing elites and the mass of Jamaica's black people. In more recent times, the designation 'coloured' has been replaced in popular discourse by the equally ambiguous term 'brown'. In many respects, brown has now become the negative bearer of some of the resentments of the mass of black Jamaicans at the way these inheritors of Independence – particularly educated, successful, professional coloured men – have come to compose the governing political and commercial class and have colonized the cultural leadership of the new nation. Although, we should note, their social advancement did not prevent numbers of them from emigrating to Canada and the US during the 1970s at the prospect of a radical turn in Jamaican politics. Today the resistance to this brown hegemony, some suggest, is voiced most vividly through the 'rudeness' of a radically disaffected popular urban culture which has thrown aside all the proprieties of middle-class colonial respectability.

However, my own family represented an odd and anachronistic variant of this larger social picture.

As I've indicated, my father, Herman, was from a modest but respectable lower-middle-class family from Sav-la-Mar, in the

poorer, south-western part of the island. The son of a pharmacy owner in Old Harbour, he went to one of the 'good' but less prestigious secondary schools, did his correspondence exams in accountancy and got the job with United Fruit. I have very little sense of what his youth was like. He married my mother in 1918, on Armistice Day, and they moved to Kingston.

In the 1920s and 1930s a job with United Fruit represented a great career for an ambitious young middle-class brown man, which made him a good catch for my mother, whose immediate family were lighter-skinned and considered themselves of a higher social position, but whose commercial prospects were not as promising. Hypergamy – 'marrying upwards' through the colour-class ladder – was a recognized form of social mobility. My father spent much of his career as a respectable company man, although after retirement he worked in a public capacity for the local banana small producers' association. His life was work-oriented. He was the first Jamaican (that is, non-white) to occupy each of the positions in United Fruit to which he was promoted, ending as chief accountant. He was a model of probity in every department of his life. I would be shocked to hear that he had any sexual relations outside marriage. The annual visits of the United Fruit accountants from Boston were the high point of my parents' social calendar. However, I suspect that his intermediary position as a brown man may have limited the appeal which the moderate version of Jamaican nationalism – attractive to some of his peers – held for him.

Hard-working, financially cautious, self-effacing, smoking his stubby Jamaican (on special occasions, Cuban) cigars and regularly sipping a rum-and-ginger of an evening (on special occasions, whisky), he wanted nothing so much as a quiet life. My mother's social striving did not come naturally to him. Nevertheless I resented his social quietism: the fact that he went along with her project for us without complaint, and that he tolerated the way he was patronized by the men he drank with at his cricket club – which, on these personal grounds, I refused to join. Consequently, although he was a well-loved, kindly and benign figure in the domestic setting, he was also an absent father in my emotional formation.

The family's income was secure, although never high enough to match that of his professional friends in dentistry or the law and certainly never enough to maintain the imagined social position to which my mother aspired and to which they could never properly belong. They seemed always to be quarrelling about money, which may be why I still find it such a difficult subject to talk about. It formed the distorted parental culture of aspiration which appeared to encapsulate my destiny.

My mother had imbibed all the habits of her adopted class. Her image of the good life, her standards of decorum, her style, manners, dress, instinct for commanding everybody around her and her ambitions for her family were shaped by – and remained locked into – the template of that already dying estate world of her privileged childhood. She brought all those illusions into the heart of our family. Improbably, she continued to think of England as her real home. She never used a hairbrush which wasn't an imported Kent, or any face cream but Nivea, or washed with anything but Yardley's soap. When we visited my grandmother's more modest house in the country, my mother was received like the *grande dame* condescending to visit the poor country relatives. I hated every minute of this performance.

Her sister Inez ('Hoppy'), who stayed at home, was a very different sort of person: opinionated, rather masculine, troubled by a smoker's cough, unmarried, not well groomed like my mother or with my mother's feminine stratagems, but independent. She lived in our house for several years, but the two of them did not really get on. Hoppy had a responsible position in the Standard Fruit Company, another US-based banana business, and, unlike her sister, she worked all her life. She was more a prototype of the independent middle-class working women who dominate the scene in Jamaica today.

My mother Jessie not only kept servants, as was common in her social circle (even poor but respectable people often had at least one); she also masterminded a retinue of odd-job handymen to whom she paid nothing so vulgar as a 'wage for the job', but rather a sort of gift for feudal services rendered, which she thought were hers by natural right. She was outraged when, after Independence, the term 'servant' was declared demeaning and was replaced instead by 'helper'. She expressed bewilderment, too, at the government's idea that they might have to be paid a minimum wage.

Jessie was a handsome, elegantly tailored, self-driven person

who managed us all – my father included – with a passionate exercise of sheer, obstinate willpower. She tried to inject her old-world values into the faster, more commercial circles into which my father had moved. She vigorously defended them within the family and their close circle of Jamaican friends. And she tried to impose them, with an indomitable will, on us. Disastrously, she made the family her career.

We lived in a sprawling bungalow situated on half an acre of land in the residential brown middle-class area of Kingston, St Andrew's, on Trevennion Park Road. Though my mother was proud of the fact that she had done the designs herself, the house was not conveniently laid out. It was located off the Half Way Tree Road, at the hinge between the retail, commercial and shopping sectors by the port downtown and the middle-class suburbs expanding uptown. It had verandas on three sides. It was fronted by specially nurtured flowerbeds, the tending of which my mother supervised. At one side the bedrooms looked out on a carefully selected plot of fruit trees: grapefruit, orange, lime, soursop, fig, Bombay mango. Towards the back there was a chicken coop.

The backyard proper belonged to a different world, that of domestic life and the servants. Here, the 'staff' ate their midday meal: a mountain of food – starchy carbohydrates – with the occasional helping of salt-fish or pigtail. They did the household laundry in washtubs in the open air, laying it out to whiten in the sun; and pressed clothes with irons heated on open coal pots in one room of a little wooden hut which was their base. My mother insisted that the electric iron be kept indoors. In the house the housemaid cleaned, tidied, made the beds, served at meals and performed a myriad of other domestic tasks. A room was reserved for our cook, Ethel, to sleep in after serving supper, when it was too late for her to get home to Trench Town and return next morning to make breakfast before my father's departure for work.

Some of these servants inhabited that 'other', darker Jamaica. One was Cecil, the man who worked in our garden all through my childhood, who turned out to be a leading figure in a native Baptist Revivalist sect. On Sundays he led his people up to Hope River, where he conducted mass baptisms. I discovered that Ethel and other domestic workers would sometimes stop off on the way home, very late at night, at one of the open Pentecostal yards, where an eschatological version of the message of black redemption was being preached in the heart of downtown Kingston. I guess their weary bodies and tired spirits were lifted for an hour or two.

This other Jamaica remained entirely invisible to my family. It was occasionally written about by a few intellectuals, but in what were effectively specialist anthropological treatises. Aside from its function in giving life to ancestral racial and class fears, its conscious presence in my family was all but absent.

Installed on a stool on the back veranda which looked out on this backyard, my mother would sometimes supervise the cooking of special dishes and make cakes or rum punch or mix-up-matrimony (sweet-sop, oranges, condensed milk and ice) or eggnog (a Dickensian import). Otherwise she never really cooked, certainly not in the kitchen, which was Ethel's kingdom, where she made wonderful, creole-spiced meals on an old open wood stove in a sweltering, dark interior. Nevertheless this became a sort of haven or free port of call for me. The rest of the backyard was quite wild, with large fruit-bearing breadfruit, mango and avocado trees. When later, in Oxford, I had to cook for my student household, my culinary efforts proved sufficiently popular that I was invited to take on the role of cook full-time, which I more or less did. So much for the research! I tried to remember what Ethel had done and which spices she used, and to adapt my cooking to what was available in England.

However, the prime space at Trevennion Park Road was on the fourth side of the house, where my mother determined to lay out a tennis court, ringed by magnificent Bombay mango trees and contained within wire netting. She laboured long and hard over this project, her pride and joy, watering it continuously with a sprinkler to induce the grass to grow, measuring, marking out and refreshing the baselines with quicklime. She staged tennis parties. The men, including my father and my brother George – who could hardly see the ball – wore long whites, the ladies tennis dresses. I was sometimes allowed to be a ball-boy but I was never invited to play, even though I was captain of my school team. I resented this slight while accepting it as normal in our household. Besides, I had a ferocious first serve with which I could have inflicted useful damage! Between games, large jugs of iced lemonade were triumphantly produced by 'the maid'. After the game the guests repaired to the house for drinks. This gross colonial simulacrum of upper-middle-class England seems so bizarre today that I find myself wondering whether it really happened or if it is only a scene from some pre-war film I saw.

The family entertained. The centrepiece was the rum-punch gathering of friends on the veranda late on Sunday mornings, 'after church', as some of the guests would claim, though none of them had darkened a church's doorstep for years. My parents rarely did. I, however, was often sent on Sundays to represent the family. My very dear friend and surrogate older sister, Doris Lopez, who lived with us for a while, sang in the St Luke's choir. I had been confirmed and knew the Anglican catechism by heart, but can't say that its formalities produced anything like a spiritual experience.

Sunday morning veranda talk was a distinctive genre: a melange of politics, social affairs, gossip and scandals embroidered with sexual innuendos. They were a sophisticated crowd, a Kingston 'set' familiar with the ways of the world of which Jamaican country people would have disapproved. But as a small boy I drank in this inconsequential chatter with rapt attention. Sex hovered tantalizingly at its edges.

For a year or two I joined a Christian youth group run by Christian Endeavour, one of the many American evangelical organizations. I had been baptized and liked singing hymns at church, but I had no strong religious convictions. However, by this time, chasing girls as I was, I was also prepared to chase God. We used to travel in a bus to small towns and villages around Kingston where Revivalist meetings were held and the visitors would sometimes lead the services. Occasionally I was invited to give a talk or to preach. Responding no doubt to what I could see around me, I frequently addressed the social themes of the poverty and oppression of the people and asked whether this was really God's design for them. Not quite what was required. The episode didn't last long, but it took me to places and introduced me to the sort of people most of my family had never seen or met.

When I was young we played elaborate imaginary games loosely based on the last cowboy story or Hollywood romantic action film we had seen, with its Oriental hordes and harems to which the girls in the group were willingly recruited. We went to the cinema religiously on Saturdays, out partying in groups, often to one another's parentally well-supervised parties, with a lot of dancing. There existed a surprisingly eclectic touch of middle-class American adolescent culture. We waltzed, jitterbugged to big-band swing, mamboed to Latin rhythms and slow-jived and wound our hips in sexually suggestive ways to Jamaican music. There was a lot of early sexual experimentation, both in the dancing and the post-party snogging, more purposeful as time passed and puberty advanced. My name was coupled with that of several young ladies, but none of these turned out to be serious or long-lasting.

Sex never surfaced as an overt topic of conversation or instruction in our family. Elaborate strategies were deployed to skirt around the subject. Most of what I knew about sex – including a lot of misinformation – I picked up from the garbled chatter of school friends, so I was sexually pretty miseducated. More significantly, I experienced my family and home as, to all intents and purposes, having somehow bypassed sex. My parents were middle-aged and I could not imagine them making love. They seemed too socially driven, too preoccupied with rowing about money and status, to have time for any of that nonsense! My brother was twelve years older than me, in his twenties by the time I was an adolescent. But because of his restricted social life he never seemed to have brought girls home and, as far as I knew, may never have had a sexual relationship until he went to university in the US. My sister was more adventurous; she and her school friends talked about and fraternized with boys. However, she brought few eligible young men to the house either. So there were no charted pathways for the youngest – male – child.

I dated some of the young women in my friendship network. We went to Saturday afternoon matinees, snogged on the balcony, then to the ice-cream parlour for gigantic, syrupy American sundaes and a lot of flirting and fiddling around. Only one or two of these developed into something more serious. The women who interested me rarely met my parents because only the daughters of family friends – whom I mostly didn't fancy – were invited to the house on special social occasions, like a birthday or weekend parties. The women I liked belonged to a fundamentally different order of social life from that characterized by my family. They were a guilty secret. Not a good way to make a start.

I am trying to describe something other than the usual restraints, evasions and boundaries, particularly about sex, common among respectable Jamaican families. A double standard prevailed where much more was understood than was ever said or acknowledged, but in which everyone knowingly colluded. This was a system my male friends learned to negotiate without difficulty. I sometimes think of it as being at the heart of the secret bonds between middle-class Jamaican men and their mothers!

My family scene, however, seemed to be something more: emotionally drained, lacking in bodily or sexual texture or energy. I don't think I ever heard the physical aspects of sex directly referred to in our house. Certainly no one took me aside for a chat about the birds and the bees. It was as if my parents had no conception of what it was like to have a young, male adolescent under their roof. I must have started masturbating around this time. But when my mother discovered this she consulted not me, but the English family doctor, Dr McCrindle, who lived in the dark, shuttered house next door, and on whose advice I was duly circumcised!

Such was the ethos of my immediate family. I can't recall a time – although who knows? – when I experienced this social arrangement as right and harmonious, or as a haven in which, by rights, I belonged. There was a family joke that the first time my sister saw me as a baby, she is reputed to have asked, 'Where did you get this coolie baby from?' 'Coolie' is the degrading term which used to be common in Jamaica to refer to impoverished, brown Indian peddlers. I began to feel and behave more and more like an inside-outsider, 'the coolie of my family'. As in many self-fulfilling prophecies, I acquired an overwhelming sense of being 'out of place', which is the brilliant title that Edward Said gave his autobiography. I was labelled by my parents – as Said was – 'the naughty one'.

My disaffiliation from my family can be charted along a number of vectors which, in sum, constitute the story of my early life. At the same time, there were occasions when I felt conscious of – and drawn to – that other, darker Jamaica of the multitude. These turned particularly on its sounds, which operated not only 'out there' but inside me too.

The black Jamaican sounds that attracted me were, emphatically, from *elsewhere*, from another Jamaica I didn't inhabit and that was not mine: drumming in the countryside, rising up out of the hills and valleys around the towns; religious music, people singing Baptist, or Moody and Sankey, Christian hymns in the Revivalist and Pentecostal churches, but in that 'African' way, the voices getting deeper and deeper, slower and slower, the rhythms more grounded, closer to the earth.

There's one memory which still holds me. My grandmother lived in a house in Old Harbour right next to a Pentecostal church. My father's family was divided by religious affiliation, part Catholic, part Anglican. My grandfather, who died before I was born, had converted to Catholicism. So on Sunday mornings the members of the family set off to their respective churches. We'd return to my grandmother's house – a place I absolutely adored because it was so different from the middle-class milieu of our Kingston family home – to a lavish, welcoming lunch. The house was small and Victorian-colonial. It had verandas on two sides, framed photographs on the tables, antimacassars over the chairs and a piano in the drawing room. There was little income, so it was modestly furnished and quite small. It was situated in a poor part of the island, away from the more immediately alluring north coast. The south of Jamaica is flat and dry and dusty. But I found the house an open and loving place to be, filled with passing friends who stopped off on their way to Kingston and many neighbours too, enlivened by the stories and gossip of my aunts. It offered a bountiful hospitality over which my grandmother, 'Mammy Hall', presided. I remember after all these years her nut-brown face breaking into a chuckle. I am privileged, since her death, to wear her wedding ring in memory of her.

I never figured out where my many aunts slept. My Aunt Iris, who worked at the post office where the main highway and the road to the south-coast fishing village met, would often be tempted to climb into the back seat of a friend's roadster and simply take off for Kingston to spend a few days with us.

Aunt Gerry took on the supervision of many of the domestic tasks when my grandmother became too frail. My grandmother had built a small, two-room school in the backyard next to the mango trees and taught children from the locality, preparing them for secondary school. She opened the school when she was nineteen and was still teaching spelling to a selected few children on her back veranda when she was past a hundred. Aunt Gerry also took charge of my cousin Clare's education, successfully guiding and mentoring her through Immaculate Conception High School, one of the renowned Jamaican elite girls' schools; to college in the US; through her entry as a nun into the Franciscan Order and her astounding success as the headmistress of the school where she'd once been a pupil; and on to her work as a regional representative of the Caribbean and Latin America on the Franciscan Order's council, and her leadership of the Immaculate Conception convent community. Stern disciplinarian as Aunt Gerry was, and devout in her Catholic faith, she provided the household with moral backbone. This was allied with a loving and caring spirit.

My Aunt Mavis, who lived in Kingston and worked at my father's office, was a sophisticate – exotic, Spanish looks with black hair and plucked eyebrows, whose dressing table was covered with a thousand cosmetic preparations. She always arrived at Old Harbour by train from Kingston at the weekend with a basket full of specialities for the household, such as good honey or Syrian bread. For many years, she used to take me to the matinee movies at the Carib Cinema in town every Monday afternoon, before it became a somewhat more grown-up, regular Saturday afternoon haunt of my school friends and the site of their budding romantic explorations. I was raised on the great heartland of American popular cinema: musicals, romantic comedies, melodrama, films noirs, thrillers, the 'better' sort of westerns.

Aunt Ivy was reputed to be harum-scarum, and walked the little town a bit too freely for my grandmother's liking. But she knew and looked out for everyone and had a mischievous sense of humour and wicked smile which enlisted me with ease into her schemes.

Only one of my aunts, Aunt Ionie, was married. Her husband was Harry and they had two children, my cousins Gloria and Jimmy Sherlock. After they married they moved to Brooklyn for a while where the children were born. But Ionie had problems with her health and Harry's work wasn't secure, so they returned to Jamaica just before the First World War. Harry took up carpentry but died relatively young. We weren't close, although it seems that Ionie and Gerry got on well. By all accounts Ionie was devoted to her children and in difficult circumstances proved herself to be a good, resourceful mother.

Next door to us in Old Harbour the Pentecostal church would not convene until noon, so by the beginning of lunch the singing would be in full swing, starting quite high and energetic and gradually becoming slower, deeper, more rhythmic. In retrospect, I came to see that I'd been witnessing English Protestantism undergoing creolization, within earshot of my grandmother's home. Both the Anglican vicar and the Bostonian Jesuit priest were regulars at my grandmother's table, where the beautifully polished wood would groan with chicken and rice-and-peas and plantain. The rival vicars of Christ loaded up their plates with the tasty food and modestly consented to having their glasses refilled with my mother's potent rum punch, brought triumphantly from Kingston. Only two topics of conversation were forbidden at table by my grandmother: religion and the abdication of Edward VIII! Throughout lunch I would listen with one ear cocked to the sound of what I perceived as a distant Jamaica starting up right next door. I was perfectly aware of the contrast between the colonially inflected, creolized, Westernized manners and customs of the respectable, brown Jamaican 'country' family around the table, and this other Jamaica of the poor, rural folk – the latter represented by this deep, rhythmic, powerful religious wail of trouble and tribulation, raising its collective voice to the rafters.

By the time I was born in 1932, Jamaica and the Caribbean more generally were well advanced in the formal and informal prerequisites of breaking with colonialism. The close proximity of the other Jamaica, darker and less subservient to the sensibilities of colonial order, came to a head in public life in the labour rebellions of 1938, when it spilled over and threatened to destroy the social propriety which gave meaning to my family. Or so it seemed at the time. Jamaica was torn apart by insurrections which inaugurated the drive for self-determination and eventually Independence. That was when this other Jamaica publicly, dramatically asserted its presence.

The unrest of the late 1930s was the outcome of profound crises which had accumulated over many decades. Economic dependency and the exploitation of labour had done their inexorable work. In the eighteenth century the Jamaican plantocracy reaped the economic rewards. 'King Sugar' reigned supreme. But after Abolition in the 1830s West Indian sugar was increasingly replaced by reliance on the cheaper sugar beet. The British government paid the planters compensation for the loss of 'their' property – that is, the enslaved: a bounty for their acceptance of the end of slavery. The planters looked elsewhere for more profitable investment. Jamaica became an economic backwater. The development of the US-owned banana industry did something to revive its fortunes, but left the majority of the working population untouched. By the Depression of the 1930s, the living standards of the masses had collapsed and unemployment was rife. These devastating consequences erupted politically, driven by intensified trade-union activity and by general, deep-seated social discontent – conditions which formed the historical background to the labour rebellions of 1938.

By the 1930s economic dependency had become ruinous for the majority of ordinary Jamaicans. The Depression ravaged the country. Its immediate effects were evident everywhere, visible in the poor parts of Kingston, in the towns across the island and throughout the countryside. Banana disease and competition from other sugar suppliers threatened the two main exports. The sugar price had collapsed, and the downward trend seemed never to end. But once the right of workers to combine to defend their living standards had been conceded, the unions began to organize, especially in the docks, on the sugar estates and among the unemployed.

A number of different elements fused and condensed, in what we would now call a conjunctural crisis, which represented a step change in the evolution of the Jamaican state and quickened the pace of the Independence movement. It reached a high point in Jamaica but it was in fact a Caribbean-wide, regional phenomenon. I very much regret that so few Jamaicans in the diaspora today know much about it. It's fast fading from collective memory.

Around the world the tempo of anti-colonial struggle was quickening, and this had a radicalizing impact on the politically conscious social groupings on the island. Colonialism began for the first time to be openly identified as 'the enemy'. A black consciousness had begun to surface too, although only a minority spoke publicly of a race politics, and of its roots in slavery or in our African ancestry. However, across the metropolitan world the two previous decades had witnessed an escalation of anti-imperial activities and organizations in which West Indians were extensively – disproportionally, perhaps – involved, particularly in the UK, France and the US. The call for self-determination can now be seen as part of wider global developments which eventually brought the curtain down on the old empires and helped new nations into being; although we have to acknowledge that Anglo-Caribbean decolonization turned out to be a less radical, more limited and protracted process than anyone guessed at the time. But whatever the result, any astute observer could have seen that the events of 1938 gave warning of a political hurricane sweeping across the whole region. In Jamaica, as had been the case earlier with the struggles against slavery, popular resistance made the wheels of history turn faster.

In the US, for example, following the great migration of blacks from the Southern slave states to the cities and factories of the North, a host of Left, radical and black-pride movements sprang up, sponsoring a flood of activities, campaigns, organizations and publications in which West Indians played a significant part. Marcus Garvey took the United Negro Improvement Association (UNIA), which he had launched in Jamaica in August 1914, just as the First World War was breaking out, with him when he migrated to Harlem. His 'black independence' philosophy inspired the first African-American – or New World – mass political movement of modern times. Robert Hill, who has devoted so much of his life to researching Garvey's biography, papers and influence, is of the opinion that he produced 'the first felt sense of national consciousness', both in terms of a wider black nationalism and as a powerful element which has run through Jamaican – and Caribbean – politics.

This was matched by a host of different, politically diverse strands which developed in the Garvey years, including the black self-improvement legacy of Booker T. Washington, the Pan-Africanism of figures like W. E. B. DuBois, the broad-based, reformist National

Association for the Advancement of Colored People and a variety of worker-, socialist- and Marxist-Leninist-oriented currents, as well as the vibrant cultural movements of the Harlem Renaissance. The Caribbean presence in these political organizations was enormous. Caribbean politics was active in the diaspora. Domestic Jamaican politics could not remain immune from these developments, which shaped and radicalized political life back home. The events of 1938 marked the birth of modern Jamaican politics.

In 1938 lay the roots of Jamaica's political settlement, in the period leading up to and following the arrival of universal adult suffrage in 1944 and Independence in 1962. This is personified in the figures of Norman Manley, the People's National Party (PNP) leader, and Alexander Bustamante, the leader of the Jamaican Labour Party, the JLP. The dominant social forces which animated the new politics were composed of the coloured middle classes and a professional leadership elite, the small but industrially strong organized workers and the volatile mass of the urban poor and unemployed. The latter were more an underclass than a working class, defined primarily by permanent or serial unemployment and conditions of grinding poverty. They were black, of course, as the great majority of the poorer classes are in Jamaica: the multitude who were the social constituents of that other Jamaica, and for whom Independence brought precious little material or social advancement.

The political system which had been inaugurated in the struggles of the late 1930s has had a remarkably long life. Jamaica has been, until recently, one of the most stable two-party systems in the world. Many believe it has outlived its usefulness with the waning of the nationalist moment and the dawn of the era of globalization. But it persists. It proved itself an effective system, even with its many limitations. The strength and weakness of Independence were in part attributable to this structure. The polarization of the political field into the two nationalist parties, the PNP and the JLP, paradoxically worked to capture every social group within the political system. Political life in Jamaica seemed to be comprehensively representative. The PNP, founded in 1938, was pro-self-government, social-democratic, worker-oriented but –

its dominant tendency – a reformist party, strongly influenced by Fabian traditions. For a short while it held within it a powerful, neo-Marxist minority which in 1954, in the climate of the Cold War, the leadership expelled. The JLP was a pro-self-government, free-market, business-oriented and populist party of the Right.

Both had middle-class support (the PNP from government and public employees; the JLP from small and big business); both had popular class support (the PNP more among the urban and organized workers; the JLP among the dockworkers and in the countryside); both had rival trade unions; both had a middle-class leadership (although the JLP leaders tended to be drawn from black professionals, while the PNP was stronger among those of the brown middle class); and, astonishingly, the two parties were led by two brown men who were cousins, although they were very different characters. Norman Manley, the father figure of the struggle for Jamaican independence, was an Oxford-educated Rhodes Scholar (he was to sit on my own scholarship committee) and brilliant barrister. He had studied law in London and married his white cousin, Edna, the sculptress, who in later years became a formidable, pioneering figure in the vanguard of the Jamaican artistic renaissance. In age, Norman loosely belonged to my parents' generation. But his brown middle-class 'country' family clearly had closer connections to England than mine, and he was significantly grander in landed status. Bustamante had grown up in Central America, where there had long been a flourishing Jamaican diaspora, and was a poorly educated but politically astute populist demagogue. Indeed, initially Bustamante had been a PNP member; but, having been jailed for three years for political subversion, on his release in 1943 he broke with the PNP and founded the JLP.

This political arrangement in Jamaica was cross-cut by deep social divisions, based on profound differences of wealth, colour, class and education, marking the unbridgeable gulf – within both parties – between the lived worlds of their middle-class and professional support on the one hand, and their popular base on the other. To some degree, these socio-economic underpinnings came to override political ideology. Increasingly large numbers of the poor and the unemployed, whether urban or rural, fell out of the bottom of the system and were effectively disenfranchised, represented by neither the JLP nor the PNP.

Here, paradoxically, vernacular lived cultures spoke more powerfully than – and as a substitute for – formal politics. Popular religion and urban culture became proxy symbolic resources in which poverty, social discontent, people's disaffiliation from the system, class interests, racialized divisions and political differences found expression. The 'revolution' which Independence set in motion was cultural, not political. The slow, subterranean emergence of a black Afro-centric consciousness, of the Rastafarians, of Black Power and of reggae, was the principal vehicle of this profound transformation.

Thus, in the end, those marginal to the political system were harnessed to the formal parties through informal rather than conventional means: through religious affiliation, the politicization of rival, and increasingly militarized, 'garrison' no-go areas, petty and organized crime, gang and community loyalties and the 'Don' systems of patronage.

The convergence of the formal institutions of the state – the two leading political parties most of all – on the one hand and the interlocking fiefdoms of the local area leaders on the other was characteristic of Jamaica's modern political evolution. Informal practices of clientelism had preceded the period of universal suffrage, but since the 1940s they flourished inside the evolving political system, and underwrote the emergence of machine politics. Local Dons organized political enclaves among the urban poor. They dispensed justice and looked after 'their own' people. They represented an informal system by which scarce resources – material, social, political – were distributed to the dispossessed, and political power was localized through an elaborate system of personal allegiances. Neighbourhoods turned into armed garrisons and political violence came to be embedded in the organization of daily life. In this way political allegiances took on a primordial quality and Jamaican politics were fought out, often literally, on the street.

In the 1970s political violence intensified, particularly during Michael Manley's first period as Prime Minister from 1972 to 1980. Michael Manley was Norman's son; he was one of our greatest and most charismatic prime ministers of the new generation and a leading figure in Third World politics. He had been an older contemporary of mine at Jamaica College, in his final year when I arrived in 1943. During his period of office the easy availability of weapons accelerated, although many believed that the guns were distributed with the connivance of the CIA in order to create unrest and to derail Manley's political authority. The rapid circulation of firearms proved a crucial ingredient in the social and political collapse of these years. The widespread practice of criminal patronage constituted the seamy underside of the 'above-ground' political system.

Eventually the links between mainstream and underground political traditions were stabilized, mainly through the connections between the Dons and the government. As the former became more independent, it was difficult to tell which was the leading player. Even so, these connections have not vanished from the political landscape and they continue to send regular waves of disturbance through official Jamaican political society.

The emergence of this system of universal, mass politics coincided with my own growing up. I had inside me the sensibilities of the colonial order of things. But for my generation, following 1938, in no way could the colonial system represent our future. We could only perceive it as an unwanted impediment. Thus the events of 1938 were formative for my future intellectual and personal life. Much of the rest of my life in Jamaica was about struggling to erase and overcome the gap between my early childhood within the enclave of my family and the tumultuous world of Jamaican society and politics outside, from which the former was designed to insulate me. If 1938 symbolized the creation of modern Jamaican politics, I was of the generation which was born to inherit the new world the rebellions had inaugurated. This new political world marshalled the historical conditions in which the very idea of politics could enter my life, and enabled me and my generation to imagine a sovereign future.

Although I was much too young at the time to understand what was happening, I can see that I was formed by 1938: I came to be of that political generation. Generation is more than chronology. It's symbolic rather than literal, relating as much to a shared experience, a common vision, or thinking within the same 'problem space' as it does to a mere date of birth.

I came to England in 1951, three years after the arrival of the *Empire Windrush* with its cargo of post-war West Indian migrants. I was of that generation too, although I was not strictly speaking a migrant. They were working people who came to find employment, while I was a scholarship boy who came to study. But so far as the broader experience of migration was concerned we belonged to the same historical moment, although my mother would have fainted at the very thought.

In UK terms I was of roughly the same generation as those Caribbean intellectuals, writers and poets whom I got to know in London in the 1950s: Vic Reid, Edgar Mittelholzer, Andrew Salkey, Kamau Brathwaite, George Lamming, Sam Selvon, John Hearne, V. S. Naipaul, Wilson Harris – all pivotal names in the creation of modern West Indian literature; and painters like Ronald Moody, Aubrey Williams and Frank Bowling. Most of that generation were, like me, products of a 'good' colonial education, but many still harboured a 'small-island' outlook on the world. As George Lamming accurately but paradoxically put it, many of us first became *West Indian* in London.

In the Jamaican context, and notwithstanding the closeness of our births, I was a generation older than cultural icons like Rex Nettleford, also a Rhodes Scholar, founder and lead dancer of the Jamaica Dance Company, trade-union educator, author of the famous text on black identity *Mirror Mirror*, Vice-Chancellor of the University of the West Indies and charismatic figure in the early post-Independence years. And, in much the same way, I was two generations older than the radicalized cohort of the 1970s, such as the group who clustered around the political paper *Abeng*. This was the generation which embraced foreign resident Marxist critics, of whom Ken Post was probably the most conspicuous; radicalized young socialist activists within the party system, who included D. K. Duncan; politico-intellectuals like Don Robotham; and future critical scholars who came out of this ferment, like Barry Chevannes, Robert Hill, Rupert Lewis and Trevor Munroe. Munroe, a political scientist and author of an early study of Jamaican decolonization, founded the most prominent of the Marxist-Leninist groupings, the Workers Party of Jamaica (WPJ). Despite their real differences, he remained throughout a close confidant of Michael Manley's, and after the collapse of the Soviet Union and dissolution of the WPJ was appointed a PNP senator. There were, too, the younger figures among whom one could include Tony Bogues and David Scott.

The year 1938, then, locates me generationally. When I was young I was often the youngest in my class. Now I am almost always the oldest person in the room. It doesn't matter. Growing old happens.

However, my generational location continues to be a source of misattribution. I find that younger people are often tempted, anachronistically, to push my chronology forwards, making me one of their contemporaries, but separating me from the time of my real historical context. They think of me as a post-colonial, as, politically, 'a product of '68', of the student movement and of the counter-culture. Really, I was formed as one of the last colonials, and politically I was a child of 1956: of Suez and Hungary, of the collapse of the Communist dream, of the Cold War and of post-war decolonization, and thus of an earlier and very different kind of 'New Left'. The distinction between one conjuncture and another matters profoundly to me. Essentially, unlike most Afro-Caribbeans of whatever generation now living in the British diaspora, my early formation was within – not 'post-' – colonialism. I came to England as a young colonial, when Winston Churchill was Prime Minister, and I had lived in Britain eleven years before Jamaica became independent.

So although 1938 defines me generationally, in a Caribbean frame, it does so in uncanny ways. Hence the feeling of being anachronistic. Or, as James Clifford puts it with insight, it signals the syndrome of recognizing oneself, strangely, as 'becoming historical'.

Why uncanny? The labour rebellions of 1938 worked their way into my psyche, and in the years that followed unsettled me in difficult, unexpected ways. I was only six at the time. But in retrospect I can see that for me, and for my family, their imprint was on us all. These seemingly distant events weren't so distant after all. In displaced form, they entered our household, and entered too my inner life.

Even though there was much I couldn't know about the insurrection, I *was* aware that something significant was happening. It turned out to be the first important political event I can recall, and so it stands as a sort of symbolic political birthdate for me. Of course, there was an obvious distance between the events and me. I was the son of a coloured Jamaican middle-class professional family, the members of which, like all my parents' class, had learned to avert their eyes from the plight, needs, aspirations and demands of the mass of black people around them. I didn't understand how my family – subalterns in the old colonial order – had invested so many of their hopes and fantasies elsewhere. Negative and regressive, my family lagged behind even their close friends and peers who, though they didn't relish the prospect, could already enviously glimpse – and had reluctantly begun preparing themselves for – a possible future as the successor class, the new post-Independence ruling elite. Which indeed they duly became. By way of a sort of negative realism, they had grudgingly grasped how to respond to the coming changes. My family did not, and in this respect were not one but *two* generations out of date.

On the day the rioting peaked I remember my father – in his quiet way, I imagine, divided internally by contending questions and loyalties – coming home at lunchtime from the office with news about the mayhem that was rumoured to be unfolding in downtown Kingston. Stores, schools and businesses were closing early. There were stories of looting, a sense of impending crisis in the air and a pervasive atmosphere of panic. Wild accounts rippled through the city about 'mobs on the loose', which struck alarm in the hearts of middle-class Kingstonians. Rastas whose unspeakable antics had put the fear of God into middle-class households were often dispatched to the city's Bellevue Asylum for what was declared to be seditious talk. Just a few years earlier Alexander Bedward, the prophetic Revivalist preacher, had been incarcerated there for precisely just such an offence. Now it was reported that the inmates had escaped confinement and were at the fence engaging passers-by in bizarre, apocalyptic disputations. Respectable society was transfixed by the spectre of a world turned upside down. Their world *was* indeed crumbling; the old order was passing. It would never be the same again. Was this, it began to be asked, some sort of final reckoning, the unfolding of a tropical *Götterdämmerung*?

It's difficult, looking back at these events, for me to get everything in a proper historical focus. On the one hand, my most immediate experience was of my family's fear of the riots as a flashpoint of militant disorder. But on the other, what had seemed like the premonition of imminent social collapse turned out, as I subsequently came to see things, as inaugurating a world of new possibilities, a world in which blackness itself came to function as a resource for the future. These contrary impulses exist in my memory as a kind of double-exposure. Even so, my childlike ignorance notwithstanding, 1938 was the significant historical event in giving form to my future, disaffiliating me from the values of my parents.

I vaguely became aware of Garveyism a little later, although I didn't know much about Garvey himself and it was a long time before I came to appreciate his influence. I knew of Edelweiss Park, where Garvey's UNIA had established itself. I'd occasionally encountered Garveyite publications. I came to understand that Garveyism had connections with larger Pan-African aspirations, and a philosophy of black independence, pride and self-improvement.

This certainly wasn't part of my family's world because they in no sense identified themselves with the black masses or with an African diaspora. Indeed 'Back to Africa' was a source of ridicule around Kingston middle-class dinner tables. It took me some time to understand the 'Back to Africa' message and its considerable resonance, not only among the urban poor and the unemployed, who were at the forefront of the industrial struggles of the late 1930s, but also among sections of the colour-conscious nationalist lower-middle classes as well. I'm thinking here of the affiliations to this kind of sensibility apparent in Una Marson, for example, who was to become an important journalist and BBC broadcaster and who was active in the League of Coloured Peoples. She was the sister of Mrs Marson-Jones, whose primary school I attended. Although I couldn't have been aware of it at the time, pockets of black consciousness were there, in the air we breathed.

'Back to Africa' was one expression of a larger mentality, not always consciously articulated and largely invisible to middle-class Jamaica: more vernacular, more syncretic, more African-derived, reflecting the outlook of poor, black Jamaicans. This vernacular culture inevitably posed, challengingly, the troubled issue of the 'African' character of Jamaican folk culture: the extent of the African elements which had survived the Middle Passage – the route by which Africans were transported into captivity in the New World – into the creolized, racially mixed world of plantation and colony, and which were active in many areas of popular rural and urban life. Traces of this 'other' world persisted in customs, in folklore, in the lived worlds of folk religion, in celebrations around the life cycle, in Kumina and other traditional festivals and ceremonies, in practices of drumming and dancing, and in the spirit superstitions and the 'black magic' customs of obeah and pocomania. These mentalities were often fused with ecstatic Afro-Christian traditions, much like santeria, vodun and other religions of the oppressed in the Caribbean region.

This fusion of African, Christian and indigenous elements led to the formation of small Rastafarian communities. Reputedly the first of these, the Pinnacle, founded by Leonard Howell in 1940, was broken up and dispersed by the local militia in 1953, shortly after I'd left for England. These scattered communities, where the Rastas with their locks spoke and 'reasoned' in apocalyptic language based on a counter-reading of the Old Testament, began to appear in small numbers everywhere.

When I was a boy there was a Rastafarian settlement by the old railway station, near what was in fact a refuse dump, known as the Dungle. These were the days before Rastafarianism became a force within Jamaican national consciousness. Rastas were regarded by polite society as menacing, excluded outcasts roaming the streets, begging. Some of them would occasionally wander into the middle-class residential areas, on the lookout for small acts of charity. They smoked ganja which – it was said – turned their eyes red and drove them crazy. With what was regarded at the time as an unfathomable logic, they refused to cut their hair. My mother would call me in to the safety of the house if one of them came begging at the gate. In fact they never caused any trouble. Peace and love, rather than murdering the middle classes in their bedrooms, was what they were about. But they came to be perceived as the most terrifyingly visible proof of the nameless, poor black threat that pressed in on middle-class Jamaica. The transition which Jamaica was undergoing was profoundly worrying for the class in which I was brought up. These were the classic circumstances for the projection of social anxiety onto what we subsequently called 'folk devils', and for generating an entire curriculum of moral panic.

Actually, these symbolic investments were not as far away from the palm- and bougainvillea-fringed gardens of Kingston suburbs as I had once imagined. I've already referred to the roles in the household of Edith, the cook, and of Cecil, the gardener, who went about their work for my mother with, I suspect, quite contrary, unthinkable reveries occupying their minds. There were also obeah practitioners in the poor areas of the city and in the surrounding hill villages. On the fringes of conventional Christian religion, already itself creolized, a whole world of deeply syncretic religious practices flourished. Even today, the neighbourhoods of the Kingston underclass are sometimes only a few roads away from the wealthier suburbs, which is why the seriously rich – of whom there are many – have migrated further out of reach, up into the mist-covered Blue Mountains which look down over the city. The sounds of drumming from the shacks buried in the ravines easily reach the bedrooms of upper St Andrews.

However, as I was growing up all this certainly didn't work for me as a form of racial consciousness, although it was difficult to miss the differences between the lifestyle and material stability of my own family and that of the urban underclasses, living in the tin-roofed, corrugated-zinc hovels and tenement yards of the city, or of the poor peasant people scraping a living in the remote hill villages and taking whatever they could grow down to market.

Yet in the 1940s and 1950s the heart of the 'other Jamaica', culturally, was rural Jamaica, folk Jamaica, the Jamaica of smallholders, peasant cultivators, landless workers and the rural poor. This world, it seemed to me, with its rich, complex and sometimes obscure religious and cultural affiliations, was not only not yet politicized but barely visible. George Lamming claimed that the great achievement of the West Indian novel was to bring 'the people's speech, the organic music of the earth' into fiction. This is an important way of thinking about the Caribbean. I loved the rural areas and always spent my summers in the countryside. But for long it had no collective political expression. Half the population lived in the environment of Kingston and in the other big towns, and during my years in Jamaica official politics seemed blind to the lived realities of the countryside.

I used to look forward to the anticipation awakened by heading out of Kingston up into the interior, over the Blue Mountains. You had to drive past steeply terraced slopes, roughly built settlements and shacks where it was hard to imagine how anyone kept body and soul together, down the other side to the coconut-tree-fringed beaches of the north coast. There was always a tempting glimpse through the trees of the rolling swell of the Caribbean Sea.

I spent much of the summer holidays in Port Antonio, on the

north-east corner of the island, once a flourishing shipping town where my mother had been born. From there one drove along through St Ann's Bay and Ocho Rios, past the newly designed American-style hotels along the coast, on through the jewel of an old eighteenth-century town and former slaving port, Falmouth, already falling apart with decay and neglect, to the other busy, 'cosmopolitan' tourist capital, Montego Bay. The memories of the landscape stay with me.

In the 1930s, the coexistence of these distinct cultures posed the question of the African, slave and creole origins of Jamaican identity, matters which couldn't yet be articulated within the discourses of the official Jamaican nationalism that was crystallizing at the same time.

It was these undercurrents which rose to the surface in 1938, the year that gave me the feeling of being consigned to a messy 'in-between' space. I couldn't then see that in this lay the potential for a new political rationale and the potential, too, for a history that I might yet make my own.

I felt estranged from the structures of disavowal and hypocrisy which flourished in my family, and from the way my parents strove to be something socially they manifestly were not. I felt an acute embarrassment at what I regarded as my parents' cringing display of a desire for social recognition, coupled with an inner rage which I found impossible to explain. In this context, I became sensitive to the psychic repression which underpinned the multiple, finely observed, racialized exclusions on which my family and class sense of complacency was grounded. I resented being invited to identify with their fantasy relationship to colonial dependency. When I look at photographs of myself at about seven or eight, I see a sullen, cross, unhappy, rebellious little boy clutching an air rifle who looks, frankly, depressed, and planning to shoot something or someone if the opportunity arose!

I'm not sure what my siblings made of it all. George, my brother, faced considerable social restrictions. As I've said, he suffered seriously from poor eyesight and he eventually became blind. This made him an unlikely model of teenage behaviour for my family.

He was the clever and much-beloved one – a kind, gentle, thoughtful, rather dreamy soul who, because of his eyesight, often looked into the middle distance as if in fond hope of catching sight of something there. He wrote short stories and poetry. He finally went to the US to study agricultural chemistry and worked for a while at Caymanas sugar estate until he went blind. Dependent as he was obliged to be, he was never in a position to be assertive and he was, in any case, by instinct conservative and compliant.

My sister, Patricia, on the other hand, had a turbulent adolescence – always rowing with my mother, although hardly ever about what I see now as the larger social matters. My mother made no secret of the fact that she only really respected strong men and took a poor view of women because they didn't really have any power. Watching her struggle every morning to tame Pat's resistant, curly hair was like observing a symbolic punishment ritual.

I've written about my sister's life before and I don't find it easy to elaborate further on a painful experience. Pat, five years my senior, began a relationship with a black student from another Caribbean island studying medicine at the University College of the West Indies. He was from a highly respectable black background which later far out-distanced my family in public achievement and social position. But my parents, or my mother, objected to his colour and to his origins. And my mother simply put a stop to it. A few months later Pat had a serious mental breakdown from which, in truth, over the many intervening years she has made only a tentative recovery.

As for myself, I suspect that I identified in a simple way with the poor and discontented, and I'd probably picked up enough about the political situation from anxious adult talk to know that, in the aftermath, 'my class' was in serious trouble. Major political upheavals threatened and social transformation would almost certainly follow. But of what sort, and with what consequences for people like them, they – and I – had no idea. Over the years, the labour rebellions of 1938 and their aftermath forced me to ask for the first time who I really was and where I belonged between 'the two Jamaicas'. I couldn't even apprehend the aspirations which the rebellions expressed. It was impossible to articulate my confused feelings in my family circle, even had I understood them better. I could not find a language in which to unravel the contradictions or to confront my family with what I really thought of their values, behaviour and aspirations. But, in one way or another, the times represented a crisis for people like my family, with their pretensions, self-delusions and fantasies.

My family, loyal, middle-class, brown colonials that they were, were schooled in the philanthropic gesture. My mother's instinct was to fall back on a condescending largesse, *de haut en bas*, towards the poor. In the fixed relationships of the old estate world, everyone knew and was still in their appointed place. What she could not tolerate was 'radical' talk about changing their social conditions as a way of dealing with their poverty. Instead, the middle classes, trapped between the brown elite and the black masses, viewed with bewildered horror the growth of a black consciousness, the rising tide of class discontent, the spectre of the poor and unemployed 'on the move', the spreading suspicion of inferior 'coloured people' like us, the palpable hostility towards the 'mother country', the general revulsion against the routine oppressions of a racialized colonialism and the growing demand for self-government. They knew things would never be the same again. It was in effect a death warrant for our complicit, perverse version of subordination. In the wake of 1938 my mother used to reflect, gloomily, 'Our Jamaica is fading away.' Our Jamaica? Which one, I wondered, was that?

I am not sure how common among my peers such feelings would have been. If I'm honest I think they would have recognized them. But many of my generation, I suspect, would tell a rather different story, reflecting on a happier experience presided over by a benign, loving and over-indulgent mother and a strong, rather authoritarian but much-respected father. My experience was very different, and more troubled.

My school friends – clever scholarship youths of all colours, shades and backgrounds – were middle-class too, but drawn from a wider spectrum, mirroring the less colour-hierarchical Jamaica that was emerging. But I wasn't allowed to bring many of them home: only those considered by my family equals in social status and of the 'right' colour. 'Not the sort of people you should be fraternizing with!' Well, I understood that code all right.

'Liberate yourself from mental slavery', Bob Marley later exhorted his fellow Jamaicans. But in my case, in my particular colonial-family situation, this did not come easily. I recall one symptomatic occasion which offers a clue as to my inner turmoil and confusion.

Much as in India expatriate families used to retire to the hill stations during the hottest season, my parents retreated from the sweltering heat of Kingston for two weeks every summer to a hotel in the cooler, sometimes misty and rainy environs of Christiana, a small hill town near Mandeville, which is the preferred area of today's returnees – no doubt because the weather reminds them of England. I was never included in this party but went instead with my grandmother to Port Antonio to stay with my godfather, Mr Geddes, custos of the parish, who owned a small estate with three plots of land. The office of custos, a remnant of medieval England which had found its way to Jamaica, was an important post in the localities which obliged the holder to carry out certain civic duties. There I used to roam about the wildest parts of the estate for hours, alone with my home-made catapult, aiming unsuccessfully – but in an inexplicable rage – at birds or anything else that moved.

Sometimes I was allowed to join my parents on one weekend of their holiday at the Savoy Hotel. One day I was playing with Peter, the son of a white expatriate couple who were also guests at the hotel, and I found myself uncertain what to call him. I couldn't read the class/colour code in play. At home the servants always addressed me, son of the household, with the respectful prefix, 'Mas' (short for Master): 'Mas Stuart'; or when addressing my father, 'Mas Herman'. Although Peter's parents were in the bar drinking with mine, I felt that, since he clearly belonged to a superior class or race, I should call him 'Mas Peter'. Uncertain what to do, I consulted my mother. She told me in withering terms what a social faux pas this would be. 'Of course not,' she said with exasperation, 'they're just like us!' But I knew they weren't. I can only remember wanting the ground to open and devour me. It was one of those moments that has stayed with me, condensing all that I found troubling and inexplicable about the life I was obliged to live.

In fact, you didn't need specific incidents to remind you of how the system worked. You couldn't miss it. Jamaica is actually a very small place, and although the interior can be remote, no corner of society, except perhaps the deepest recesses of the Blue Mountains or the inhospitable Cockpit Country, ever fell out of the public field of vision. So I was familiar with the impact which a racialized colonialism had made on the lives of ordinary Jamaicans. But I lived in a bustling, multi-class, multicoloured colonial metropolis with all its intersecting social and spatial lines and carefully constructed gradients; and in the more run-down parts of the city, the extensive poverty and unemployment of the black majority were in constant evidence.

In these ways I slowly began to piece together the true diversity and historical complexity of the nation: its deep economic and class divisions; its conflicted cultural orientations; the elaborate structure of racial and colour differences; the intricate patterns of social and cultural creolization evident in so much of our lives. I remember the traditional Anglican ethos and ritual of the official service commemorating Armistice Day in Kingston Cathedral. The contingent of cadet corps boys from my school, with me as sergeant in command, were all in uniform, on parade, alongside the resident Sherwood Forest regiment and the Scouts and naval cadets; and also the straggling followers, barefoot boys from breakaway churches and pocomania yards of the poor areas only a short distance away. The social disjunctures of this cameo have, for some reason, remained with me.

Jamaica was a land of ruts and potholes, literally and socially. How could one miss the social chasms which cross-cut Jamaican society, between the well off and the poor, the governed majority and the agents of colonial governmentality, the country people and the coloured city professionals, the cardboard tenement yards of downtown Kingston and the mown lawns and trimmed hedges of uptown St Andrews? I couldn't anticipate the later debate as to whether there were two (white, black) or three (white, brown, black) Jamaicas. But inevitably I began to feel the indigenous vibrations, vaguely to identify with the anti-colonial commitments which were becoming prevalent among the excluded classes and which were also pulsing through the wider society, and starting to find a sympathetic echo among the intellectual, politically advanced older boys of my own school.

All this became easier when I began to put my sense of alienation into practice in the form of telling my family as little as I could get away with about my private life or what I was doing. I maintained instead a stubborn, grumpy, minimalist response when asked. I increasingly withdrew, emotionally and physically, spending more time outside in dubious places, engaged in dubious activities. I suppose I regarded this strategy of emotional withdrawal as a way of punishing them. I adopted a rebellious, adolescent style; and, even more traitorously, picked up on counter-reverberations in the wider world around me, ultimately identifying politically with the emerging social forces which sought to overturn precisely those values my family stood for and embodied. In these circumstances my bicycle became the agent of my liberation!

I don't think I'm short-circuiting too much in endeavouring to read my own family situation in terms of Jamaica's momentous history, which certainly had strange repercussions in my private, domestic world. But I sometimes wonder if more was going on. I wonder if inside my family life this displaced larger history was in some way being restaged, in its own theatre, with its own disturbing psychic properties.

Maybe, though, this is how these two processes – the historical, in the conventional sense, and my own subjective development – have come together in my mind retrospectively. Yet looking back, it feels as if 1938 has come to represent the opening skirmish in my personal war of position with my family, where I was uneasily torn between the enclave of the colonial coloured family and the tumultuous world of black Jamaica against which my familial enclave was designed to insulate me.

These childhood experiences represented for me a slow disentangling of threads, a process of disenchantment and disaffiliation, pointing towards a radically different path ahead: an unpleasant experience, replete with gaps, contradictions, evasive silences, guilt and rage. But also a journey with only one possible destination: out. James Joyce, in his own situation, recommended 'silence, exile and cunning'. Indeed.

I felt like a sort of internal exile. Of course, I enjoyed many family occasions, although I often found them too formal and emotionally chilly. But I increasingly withdrew from everyday family life. I began to experience my social milieu as self-deluding, over-defensive and pathologically extreme, its conception of its social position a fantasy. This wasn't my world. I fundamentally didn't belong to it. I couldn't believe in it and in time I didn't want to.

I remember there being occasional open confrontations, although never a conclusive reckoning. But it soon became painfully obvious that I was seriously critical of, and detached from, the whole familial baggage. Some years later, after I'd left Jamaica and created for myself an independent life, a memorable showdown occurred. But the instigator was Catherine, not me.

During Catherine's first, difficult visit to Jamaica in 1965, after we were married, the whole collective family project of 'keeping up' in the class/colour game was the occasion of an angry but splendid exchange of fire between Catherine and my mother. We were having supper, served as usual by a maid dressed, as 'Miss Jessie' always insisted, in white-starched cap and apron, standing silently behind her chair. As usual they behaved as though she didn't exist. My mother was complaining (again) about the 'servant problem', and (again) about how 'the younger ones, these days, don't want to work' and were inclined to be 'uppity'. Catherine exploded. 'You can't talk like that about people who are standing right there serving you and listening to what you're saying about them!' My mother had never been spoken to like that in our house, especially by a nineteen-year-old woman, the daughter of a white Baptist minister, who'd just married her precious son! Relations between them subsequently improved but were never really restored.

By this time I had come to see that my shift of attitude existed in the undertow of the larger political realignment of pre-Independence Jamaica towards not a more equal, but a somewhat more inclusive and racially mixed society. This transformation opened up new horizons for a clever, bookish, isolated, coloured middle-class colonial youth like me, hungry for new experiences but unsettled in 'the castle of my skin'.

I came to understand that my world, too, was constrained by those multiple grids of class, status, colour, subordination and dependency which were the lifeblood of the subaltern middle-class imaginary. What I lacked was the perspective to understand the psychic costs of being brought up, at a moment of momentous historical change, in a family devoted to these anachronistic, deeply contradictory aspirations and identifications. Looking back, it seems to me that the larger social tensions of the nation were displaced onto, and re-enacted in, the 'little theatre' of family life.

Following my sister's breakdown I used to visit her in hospital on the heartbreaking days between bouts of shock treatment, watching her terror of anticipation before treatment, her distress as her personality was remoulded afterwards. In later life she not only devotedly looked after my mother, my father and my brother until their deaths, but she came to idealize and identify with our family and its past, which are still the memories she lives by. Regrettably, this has erected a difficult emotional barrier between us. She must, I feel, have *known*.

As it happened, I was reading Freud and psychoanalysis at the time and was beginning to have a harebrained scheme about doing medicine at university in order to become a psychoanalyst – a crazy notion, since the breed was largely unknown in Jamaica. In fact, the experience of watching my sister fall into illness, together with my poor performance at school in the sciences, put paid to that idea. However I not only identified her particular form of obsessive neurotic disorder, but came to absorb a much deeper and more sobering lesson. I grew to understand that she was a prime example of the process by which a casualty of the whole colonial racialized system lives out, in the interior of the family and in the collapses of her mind, the trauma of a colonial culture, condensed into and expressed through the psychic intimacies and emotional intensities of the colonial family. Which, in different ways, both Freud and, much later, R. D. Laing explored.

Partly as a result of this experience, I have never been able to make that distinction on which so much conventional social science depends, between the 'objective' and the 'subjective' aspects of social processes, the interior and the exterior social worlds. Another way of putting it is that this may have been the origin of my subsequent intellectual interest in the relation between the social and the psychoanalytic. They are different domains, to be sure, with their own rules, modalities of being and conditions of existence. But they are also reverse sides of the same coin.

The main lesson my upbringing taught me was the way the tensions, ambivalences, fantasies and anxieties of a colonial culture, deeply divided along race/class/colour/gender lines, are lived out subjectively and internalized in the intense, emotionally charged, pathological world of the colonial family. My life represented a distorted version of what Françoise Vergès has called, after Freud, the 'colonial family romance'. In this argument the coloured, or creole, son fantasizes himself to be 'really' the unrecognized literal, or symbolic, child, not – as in Freud – of some royal or princely family, but of the plantocracy, via the person of the surrogate white father. My family were willing victims of this profoundly destructive, but unconscious, structure of misrecognition.

This was also the moment when I realized that, if I ever got the chance to study abroad, I would be well advised not to return to Jamaica lest it consume me. Winning a scholarship to Oxford in the late 1940s was regarded by my parents' friends as representing the triumph of, and justification for, my upbringing. But I knew in my heart of hearts that it was the beginning of a lifelong escape attempt. Did I believe that escape was possible? I suspect not. But I had no option but to proceed as if it were.

3. Thinking the Caribbean: Creolizing Thinking

I came to understand that, as a colonized subject, I was inserted into history (or in this case, History) by negation, backwards and upside down – like all Caribbean peoples, dispossessed and disinherited from a past which was never properly ours. We were condemned to be out of place or displaced, transported to a phantasmatic zone of the globe where history never happened as it should. We were conscripted into modernity as peculiarly wayward footsoldiers. My family was testament to the degree to which this waywardness organized our inner lives.

This mode of being, as I've explained, produced a profound nexus of silence, evasion and disavowal. It was the mental and emotional world into which I was born and it remains inside me, all these years later, an unwelcome reminder of what I had been destined to be. In part my purpose in this chapter is to emphasize that these evasions and disavowals, which worked to deny the colonized any hold on history, themselves possessed a history. Our sensibilities derived directly from colonial subjugation and from the long history of racialized enslavement. It's important for me to acknowledge, personally, that the pathologies which accompanied my upbringing weren't peculiarly mine, and need to be located in their larger history.

To evoke my mental world in this way is to follow history from its 'bad' side, as Brecht has it, focusing on the afflictions which were lodged in our inner lives. This is the story of colonial oppression. But while true, it misses an important dimension. Intellectually there were also virtues in our capacity to see the world askew, from below or backwards, or from below *and* backwards, free from the desire for domination which characterized the imperatives of the colonial order. This was to live W. E. B. DuBois' 'double consciousness'. We never *could* subscribe to 'the rational madness' (in Derek

Walcott's words) which conceived of progress as a programmed sequence leading us to 'a dominated future'. Walcott believed such an idea to be 'the bitter secret of the apple'. We grew up knowing the contingencies, the out-of-placeness, of history. For us history was the carrier of no absolutes and conformed to no overarching scriptural commandments. Nothing was ever codified as having its correct place and time. In a suitably paradoxical formulation, displacement moved to the centre of things. To think in this manner enabled us to catch the world in all its unpredictabilities. Out of our subaltern position there emerged the possibility of engaging with history anew. That colonialism, despite itself, bequeathed to us this way of seeing indicates that within what I've identified as the 'bad' dynamic of history, contrary and liberating forces were also generated. As the Lévi-Straussian in me later came to realize, the Caribbean has been – for me, personally speaking – good to think with. My understanding of the world was creolized from the start.

At this point in my story the angle of vision needs to shift, if just a degree. In the last chapter I tried to explain how, late in life, I look back on growing up in colonial Jamaica as one of the emergent brown middle class. As a boy there was much that I couldn't understand and much that troubled me. I sought to convey what it was like to be formed in a social world particularly when, after 1938, it was dramatically apparent that there was no future for colonial rule. This was how I encountered the world: instinctively and spontaneously to begin with, and later, as I became older, more consciously and determinedly. When I embarked on recounting this time of my life I also hoped to unearth some of the principal relations between the emotional travails of me and my immediate family and the larger impulses of a society still subject to colonial jurisdiction, but one in the midst of being carried forwards to universal suffrage and Independence. But in this chapter my focus has to change: from my lived experience of growing up in Jamaica to the ideas which those experiences activated. What of the social theories which I later came to espouse? How were my intellectual attachments formed and where did they lie?

As I said at the end of the last chapter, I've never been persuaded by the orthodox social-science division between the 'objective' and the 'subjective'. It's always seemed to me that even the most abstract theories are, to varying degrees, informed by their subjective conditions of existence: by, that is, the inner psychic dynamics of the theorist. I've felt this to be true of my own life. And this book stands as an experiment in drawing out what connections I can between my 'life' and my 'ideas', in so far as these are ever separable.

Much of my professional life has been concerned with the politics of who we think we are. I've been riveted by the question of how we can understand the chaos of identifications which we assemble in order to navigate the social world and also how we seek to reach, somehow, 'ourselves'. Of course this arrival never occurs: we'll never be ourselves, whatever that could mean. To recognize that this is so makes the idea of drafting this record of a life a curious thing to do. It requires diversions, explanations and reflective detours which more mainstream accounts can forgo. Identity, in the singular, is never achieved with any finality. Identities, in the plural, are the means for becoming. The narrative I'm mobilizing here will never reach its destination, even if I were to live long enough to complete it and, with a flourish, add *finis* to the final page. Which is unlikely. So in this chapter I'll address the question of *how we think* 'where we are from'. Or, to put this more precisely, I'll attempt to show how I think 'where I'm from'. This is inseparably a historical and a conceptual issue. We need to consider how we are inserted into the social processes of history and simultaneously think about the mental means we, as subjects, employ to explain to ourselves where, in history, we find ourselves.

In so doing we must remember that the entire social system of Jamaica was inflected by the full force of white bias: by the tilt of the social structure towards a reverence for, or an identification with, everything associated with the 'mother country', and with her earthly representatives on Caribbean soil. Jamaica was imagined as something other than itself. This decentred relationship invited the mimicry of the white metropole, which worked as a live current running through our lives. This 'other', in all its facets, constituted *the* absent-present of colonial Jamaica and formed its 'constitutive outside' – fantasy supported by a largely delusory picture of what life was *really* like 'over there', where civilization *really* belonged. Implicitly, this made West Indian societies second-rate simulacra of 'the real thing'. We can only speculate at what cost people endured – as Althusser would say – their relation to their real conditions of existence through this disjunctive imaginary relation to the white world. The damage this did to the prospects of developing an independent, indigenous culture is hard to overestimate.

Twentieth-century Jamaican society was structured around the main social divisions – class, race, colour and gender – but in its own peculiarly colonial way. Not one of these dimensions prevailed or, as Marxists would say of the economy, determined everything in the last instance. They were interpenetrating, mutually reinforcing as well as mutually destabilizing, productive but also disruptive and contradictory: vectors which were overdetermining, without losing their specificity of form or effect. There was no perfect, or legally enforced, match between them such that they could be read off, one against the other. Indeed, markers of social position were 'traded' as identifiably different social goods in the complex marketplace of Jamaica's social system. Thus, for example, black men could achieve social mobility through marriage, or by offsetting the negative attributes of wiry hair or dark skin colour against the positive virtues of being well educated or having a professional job. When my father 'married upwards' into Port Antonio 'society' his position and prospects immediately improved, although there is no evidence that this was ever his intention.

Caribbean social complexity derived from the peculiar evolution of these vectors of difference, consolidated in the long period of colonization and in the era of plantation society. They reflected the distorting effects of the colonial relationship, as well as the contradictory ways in which these hierarchies worked with and against each other.

Class and race/colour were what everyone was talking about, whether overtly or not. Jamaicans are great talkers, self-dramatists and narrators. They can argue all day about politics, and love to stage dramatic and voluble altercations in public, as well as to gossip and to scandalize. The intricacies and mismatches of the social distinctions were often either the essence of the scandal, the necessary scaffold to the joke, or the unidentified but piquant and widely appreciated point of the whole story. But no one could actually say that this was so.

None of us was outside this structure of feeling. We knew the system instinctively. We imbibed it, as they say, with our mother's milk. It was in the air we breathed. It provided the prism through which every social relationship, occasion or event was seen, interpreted, lived, depended upon and made sense of. It composed the social map of meaning on which we all – both the subjects and objects of this discourse – depended in order to interpret our world. Everyone assumed this was just how everybody else thought, how people spoke, how society worked, how things were. It had become sedimented in Jamaican common sense. Class discrimination and racialized differentiation were ubiquitous. I won't speculate here on what it does to a young person's head to have the mind furnished in this bizarre, pathological way.

I will bring colonial and enslaved Jamaica into sharper focus in order for readers better to understand the world which created inside me the deep-seated disorientation I've been evoking. The historical facts of colonialism and slavery come to be dominating, recurring issues: not simply as events which occurred in the distant past, but as histories which eat into the present and whose afterlives still organize our contemporary post-colonial world.

But what do I mean by saying that we were inserted into history backwards, or the wrong way round? Just think of the manner in which the colonial order first arrived. On his ill-fated voyage westwards, Columbus – we are obliged to begin with Columbus! – discovered New World 'Indians' *by mistake*, thinking that he'd arrived in the East. From the start the Caribbean was in the wrong place.

The making of the New World was not only a feat of navigation, it was an epistemological event. Columbus persuaded himself, as Europeans did later in North America and in Australasia, that the land had been 'empty'. Indeed, the explorers constructed an imaginary America – John Donne's newfoundland – out of the most far-fetched farrago of 'facts', images and expectations from diverse and myth-driven sources like Herodotus, Pliny, explorers' diaries and travellers' tall tales, such as the exploits of Sir John Mandeville, which they read long before they actually arrived. The New World thus *already* existed in Europeans' imagination before it had been discovered and was as much a product of that as of their scientific or maritime achievements.

In this context I always think of Theodor Galle's later engraving of Amerigo Vespucci 'discovering' America. Vespucci appears as the all-conquering male, while the female 'native' – actually becoming in this very instant *a native* – lazes in her hammock and impassively waits to be conquered and possessed. On the horizon the conquistador fleet advances menacingly on the 'empty' lands, ready to claim the territory for Ferdinand and Isabella of Aragon and Castile.

Indeed, Charles V – from 1519 simultaneously both the Holy Roman Emperor and Charles I of Spain – convened what came to be the famous theological debate, in Valladolid in 1550, as to whether 'these natives' could be conceived of as human beings at all, or whether they were born of a different creation. A sympathetic priest, Bartolomé de las Casas, debated the matter with Juan Ginés de Sepúlveda who, drawing from Aristotle's *Politics*, proposed the notion that the indigenous Amerindians were 'natural slaves'. This was an ominous moment.

Locke was subsequently to espouse the idea that America represented a snapshot of all humanity as it had been in the past. He called this world 'the childhood of mankind'. 'Thus in the beginning', he concluded in a breathtaking flourish, 'all the World was *America.*' This was historically of the first importance. It provided the philosophical means for imagining the displacements which from the very beginning of the colonial order defined what the Caribbean was.

A decisive evolution of this manner of thought occurred later, in the Enlightenment and after, elaborating the notion that there existed a fixed sequence of stages through which humanity must pass in order to rise from hunter-gathering to modern civilization. The belief that the Caribbean was 'not yet civilized' derived from the natives' observable – conspicuous, even – lack of civilization. How *could* they be civilized when they had no conception of private ownership, of organized government, of advanced modes of subsistence, of marriage, of refinement of manners, of sexual modesty or of clothing to hide their nakedness? Such conceptions of civilization, valorizing an overriding, singular story of modernization, can still be heard today; and when they are resurrected, as they regularly are, they remain – politically – highly charged.

When I was growing up in Jamaica there existed only the ghostly traces of the indigenous inhabitants, long since extinct. The great majority, dragooned initially as forced labour, succumbed to the harsh regimes and to the diseases which the early colonizers introduced and within decades were all but wiped out. Peter Hulme, the voraciously well-read and insightful scholar of the Pan-Caribbean region, tells the story that after Independence Alexander Bustamante, the Prime Minister, was keen to embellish the national emblem with 'Amerindian' motifs – figures in feather headdresses, alligators slumped out below, a profusion of pineapples. The citizens of the new nation were puzzled as to whom, in modern Jamaica as they knew it, such representations could possibly refer.

Jamaica was first conquered by the Spanish, and then for long – as in much of the Caribbean – Spain and Britain fought for the spoils. The modern Caribbean came to life in a prolonged battle between Spain, France, Britain and the Netherlands, predictably with much bloodshed. The story of the Caribbean is the story of violence. And, of necessity, this is my story too and that of my family, even when – particularly when – it remained unspoken. We don't choose our histories.

Until the seventeenth century the Spanish had been the only Europeans actively occupying the islands, though even then only the largest ones. For Spain the Caribbean functioned as a strategic relay station to the Americas and the entire region proved militarily important. The geopolitics of the area shifted when, late in 1655, Jamaica was captured by two of Cromwell's military adventurers,

Admiral William Penn and Colonel Robert Venables. The British had begun to settle in Barbados from 1627, and in Jamaica their arrival as settlers coincided with the beginnings of the sugar plantations and of the system of enslaved labour on which the plantations depended. This marked the fateful historical transformation, for the Caribbean certainly, and less visibly – screened out of sight and 'far away' – for Britain too.

For a while the planters tried, unsuccessfully, to maintain the workforce supply with convicts and war captives. But they also quickly succumbed to the murderous labour regime and to disease. When in 1713 the British broke the Dutch monopoly of the African slave trade as a result of the Treaty of Utrecht – which gave Britain the right to sell slaves to the Spanish colonies – they established a dominance in the Atlantic slave trade. This signalled the making of the Atlantic world, a powerful element in the constitution of what we call modernity.

By the end of the seventeenth century the planters, as an emergent social stratum, had developed an intricate mercantile system linking Jamaica and London, establishing significant leverage in political and financial circles in the English capital. Their influence was evident in the decision by the metropolitan government – after heavy pressure from the free-traders – to abolish the Royal African Company's monopoly on the slave trade, colossally increasing the number of slaves bound for Jamaica. The Jamaican Assembly introduced a comprehensive slave code, based on the model of Barbados, such that the management of the slave population came to be a public matter, affecting the very lifeblood of the island. Sugar promised many quick fortunes to the planters, although the vulnerabilities of the crop, and the costs of the human means required for its production, spurred the creation of elaborate networks of credit. By the early eighteenth century the slaves outnumbered their masters by a factor of eight to one. When the European powers signed the Treaty of Utrecht, Britain's plantations in Jamaica were well advanced, forming the indispensable core of the island's economic and social structure.

The planter class was composed not only of those who held titles to the land and to the slaves. They were in turn supported by an entire social stratum who serviced the plantation in less exalted roles: the overseers, estate managers, attorneys, factory supervisors and book-keepers. Often such functionaries had been sent to the Caribbean to make their fortunes, and the successful among them started by buying land and hiring out slaves during the busy crop-over season. Because their reference group was composed of whites they mixed socially, and identified their interests, with their richer employers and exercised the same social and sexual privileges towards the enslaved.

Yet the actual workings of the plantation were subject to the inevitable contradiction between abstract capital – the slave as a unit of production – and the daily realities of the living, sentient souls who contended with their fate as enslaved beings.

Slaves were constantly running away – the practice of *marronage* – from the plantation regimes. Some, like the original Maroons, managed to escape to the remote mountains and establish villages of their own, such as Maroon Town and Accompong, where memories of African ways of life were able to survive with a relatively deep resonance. They fought three wars with the British and established a degree of autonomy. Escapees were constantly recaptured and returned to the compounds to face the whip and branding iron, on occasion tracked down with the help of the Maroons themselves. When conditions became too much to bear, the enslaved confronted their masters or fled, on the elemental calculation that enough was enough. There were frequent uprisings. Rebels were punished by means that were designed to create terror: currents of unrest had to be suppressed. As Abolition approached, resistance came to be more organized and the revolt of 1831, Sam Sharpe's Rebellion, was critical in achieving Emancipation. Acts of insubordination, uprisings and flight punctuated the life of the plantation, while merciless discipline redoubled. Such was 'the recurring dynamic' of the plantation.

To emphasize the social relations of violence on the plantation in these terms allows us to grasp the specificities of a mode of production based on slavery. Yet it's clear that the bid to transform humans into property entailed perpetual, systematic and violent struggle, which was exactly the reason for the existence of the plethora of statutes and codes. I have in mind particularly the analysis of the Jamaican social theorist Orlando Patterson, whose idea of the 'natal alienation' of the enslaved sought to define a structure distinctive to New World slavery as a social relation. Condemning the mass of the population to the phenomenon of 'natal alienation' was to have profound consequences on later generations, long after the formalities of enslavement had been abolished. Much of the disavowal I experienced when young represented the endeavour to live with – or rather, not to live with – this traumatic breach in our nation's past.

Patterson draws from Marx in the *Grundrisse* in order to focus on the peculiarities of violence in the slave system, while recognizing that force has been an essential element in all societies. He confronts the fact that on the plantations, non-slaves had to be transformed into the social being of the slave, signalling the *work* – the pre-conditional absolute, the historical mission – of the planter class. It proved necessary continually to repeat the founding act of violence, ensuring that the transformation of the freed person into the slave became a daily task. All of which was conducted under the banner of race. The social code notwithstanding, the calculus determining the degrees of pain and humiliation to be distributed ceased to have any meaning or any given social referent. The primary purpose of the violence inflicted was to impress upon the slaves the knowledge that they had being only as that: as slaves, with no existence conceivable except as an appendage to the master. The violence was not principally a matter of punishment, dependent on its own brutal calculation. Within this crazed logic, the quota of violence meted out could never be too much.

It's for these reasons that Patterson conceptualizes slavery as a form of social death. Within the mental imperatives of the plantation the slave could not even be *comprehended* without the presence of the master. He or she could not properly exist. Slavery worked as a kind of 'conditional commutation' in which the moment of execution could be suspended for the span of an entire lifetime.

This is what Patterson means by 'natal alienation': that those born into slavery were, from their very first minute in the world, alienated from all rights of birth. Genealogical and historical memories were cauterized from the lives of the enslaved, at least in intent. The threat of forcible separation from parents and children, from lovers, from kinship networks and friends, was constant. So too were enforced sexual couplings in which the power of the master was systematically reasserted. 'Natal alienation' signified a situation in which the elemental ties of birth were severed, and the enslaved were forcibly separated from the dynamics of those human qualities which, otherwise, we imagine to be bestowed on us when we are born.

It's not easy to comprehend such a world, even though it was generated and sustained from deep within the heartlands of England's civilization. It's difficult, too, to work through the question of how these pasts inhabit the historical present. Via many disjunctures – filaments which are broken, mediated, subterranean, unconscious – the dislocated presence of this history militates against our understanding of our own historical locations. But these lived histories nonetheless still reverberate unbidden in the collective psyche today. They account for the radical puzzlement that accompanied my childhood. Within the colonial order of Jamaica a chaos of disorder was evident. But what of the disorder inside us all, parents and children, families and friends, which in its own way was palpable but could never be voiced?

This disorder is particularly active in the domain of gender and sexuality. The stereotypes of male and female were polarized through every social category. Rich and powerful white men dominated the plantation economy, governed the slave family as well as their own enslaved workers, administered reward and punishment and organized those under them to labour profitably. The master was serviced by his wife and servants in the domestic world, often took favourites into concubinage and enjoyed the sexual exploitation of enslaved women as a right of ownership. White women, though subordinate to him, in their turn governed the domestic sphere, the servants and house slaves, organized family life and the round of social entertaining.

That the sexual and gender customs of the planter class mirrored those of the home country was taken as given. As such, often in heightened form, this was a social system which reinforced social stereotypes, legitimated the sexual exploitation of women, licensed masculine aggression, normalized patriarchal attitudes, confirmed women's secondariness and conspired with female confinement to the familial and domestic sphere. This was a culture which generated, within and across the classes, displaced, intimate feelings of resentment and betrayal which could rarely be directly expressed. These patterns of behaviour function not only as traces of the past; they continue to be active, divisive and formative in contemporary Jamaica's lived cultures.

Yet even though there existed shared customs between colony and metropole, or more exactly a shared code of ethics – at least formally – between the colonial planters and their metropolitan counterparts, strands of public opinion emerged in Britain asserting that the West Indian planters were given to a wanton libertinism, and calling attention to their social mores as debauched and corrosive of all meaningful systems of social solidarity.

The view in England that colonial life had corrupted the white plantocracy, particularly in sexual conduct, and that, in a paradoxical twist, the planters were themselves in danger of 'going native', gathered force from the late eighteenth century. The notion that the planters could turn Jamaica into a polite rendition of an eighteenth-century England over-exercised by matters of taste and discrimination was, as many at the time appreciated, a crude joke with no semblance of truth. Evangelicals were shocked by the degeneration of sexual morality in Jamaica and wrote passionately against it. Indeed, the planters' sexual licentiousness (bolstered by an anxious estimation of their bonanza of untold riches) became a significant impetus for the emergence of the Abolition movement.

In Jamaica the planter class gained a reputation for shameless vulgarity. They, and their mercantile partners in collateral businesses, constituted the core of the powerful and successful West Indian parliamentary lobby, and a major force in organizing public opinion during the struggle over Abolition.

In this sense, by the early nineteenth century the planter class, for all the power of the West Indian lobby, was hardly a historic or ruling class at all. It had neither the will nor the authority to shape the people in its own image, and lacked a reservoir of moral and intellectual leadership on which to call. It was a corporate, sectional body, ruthlessly pursuing its own ends. It embodied the internal disorganization of the colony as a whole.

I've already suggested that my mother retained some residual attachment to the ethos of plantation life, 'long ago', 'when all was well'. I'm sure that in her mind this never functioned as an endorsement of slavery. The enslaved had slipped out of memory. It was rather to subscribe to the culture of 'the estate', the social successor to the plantation, where – as my mother liked to imagine things – all the daily turmoil of colonial Jamaica had been magically resolved, leaving only a time of emotional plenitude and order. It was an attachment devoid of any historical reality. Despite her social ambition, neither she nor my father was descended from the planter class. In moral conduct the behaviour of my family always respected a certain propriety, far distant from the libertinism and vulgarity popularly associated with the planters. I don't know whether their incapacity to acknowledge the erotic dimensions of their life, or indeed of their children's lives, was in some manner a reaction to what they'd learned about plantation Jamaica. In our family (and I'm sure we were not alone in this), that past was disavowed and heavily censored. It was not to be talked of. It existed like a pall of mist, enveloping us all, which no one could admit was there.

Later in my intellectual life there was one aspect of this past in particular to which I found myself returning. At special times of the year the slaveholders permitted the enslaved occasions when they were allowed to dance, sing, dress up and celebrate – for all the world as if they were free. Slaves embraced these pantomime moments to act out, or to rehearse, the dream of freedom to which they remained tenaciously wedded. The celebrations acquired something of what Bakhtin identified as the carnivalesque anticipation, in masquerade, of the day when the world would be turned upside down and slaves set free from bondage. Threaded through these festivals of artfully concealed mimicry were the manifest ridicule and contempt with which the enslaved – out of earshot, but 'speaking' through the distorted codes of the masquerade – regarded those above them. They signified through indirection what they actually thought of the customs, antics, dress, manners, habits and pretentions of their masters and mistresses.

This is a prime example of creolization. The subordinate classes mimicked the modes of expression of their masters and played out the required performance of obedience, while *simultaneously* they mimed, caricatured and appropriated dominant ways of speech, dress and behaviour, adapting them to their own purposes and meanings in order to free themselves – if only fleetingly – from the daily imprint of subjugation. This is the spirit of the carnivalesque: the world seen from 'below', imagining from within the system of signs a world turned upside down. Through caricature and exaggeration the enslaved were able to create a measure of distance between their own lives and the symbolic and actual hierarchies which ordered the plantation-colonial order.

Dressing up in imitation of their 'betters' was a particularly complex and piquant, doubly encoded performance since at one level it manifested the 'respect' required, but at the other it sent up in an excessive manner the imperatives of the situation in which the enslaved found themselves. Their masters and mistresses could never be sure which was which. Indeed, that was the whole point of the exercise. Skip Gates ironically called these strategies those of the 'signifying monkey', and 'signifying' remains a central impulse in African-American humour today, commonly observed in black comedy, street speech and jive talk. It's also what Kobena Mercer has located as the essence of diasporic discursive strategies. This is the source of that complex 'double language' so commonly observed in the behaviour and speech patterns of black New World cultures after slavery. Traces of these strategies were still evident during my adolescence, more than a century after Abolition as, redeployed for different circumstances, they still are.

The enslaved were customarily forbidden to speak their own

languages for fear that this would facilitate collective forms of resistance. Being always in a subordinate relationship to Europeans, however, enslaved Africans were also required to understand enough English to obey orders and to service their masters and mistresses. But few were taught English, although the missionaries, when they arrived, insisted that they know enough to be able to read the Bible for themselves. Which they duly did, although never in the terms which the missionaries had foreseen.

A result of linguistic fragmentation and 'compelled acculturation' was the emergence throughout the Caribbean of an indigenous *creole* or *patois* – or 'nation-languages', to use Kamau Brathwaite's formulation – a version of which is understood by everyone today, although for long the aspirant middle classes frowned on its use. Language-teaching in my school consisted of 'ironing out' the broader vernacular traces among the students' speech, a practice my parents consistently re-enforced. Nevertheless, all of us spoke a moderated Jamaican patois and used it informally among ourselves.

Jamaican patois was a hybridized compound of English and African vocabularies and phrases, organized by syntactical rules which utilized versions of both grammatical systems. This is best described in J. J. Thomas' pioneering *The Theory and Practice of Creole Grammar*, first published in 1869 and made available in our own times thanks to the inspiration and determination of John La Rose and Sarah White's New Beacon Books. The result is a vigorous, richly creative, humorous, lively, supple mode of expression which is capable of capturing – as standard English, in any of its received local variants, is not – the emotional inflections, humour and nuance of local life. As a consequence Jamaicans prove themselves accomplished raconteurs of everyday life.

In these older social forms lie the origins of specifically *Caribbean* modes of expression. Language systems emerged in which necessary truths could be expressed and collective aspirations take shape and be spoken.

My experience of these Jamaican linguistic practices undoubtedly came to inform my later understanding of how cultures work *in general*. The predominant academic conception I'd initially inherited envisaged cultures as settled, stable, traditional and continuous with their origins: what we could call a 'roots' conception. Paul Gilroy, particularly, criticized this as generating a mode of thought which he believed carried with it an inevitable commitment to a cultural or an ethnic absolutism. This critique made it possible to reimagine cultures as what James Clifford and others designated 'travelling' ones: cultures 'on the move', constantly reconfigured through 'discovery', conquest, migration, adaptation, enforced assimilation, resistance and translation. In other words, a culture not of 'roots' but of 'routes', which invites a mode of interpretation which I have been designating here as diasporic. Migrations by Jamaicans to other places – to Cuba and Panama, to Central and South America more generally, to the UK and to Continental Europe, the US and Canada – should thus be understood as further instalments of this 'diaspora-ization' of the colonial project, ugly word though it is. This perspective not only provoked a shift in my thinking but turned out to be a problem with which Cultural Studies itself has had to wrestle.

I shifted from thinking of theory as the search for the certainty of all-embracing totalities (which is how a generation of us originally encountered Marxism), to the necessity of recognizing the power of contingency in all historical processes and explanations (which is how we went on to understand it). Or, in other words, of recognizing that the dynamics of displacement underwrite all social relations.

There's also a conceptual question behind this which concerns the historical times of slavery. Abolition marked a great social triumph. But the story becomes more complex when the history of slavery is approached not only as a particular form of social organization but as one instance among many collective experiences of 'unfreedom'. Slavery not only coexisted with other forms of unfree labour; its collapse generated novel manifestations of social unfreedom. I'm thinking of the temporary system of apprenticeship that followed Emancipation, which institutionalized a finely attuned repressive code, and then also – later – of the practices of indentured labour that stretched into the twentieth century. The freeing of labour, in other words, brought with it a new mental world, a new episteme with real effects, in which the constituents of coercive social discipline – far from disappearing – assumed a new configuration, less immediately visible in the social landscape but powerfully present for all that.

If our concern is not only slavery itself but also its various, continuing afterlives, then recognition of the imposition of different systems of unfree labour, and of the emergence of new forms of coercive, state-sanctioned disciplines, unsettles the received story of both Emancipation and its aftermath. It's not that there had once been plantation terror, which on 1 August 1834 turned into the beneficent world of free labour. This 'romance' of Abolition disguises more than it explains, and produces its own mechanisms of amnesia – as it still forcefully does in public life in Britain, with the invocation of 'Wilberforce' as the archangel of liberty.

Catherine's work on the place of Abolition in the metropolitan imagination demonstrates that it served (as it still does) as a screen which enabled Britain's involvement in, and responsibility for, slavery to fall from memory, leaving only the cheering story – the romance – of Abolition. With different rhythms, what is true of Britain is true of Jamaica.

Emancipation itself had been preceded by incremental self-purchase and manumission of portions of the enslaved. The period after slavery – or, more accurately, the final decades of the existence of the slave plantation and the early decades following Emancipation – did indeed witness the emergence of an entire new network of prisons and other carceral institutions. This is well explained by Diana Paton, who examines the longer historical duration from 1780 to 1870 rather than positioning Emancipation itself as the crucial pivot. Indeed, the object of her study is exactly the connection between practices of punishment and market discipline or, as she puts it, between 'whips, wages and prison'. In her telling, there's no simple evolution from 'whips' to 'wages'.

The temporal dimension of memory, too, is of the first importance.

It allows me to place in sharper historical contextualization my own story of growing up in Kingston. Memory, in this instance, I take to be a means by which history is lived. From the 1920s and 1930s in Jamaica the Garveyites, and the initially small, derided *groupuscules* of Rastafarians, imagined bondage as the central, continuing experience of the social life of the black masses. The slow and complex transformation of the collective black imaginary, from the labour insurrections of the 1930s to the Black Power years of the late 1960s and 1970s, represented the medium by which the shared experiences of slavery could enter public and private consciousness, and in which these experiences could be spoken of.

Only recently, long after Abolition, has the issue of reparations entered the field of politics. This signals the long-delayed working-through of what can properly be called the trauma of the slave past, which Freud understands as the dynamic of 'afterwardsness', and which undoes any simple 'before and after' historical sequence. Thus the aftermaths of slavery live long in people's mentalities. But the slave past was also critical in the organization of the social structures of Jamaica long after Abolition; this in turn underlaid the shifting political settlements through the later nineteenth and twentieth centuries. It's partly the unfinished, stalled nature of Abolition which helps us make historical sense of the Morant Bay uprising in 1865, of the labour insurrections of the 1930s and of the later Black Power movements. Indeed Michael Craton, in referring to Morant Bay, points out that the rebellion was 'essentially similar to the late slave rebellions, signifying how little conditions had actually changed with formal emancipation'.

As Robin Blackburn demonstrates with finality in his compendious *The Overthrow of Colonial Slavery*, an overriding factor in the slow destruction of the slave system was the social agency of the enslaved themselves. In the Caribbean, if not in Britain, the collective memory of slave insurrection retains some kind of hold on contemporary popular life. Yet having said this, when slavery was abolished the British government raised the colossal sum of £20 million to compensate the slave-owners for the loss of 'their property', 'their' enslaved. This represented an eloquent example of an unbrokered historic compromise between the two leading, contending political forces: on the one hand, the enslaved who were accorded legal freedom, and allowed to enter the labour market as unencumbered beings, with nothing to sell but their labour power; and on the other, their former masters and the wide network of those who invested in the slave production of sugar and who found themselves enormously enriched.

I should at this point weave in a personal story. It's a curious thing. I'm a Jamaican who's lived in Britain for more than fifty years. As such, I've been peculiarly aware for most of my life of the mutual interconnections binding together Jamaica and Britain. But I only became fully conscious of the deeper, denser links spanning the longer history when Catherine began researching the relations between Britain and Jamaica in the mid-nineteenth century, from Abolition to the rebellion at Morant Bay in 1865. She explains in the preface to the book which resulted, *Civilising Subjects*, that it was her discovery that a small Jamaican country town was named after the town in England where she'd been born – Kettering in Northamptonshire – which first prompted her to explore these entangled intimacies.

We were on holiday in Jamaica with our children in the summer of 1988, when they were of an age when they had other things on their minds. It was one of those holidays which has lodged in the family memory, for all its good times and pleasures, as troubling. I fear that I wasn't innocent in all this. Catherine provides a clue in her preface. She reflects on the fact that back in Jamaica, I 'was fighting with the difficulty of accepting that [my] ways of being' had 'identified [me] as one of those migrants who had lived in England for longer than in the land of their birth, who, in the language of Jamaicans, "came from foreign"'. Once more I was out of place, this time – again – in my native land.

We were driving along the north coast of the island when we came to a village called Kettering, in the centre of which was a large Baptist chapel. This was strange to say the least. Why was it called Kettering and why did the chapel occupy pride of place? When Catherine was born her father was the minister of the handsome Baptist chapel in the centre of the English Kettering. This was the beginning of her effort to recover lost histories connecting Jamaica and England, histories organized by their profound – if always unequal – relations.

Over a number of summers which followed we found ourselves off the beaten track, traversing the hills of rural Jamaica in search of the 'free villages' which had been established after Abolition by those who had been emancipated. We navigated steep, potholed roads, one of us driving, the other trying to make sense of the maps which never seemed quite right. Many prolonged conversations with passers-by ensued, bringing into my line of vision a Jamaica which for an age I had barely encountered. We visited many non-conformist chapels that had been erected at the highest points. These had generally been founded by Baptist and Methodist missionaries in the expectation that such prominent places of worship would encourage the newly freed slaves to build industrious, monogamous, godly communities. Many of the 'free villages' which the black Baptists helped to found had English names, their chapels, schools and cemeteries bearing inscriptions in memory of significant local pastors or British missionaries who had opened the schools or who had ministered there.

Moving from one back road to another, we were, step by step, tracking the processes of the entanglement of Britain and Jamaica through space and time. Our journeys helped us rediscover a vanished past; and they represented for us memory acts which resurrected, and worked with, forgotten histories. It also seemed that the more we explored, the more we came to realize that few Jamaicans visited these places or seemed aware of their larger historical significance. The remaining material traces of this history were either ignored or forgotten by the local villagers or, perhaps, located in a different historical memory which wasn't open to us. But for us they were evocative. It proved a moving, shared experience. It marks the moment when Catherine first immersed herself in the history of the Caribbean. But it was also important for me, bringing me face to face with a history that only had a distant, hazy presence in my mind. An entire dimension of Jamaica's past moved full-force into my consciousness. It wasn't only the relations between Jamaica and Britain which were impressing themselves inside me. I was also coming up close to the histories of that other Jamaica of which I had always been aware, but known insufficiently.

It is simply a fact of our life that Catherine knows more about the history of Jamaica than I do and has helped me to understand better the history of my own native land. Her current project is exemplary in demonstrating the deep inner connections between colony and metropole, throwing into relief the processes by which each existed inside the other.

At the time of Abolition, as I've already stated, all who had a financial stake in the slave system could apply to the British state for financial compensation, from widows of modest means, say, who owned a single slave, to the super-wealthy. The economics of this social transformation is convincingly described by Nicholas Draper in his *The Price of Emancipation*. The records of these claimants offer an invaluable snapshot of who the investors were and what they did with their financial compensation. The website (www.ucl.ac.uk/lbs) created by the Legacies of British Slave Ownership group (LBS) – Catherine, Nicholas Draper, Keith McClelland and their co-workers – offers an extraordinary vision of this world, which was located at the heart of the economic and social dynamic of nineteenth-century Britain. A good proportion of the capital accrued was reinvested either at home or elsewhere in the empire, particularly in shipping, transport, railways, merchant banking and marine insurance. Smaller amounts of compensation went to widows, for example, who might have inherited annuities dependent on the labour of the enslaved, a vivid illustration of the pervasive nature of the economics of slavery. Significant reinvestment was diverted to the new businesses which pioneered Britain's industrial transformation, a thesis first formulated in 1944 by Eric Williams in his *Capitalism and Slavery*. As the LBS work has now demonstrated, the significance of the wealth derived from slavery continued on into the later nineteenth century.

Nor was this the only legacy of the slave-owners' power. They and their descendants were active agents in the reconfiguration of a continuing faith in the 'truth' of race which redoubled throughout the empire in the latter part of the nineteenth century.

Jamaica's intricately articulated social hierarchies were characteristic of what Mary Louise Pratt calls the colonial 'contact-zone', in which different national, social, economic, ethnic, gendered and racially defined groups were obliged by the imperial system to inhabit the same space. But as these systems evolved, they did so in deeply unequal relationships to one another. It was the Martinican theorist Édouard Glissant who suggestively coined the term 'entanglement' to capture these historical realities. Jamaica and Britain undoubtedly were 'entangled'. But unless we are careful, to think in these terms may underplay the violence, compulsion and inequality that the 'entangling' process entailed. Encounters in the colonial contact-zone always depended on – as I've argued elsewhere – 'inequality, hierarchization, issues of domination and subalternity, mastery and servitude, domination and resistance. Questions of power, as well as issues of entanglement, are always at stake.'

I think that from this vantage point, my own social situation as one of the brown middle class in the 1930s and 1940s can begin to take form. The social hierarchies remained much the same after Abolition as they had before. The re-formation of the plantocracy, in its protracted and incomplete march out of history, dominated political life for a full century after Abolition.

Jamaican white and mixed-race creole peoples were thoroughly Anglicized in orientation, habits of thought, behaviour and – with local inflections – speech. Early on they were often sent to visit relatives living in Britain, although this was not always a gesture welcomed back home. In truth many of them found themselves out of place, as colonials, in London society. In Jamaica, however, they represented the apex of power and summit of civilization. They continued to be the 'bukras': the colonial governing class that topped the social hierarchy. The fortunes of their class were tied to sugar. These were hit badly when, after Abolition, the value of sugar fell drastically. The banana industry did something to revive

Jamaica's wealth, but only for a minority. The island, and the region as a whole, became an economic backwater and continued to be so for the duration of colonial rule. It was hammered by the Depression; poverty and unemployment were widespread. Even so, in wealth, exercise of power, style of life, habitus and status, the descendants of the plantation class still formed their own exclusive social club and were involved only to a limited extent in local Jamaican life. By the 1940s they were visibly, though, a declining social force.

Their ranks had been swollen by the incorporation of a few wealthy, sometimes landed, upwardly mobile 'free coloured' creoles. That is, by light-skinned, illegitimate offspring of miscegenation between the planters and enslaved women. The immediate descendants of these – usually enforced – unions were on occasion recognized by their white fathers and given land, hiring out slaves themselves. Indeed, more than 40 per cent of the claimants for compensation in the Caribbean were women, the vast majority of whom were of mixed descent. Some were sent to England to be appropriately educated; some were taken into the household in domestic roles. Considerable numbers of coloured women were able to establish themselves independently in the towns as hotel, lodging house, bar, brothel or saloon keepers. It was the 'free coloureds' who were, in time, to become the leading element in the brown middle class, which was the ethnic and social formation into which I was born. Politically the voting criterion was based on property ownership, not on ethnicity or race, and after the reforms of 1829 Jamaican 'free coloureds', after a lengthy struggle, won considerable civic rights and privileges within the system, including representation in the House of Assembly.

Some of the free coloureds did well for themselves. They were socially and economically upwardly mobile, accumulating wealth, buying or inheriting land, entering the older professions like the law and medicine, and building large town residences. As the local economy diversified, the upper elements of this middling stratum seized the new opportunities for small-scale capitalist enterprise. They went into medium-sized farm production or local – and eventually foreign – markets. Or moved into a variety of businesses: construction, outlets at the upmarket end of (imported) retail, trade and commerce, increasingly into small manufacturing, civic administration and the public services. Over the years the most successful established themselves close to the apex of Jamaican society. Their descendants are among the core of Jamaica's commercial and civic administration today.

The lower-middle classes were employed in the poorer ranks of the occupational scale – as clerks, nurses, teachers, ministers, salespeople, secretaries and foremen. Though often struggling financially, they provided the moral backbone of respectable Jamaica. A small proportion of rising black families were assimilated into this sector, slowly diversifying its mixed-colour composition. However, the spiritual centre of local society was incarnated in the lower-middle classes. They – the women especially – were religious, the custodians of the country's moral conscience, guardians of local vernacular habits and customs, as well as experts in the cuisine.

These ranks of the middle classes were further swollen by a small but significant minority of other ethnic groups which, at different times, had arrived in the island in search of work, or as refugees from religious or political persecution. Many of these minorities, such as Syrians, Lebanese and Hong Kong Chinese, were drawn into commercial activities and eventually into the professions. Others, like the East Indians – descendants of those indentured workers who had been brought in after Abolition as semi-bonded labour to replace the enslaved – started as poor peddlers but graduated to shop-keeping, and later to more ambitious commercial ventures, particularly in retail.

When, as a child, I was taken by my mother shopping to King's Street, downtown Kingston to buy clothes or materials, we invariably went to one of the big Lebanese or Syrian stores owned by people with well-known names like Hanna, Issa, Zaidie and Seaga – the latter the family name of the island's subsequent Prime Minister, Edward Seaga. The East Indians owned some of the largest retail stores. However, the grocery shop in our area and others like it were widely known – in the vernacular of the day – as the 'Chinee shop' because of their Chinese ownership.

There was at least one member of every one of these ethnic groups in my class at school in the 1940s. Dick Mahfood, from a Lebanese family, owned a ferocious motorbike on which I rode pillion in our ever-widening explorations of Kingston nightlife, including its seamier sides. He became a close friend. He often dropped by my house to collect me for some new adventure (venue unrevealed), but I was never invited to visit his house or to meet his family. Whatever his origins, he figured in relation to the Halls as an 'honorary white'.

Ethnically diverse and penetrating into Jamaican civic, public and commercial society, the upper end of the middle classes slowly began to assume the leading role in local Jamaican economic, cultural and social life. This precipitated a slow shift of power from rural to urban, and from white to coloured, giving social and cultural leadership a peculiarly subaltern component.

This brief reprise begins to outline one pole of the two Jamaicas which I've been describing. Then there was the other Jamaica.

When I was young it was the popular social stratum that was thought to constitute the 'real' Jamaicans, perhaps informed by a well-travelled if threadbare romanticism which offset the abjection which governed the actual lives of the black dispossessed. Of course such a designation was alive with simplifications. And the popular classes defied simplification. In the urban areas, for example, these amorphous sectors included groupings as different as the very poor, the urban underclass, the unemployed, dockworkers, small-time craftspeople mending clothes and shoes outside their one-room workplaces, untrained mechanics and the legion of repair people I mentioned earlier. And no doubt many more.

The term 'real Jamaicans' also covered the 'country people' and peasant farmers scratching a livelihood on smallholdings or in the steep hillside villages, or those who serviced the daily lives of the poor: the provisions and rum-shop owners and the all-purpose shopkeepers. Some were low-grade workers of the small industrialized sector: the day-rate cane-cutters, banana-growers and bauxite-miners. Substantial numbers of these men and women, whether in country or town, were engaged in manual work or in tilling the soil, growing on their tiny family plots anything that was consumed within the family or could be sold at the weekly market. Racially, the overwhelming majority were, directly or by some more circuitous route, of black African origin. However, the term African was not widely used as a self-description; to be used culturally and politically, as it is today, it would have had to cover a broad band of the colour spectrum, and reference the cultural, political and religious customs characteristic of the different parts of Africa from which the initial captives had been bought into enslavement.

Broadly speaking, the habits, customs, daily rituals, socio-economic conditions, religious and cultural practices, pleasures and tribulations of this diverse class at the broad-based bottom of the social pyramid constituted the foundation of Jamaican life. It was their labour which sustained the whole socio-economic edifice. The masses lived for the most part mired in persistent poverty. Culturally, however, they drew from – to different degrees, in different areas of daily life – the extraordinary mix of African and European cultural repertoires, fusing contraries into new formations. So deeply did this syncretism run that by the twentieth century no one could any longer tell precisely where the inherited cultural lines criss-crossing the nation could be drawn. Yet despite this profound and long-lasting experience of *métissage*, after Independence Pan-Africanism has been the prime motivating political force in the collective consciousness and freedom struggles of the black populations of the Caribbean, and so too of the New World more generally.

In this sense, respectability as a social value has its reverse side: an attitude of simmering resentment, resistance and insubordination which smoulders beneath, but is never far from, the surface. The attributions of 'attitude' and 'slackness' in daily popular life are transformed manifestations of this older historic inheritance. As I feel I must reiterate, when I was growing up the majority of black people wouldn't have called themselves black. Nonetheless, they were fully conscious of their racialized background and inferiorization. Blackness had been so remorselessly stereotyped – so degraded and abjected, its negativity so built into social attitudes, so embedded in common sense, so negatively reinforced at an unconscious level, so connected to unresolved psychic knots and defences – that it was perpetually visible. But at the same time, within the terms stipulated in the dominating social matrix, it remained unspeakable.

There was a powerful ideological fallout from the triumph of Emancipation: its respectable, nonconformist supporters took it to represent the *restoration* of the properly virtuous gender roles which the plantation, during its long history, had degraded. A common conviction rested on the assumption that enslavement had debased womanhood, and consequently compromised the possibility of an enlightened relationship between the sexes – a conviction which, when Abolition occurred, had all too real effects. The gendered norm – the idealized gendered norm – sanctioned the virtue of patriarchal authority within the family. This assumed that men could provide for their families and children, which they rarely could, and contributed too to the invisibility of women's work outside the home.

After Emancipation men often worked seasonally away from home. In reality women, in addition to bearing the brunt of family responsibilities, became the necessary, stable force in the domestic economy and the focal point of rural family life. They laboured for economic survival by tending the smallholding, carrying on their heads its produce – generally their only livelihood – often many miles to market. This gendered division of labour constitutes the basis of what anthropologists call the 'matrifocal' orientation of family life in Jamaica, with the woman for all practical purposes at the centre of things. When the man was present, customarily he would have exercised authority, received the lion's share of food and enforced sexual discipline.

In a strange repetition of this habituated practice, even today it is common to find middle-class families in which women work outside the home – they may be better educated than men, more independent, rising to senior positions at the top of their professions or holding down more responsible jobs than men – but in which, at home and in the domestic sphere, they still settle for the more subservient 'feminine' role.

Caribbean men have a reputation for absenting themselves from their obligations to, and responsibility for, the women they live with and the children they've fathered. That such collective perceptions arose, and came to be grounded in everyday mentalities, is not surprising. During the years of slavery fatherhood had accrued no social rights or responsibilities. In general, enslaved or colonized black men have often been psychically infantilized and symbolically displaced by the so-called 'absent white father'. One speculation is that, diminished in self-respect in the wider social system, men – some men – may have compensated in the sphere of gender and sexual relations, one of the few areas left to them by the so-called 'absent white father' for the exercise of surrogate and inverted modes of authority. This speculation may to some extent help us understand – though it does not in any way explain away – the casual aggression and violence shown towards women and male homosexuals in Jamaican society, and the more calculated exercise of male power through the means of rape. This degraded inheritance has become deeply embedded – and on occasion a matter to be boasted about – in the nation's sexual culture.

The religious sensibilities cast in slave times continue to retain their hold on the popular masses. The subterranean histories of these uneven, broken but nonetheless consistent symbolic attachments are of great significance. They bring to mind Antonio Gramsci's reflections on how political ideologies are formed and take root in popular life. They do so, Gramsci claims, 'by a creation of a concrete phantasy, which acts on a dispersed and shattered people to arouse and organise its collective will'.

Patterns forged during slavery, associated with the ambiguous role and influence of the dissenting churches and sustained through colonization, have had a significant popular purchase on Jamaican society. They are also to be found in other societies, similarly denuded of their traditional cultures and religious practices by colonization and disciplined by a particularly evangelical version of Christianity. The dissenting, evangelical, breakaway and Pentecostal churches in particular powerfully transmitted to Jamaicans, women especially, not only a deeply religious sensibility but a determination to maintain, even in unpropitious circumstances, a state of moral respectability. Needless to say, religiously informed respectability has always lived a double life cheek by jowl with the sensual, earthy, this-worldly quality of everyday popular life.

The missionaries of the dissenting churches, particularly the Methodists and the Baptists, often took the side of the enslaved even though they had to swear to abjure any involvement in politics. However, they intervened extensively in the education of the enslaved, and promoted schools and teacher-training colleges. Their religious message was widely understood to be about political, as well as other kinds of, conversion. The tensions between established denominations, with their roots abroad, and the breakaway local churches were sharp and did much to creolize the local branches, which were grounded in local conditions. The rebellion in 1831, in which Sam Sharpe, the black Baptist deacon, was a leading figure – and which persuaded the British that Abolition must follow – entered public consciousness as 'the Baptist War'. The activities of independent black 'Native Baptist' preachers were particularly influential and favoured the general trend towards sect formation, which has continued. The effects of the missionaries' vision of the free, independent, industrious and religious post-slave 'Man', which they promulgated in the 'free villages', had a long life.

Religious language and metaphor remained deeply embedded in Jamaican culture. During my childhood, the more ecstatic churches frightened their congregations into strict moral observance with threats of hell-fire and brimstone. But official doctrine and informal patterns frequently diverged. Common-law marriages and consenting sexual relationships outside marriage, for example, continued to be the norm for the majority of the poorer classes, as is so even today. The majority of children of the poor were – and are still – in a formal or legal sense, illegitimate. Even so, despite the putatively profane lives of the masses, the moral codes of the Bible still function as active reference points. The most wily of politicians seeking public office will adopt Biblical phrases and cadences, which still saturate the world of moral judgement.

This symbolic cosmos included elements from Ethiopianism, the religious movement focused on the liberation and Christianizing of Africa; Revivalism and its many sects and breakaway churches of the 'witness-to-God' variety, which swept Jamaica in the early twentieth century; and Zionism, which specialized in making sense of historical events in terms of matching texts from Biblical sources. In such a way the black masses were tutored in the essentials of a new hermeneutic, that is, in an analogical code for reading, debating and interpreting – like the Rastafarian disposition for 'reasoning'. Other components included traditional African folk religious practices, nature-worship, speaking in tongues, spiritual healing and communal dancing to induce a trance and body possession. These were all incorporated into Jamaican creolized forms like myall ('white magic'), obeah ('black magic') and pocomania, which spontaneously brought together disparate and contrary currents in a single symbolic formation.

It is a cliché to say that across the colonial world Christianity destroyed native belief systems and attempted to acculturate the subject population to European models of church organization and Christian belief. However, in Jamaica Christianity also instilled in the population a determination to maintain, even in the most brutal of circumstances, an eschatological, redemptive view of life as a vale of tears, but in which liberation was *also* located as just around the corner. At the same time Christianity encouraged a duty of social respectability as one of the main sources of the 'Good Life'. Its impact may help to explain the socially conservative stance of Christian churches across the former empire on the questions of women bishops and gay marriage.

Centuries of colonialism and slavery did indeed 'shatter' the lives of the oppressed, in Gramsci's terms. Their investment in heterodox religions, as a means of contending with *this* world, did to some extent constitute a 'concrete phantasy'. 'Phantasmagoric', certainly;

but with a significant leverage on political realities and driven by the hope of realizing some measure of human freedom in this world.

Let me pull together the threads of my argument. I began by outlining the distinctive shape of plantation society in Jamaica, and the degree to which the plantation bequeathed a weighty historical legacy. To understand this it's necessary to grasp the multiplicity of social determinations in play – and the fact that they work in combination, as an articulation of different forces. They are, in other words, overdetermined. Yet that they are overdetermined suggests, too, the constant misalignments of these determinations: one can never be matched to another, or read from another in a neat, stylized choreography. Displacement, in this scenario, is primary.

A virtue of this approach is that it accords a degree of social determinacy: it is exactly on this ground that, for example, the idea of race in Jamaica was (and is) organized. This never works as a given, or as an absolute; it's the consequence of contingent, discursive struggles. And as such, race can be understood as a decisive element in the business of determination, despite the various contingencies in play. Race, colour and class did not seamlessly translate into one another. It was more a case of what feminist theorists like Kimberlé Crenshaw, Avtar Brah, Gail Lewis and others call intersectionality, emphasizing their intimately related, but at the same time incommensurable, awkward and unsettled fit. Unlike the racialized segregation in the slave states of the Deep South or in apartheid South Africa, racial difference in the Caribbean was not legally entrenched. Voting criteria were based not on race but on property. Race formed part of an informal system and a source of tacit social knowledge. Informal systems of meaning leave a good deal of room for ambiguity and negotiation. However, it mustn't be assumed that because of this informality, infractions of the social rules had no social or psychic penalties. The situation in the Caribbean, though clear-cut and vindicated by common sense, was in practice fraught with exceptions, slippages and misreadings. The discursive negotiations which these slippages set in play were the stuff of the social transactions of everyday colonial life, animating anything from hushed opprobrium to full-volume public commentary.

I began this chapter by declaring that, by virtue of my Caribbean formation, my entry into history didn't conform to the grand European philosophies of history. I suggested also that – within these intellectual schemas – the Caribbean in particular, and the colonial world more generally, were ascribed a phantasmatic quality, on the grounds that colonial life defied the order and progress which represented the hallmarks of civilization. Not only was such reasoning heavily weighted ideologically, but I also came to learn that there exists *no* history free from disorder and displacement in either the Caribbean *or in the metropole*. To imagine otherwise is a fantasy, albeit a fantasy generated by colonialism and with its own long history. In this light the Caribbean once more provided me with the means to think about the properties of history *in general*.

And as I explain throughout this book, my generation discovered that it wasn't necessary to have to choose between the viewpoints of colony and metropole. New spaces – third spaces – were in the process of opening up and giving us a lifeline. This was certainly so for me.

The practices of social misrecognition which I've been evoking possessed, I think, a peculiarly Caribbean quality. They were both real – real enough to bump into – and curiously intangible. Traditional scholarship has been notoriously resistant in recuperating this dimension of Jamaican social life. I've recently been wondering about the depth and form of these silences, of these unspeakabilities. If in their texture they are distinctively Caribbean, why should this be so?

I'm still not sure. But I do think that the degree of the destruction of the Caribbean past, in contemporary imaginings, may have much to do with it. Certainly in Jamaica, colonial incursion broke up local knowledges and indigenous ways of life more completely than in many other colonial encounters – in Africa, for example, or in South Asia. There the nationalist movements had the advantage of a much longer pre-colonial history, enabling their independence movements to call upon a more deeply held conception of 'the people'. But in Jamaica this was not so. 'The past' was already 'missing', 'the origin' permanently deferred, the future unfixed. This abetted an acute social forgetfulness.

This loss of the past was not a matter of chance. It was due in part to the conscious policy at slave auctions to break up geographically based, tribal, linguistic, religious and family allegiances, and to destroy historical ties and memories, in order to render the enslaved more amenable to being 'seasoned' into slave labour. The violence of this social fragmentation was one of the many consequences of the nightmare terrors of the Middle Passage. The fact that enforced acculturation did not succeed in entirely erasing traditional memories in the slave population testifies to the stubbornness and adaptive powers of cultural form and tradition, not to their unchanging character. In fact the enslaved probably adapted best in the moment of creolization. Cultural translation was the price that had to be paid for even partial survival. It is only *in translation* that an assertion such as 'Africa is Alive and Well in the Diaspora' makes sense. But statements like this are consciously devised as a means of breaking into and dislodging the larger silences which prevail.

I should make one thing clear. When I talk about the past as missing, I am referring to an element of collapse in the contemporary systems of social memory. I have in mind the inhibitions which compromise the capacity to relate the past imaginatively and productively to the present. Caribbean literature of the past half-century or more derives its power from the determination of the writers to dramatize usable pasts for the present, creating what elsewhere in Caribbean life has been absent. My argument turns on what can, and cannot, be imagined. And on where the past enters consciousness such that it can, further, inform the historical present, and become worldly. In other words, it's to create a collective mentality which, far from being paralysed by the disavowals of the past, would allow new generations to engage strategically with the past, to become a properly historical force and to reach out to the world.

To say that the past is somehow missing in the Caribbean is not at all the same as saying that the Caribbean has no history, whatever that could mean. To claim such a thing carries us right back to the heartlands of colonial thinking. In *The Middle Passage* V. S. Naipaul polemically – as is his habit – condemned the Caribbean as a place without a history. This is not my view. In fact it seems to me that the burden of history is just too much for its people to bear.

4. Race and Its Disavowal

In the last chapter my emphasis shifted from my lived experience in Jamaica to the mental representations of the colonial situation; I sought to make sense of my own formation. As I explained, much of this turned on my reflections on how to answer the innocent – or not so innocent – question: 'Where are you from?' For all its apparent simplicity, it's heavily loaded. I'm reminded of James Baldwin encountering a West Indian at the British Museum in the 1960s, and his being confronted by just this question. 'Where are you from?' Even after Baldwin had set out his origins as clearly as he knew how – 'I was born in Harlem General Hospital' – his interlocutor persisted, until he finally posed Baldwin the question: 'But where were you born *before that*?' Precisely! The question can teem with a swirl of hidden, perilous pretexts.

In order to approximate an answer I needed to say something about how I was brought up to understand the ways in which I was inserted in history; and then how I learned to dis-identify from this way of seeing, and with what consequences. These are, it's true, meta questions: less immediately about my life and more about how a life should be narrated. But then, as I've said throughout, the distinctions between my life and ideas really have no hold. In recounting the story of someone born out of place, displaced from the dominant currents of history, nothing can be taken for granted. Not least the telling of a life.

There is one further detour I feel obliged to make before I pick up the story of my journeying from Jamaica to England, en route to Oxford University. I've kept returning to the issue of disavowal, and to the relations between disavowal and race in Jamaica. When I started writing, it was this which I constantly revisited, with an edge of compulsion I'm sure. In my early life the evasions and disavowals puzzled me and later caused much grief. What kind of collective psyche could invest so much energy in maintaining racial dominance and at the same time categorically deny the efficacy of race? Disavowal is not an uncommon historical phenomenon, especially in matters of race. When I arrived in England I encountered these mental reflexes again, but with a different temper from that which I'd been accustomed to. In this short chapter I address this issue. It's been central to my life, and central too to my intellectual evolution.

Frantz Fanon believed that colonial societies worked through race. By this he meant that the social relations of race – which governed the primal antagonism between settler and native – carried with particular force the weight of colonial authority. I imagine that when he wrote in these terms Fanon was thinking more of Algeria than he was of his native Martinique, although we can't be sure. Much of what I have been arguing, especially about the ways in which the impress of racial subordination left its mark on my family, would appear to bear this out. Yet at the same time the matter of race could seldom be spoken of for what it was, or barely even acknowledged. It was all around, in every respect present, but could never quite be located or articulated. At every turn we encountered manifestations of disavowal, of one kind or another, with their profound, unsettling ambiguities and contradictions. In order to uncover the dynamics of my own Caribbean formation, I feel driven to confront this disjunction which, intangible though it was, ran through daily life. I need to grasp, as best I can, the coexistence of the absolute authority of the racial order on the one hand, and its perpetual disavowal on the other.

In tracing race in the Caribbean, colour was the joker in the pack. Gail Lewis has explored the complexity of 'the skin's language and [its] social validation'. One important aspect of the significance of skin in the Caribbean was the game of hide-and-seek which race and colour played with each other in the post-slave social system, into which the stark categories of enslaved Jamaica had evolved over three centuries. In this society the consciousness of race and colour operated constantly at a high pitch. Small distinctions of racial origins and colour, as well as of wealth and social position, mattered enormously. There existed a social obsession with what Freud calls 'the narcissism of minor differences'. In order to locate an individual in a race/colour system, an optimum solution is to be able to call upon a code of differences which is immediately visible and can be read at a glance. In these circumstances visibility itself becomes a kind of truth. One needs to be able to map, structure and order what it is that one sees. This is achieved by correlating one vector of difference (say, skin colour) against another (say, race). In this strategy of social reading, the position of every individual becomes mappable, and as it does so it confirms race or colour as the salient determining factor. After all, it would never do for someone to be racially misrecognized!

Lévi-Strauss calls this way of thinking – this species of mental grid – 'combinatory', a sort of living matrix for the purpose of social placing. My grandmother on my mother's side claimed always to be able to recognize, among those most ambitious to 'pass' racially, the telltale signs of what she felicitously called 'a touch of the tarbrush'.

The articulations between race, colour and class underpinned the entire social hierarchy. As I've explained, virtually white people, or 'local whites', clustered at the top of the colonial class pyramid. Below it, the coloured, or more accurately the brown or creole middle and lower-middling strata, formed the intermediary class of the imperial system, the principal conscripts to the colonial order. At the bottom were the great mass of overwhelmingly black, poor working-class or peasant Jamaicans, urban and rural, or moving constantly between the two. They occupied a separate social world. Gender cut an independent path through these categories and possessed its own colonial specificity.

These articulations were specific to a society of this type and created any number of potential identity-positions. The situation generated a damaging double-split between self-other and here-there. Direct access of the enslaved to their former African cultural sources had been brutally and decisively truncated by conquest and transplantation into New World slavery. At the same time access to anything that might have stood for 'authentically British' had been profoundly reconfigured, not only by its transplantation into colonial conditions but by its function as part of a system of power and domination. These symbolic repertoires have left traces on the palimpsest of the Jamaican culture with which I was familiar as I was entering my adulthood. But none could claim completeness, autonomy or singular authenticity. They were neither intact, self-sufficient nor autonomous. They had produced what Salman Rushdie once polemically called cultural 'mongrels'. Their contradictory elements had all been stirred into the colonial cookpot and irretrievably creolized. The culture was never again reducible to the sum of its contributory parts. The contact zone – the 'third space', the 'primal scene' of their enforced cohabitation – turned out to provide the most compelling and influential site of change.

By my time, the elements of this indigenization process had long been fused and condensed into what we simply took for granted as the basis of Jamaican popular life. This I've called the 'Jamaican vernacular'. Those acute observers of Jamaican history, Tom Holt and Erna Brodber, in their different registers, both refer to the outcome as simply 'Afro-Jamaica'. Jamaica's modern history, whatever might now be its myths of origin, began there.

It follows that authenticity of origins in this field, as much as any other, is problematic. Little of the original cultures survived; their bearers succumbed to the harsh labour regimes imposed on them. None of those who followed were native to the region; they all came from somewhere else. This may be the source of confusion in that other contested term – hybridity – which has been used to describe Caribbean culture. Hybridity, although it catches some aspects, can also be a confusing way of referencing the society's diverse beginnings, its 'after-the-event' character. Hybridity too often seems to attribute entanglement to mixed blood rather than to the play of historical and cultural factors. For my liking, it's too close to a form of biological reductionism.

From the 1930s in Jamaica, more or less from the time of my birth, the inherited racial order began to fracture, its social power loosening – as was signified partly by 1938 and its allied transformations. One way of plotting this is to trace how the term 'black' entered the public lexicon, and how it became an impetus in the collective endeavour to reimagine how the self could be recast. The long and complex story of Garveyism, crucially, is important in this context, representing a new, emergent, symbolic formation of great power. But where this break becomes most visible is in the moment of what has been called secondary decolonization, in the late 1960s, in the Pan-Caribbean moment of Black Power.

In my youth, as I've said, the term black was certainly not used as a self-description by the middle classes. Coloured was much preferred. Black was considered too impolite to use even about those who were, in an obvious sense, black. I never thought of myself as black then, although I knew I didn't belong where I was. And none of my friends would have called me, or themselves, black. Yet the overwhelming majority of black Jamaicans clearly understood their racialized inferiorization, from the humiliating encounters of daily life to the way that society had been organized by its racial hierarchies. They knew intimately the depth of the prejudice, in some cases visceral, which white and coloured people felt towards them. However, blackness had not yet become a positive term to be claimed, or a leading category for group identification, or for collective political organization – although this was changing fast, especially among the emerging Pan-African minority. The idea of blackness had been remorselessly stereotyped and degraded; fears of blackness were embedded in the taken-for-granteds of common sense, its negativity reinforced by unconscious, hostile feelings, complicated by unresolved psychic knots and defences which were unspeakable even when fully knowable. All this is what is meant by saying what otherwise seems improbable: that Jamaica did not really think itself a black society until the cultural revolutions of the 1960s and 1970s.

It wasn't until that period, after major historic challenges to the existing racial order, that this taboo was broken. It was not only a Caribbean matter, but a global one. A new historical epoch was inaugurated by decolonization and by the emergence of new non-white – 'non-aligned' – nations, encompassing Civil Rights and Black Power in the United States; Garveyism in the Caribbean (although not only in the Caribbean), combining with Rastafarianism and reggae; the long struggle against apartheid; the black British 'culture wars' and the mobilization of anti-racist movements in the 1970s. And much more. In the aftermath of the 1960s the word black acquired its positive contemporary connotations, and profoundly transformed the possibilities for popular life. These ruptures in meaning, and the creation of new black identities, became visible day by day in alternative, cultural modes such as music, street styles and dance, where new ways of expression could be voiced, embodied and performed. Through Rastafarianism and reggae Jamaica played a disproportionate role in this global reimagining of what racial emancipation might promise.

As I've sought to explain, for my generation of brown, middle-class Jamaicans repression concealed an eloquent silence, screening out the glaringly obvious which (in turn) demanded to be heard, and was – for this very reason – unsayable. The essence of disavowal is precisely to know and to not-know at one and the same time. Foucault argues that, far from successfully repressing what is unspeakable, prohibition actually generates productive linguistic proliferation, which paradoxically signals the ultimate failure of repression. Prohibited from saying more, he suggests, we find other ways – more indirect, more displaced, but also simultaneously more insistent – of, well, *saying it*. Thus for Foucault the repressive aspects of Victorian sexual morality had the effect of stimulating a great avalanche of new kinds of erotic writing, pornography and 'talk', precisely about that deemed unspeakable, sex. Jamaica was a case not of repression as such, but of a collective psychic disavowal. Censored from speaking about the troubling existence of race, Jamaica – the middle classes especially – produced in that absent/present space not just a plethora of talk, but a thousand euphemisms, evasions and circumlocutions. The more society tried to avoid it, the more expansive and refined the terminology became, and the more effectively it opened the door for the racial unconscious to enter the social language. Catherine, in her study of Lord Macaulay, has argued that in colonial discourse this forgetting is a form of 'racialization without race'.

It may be useful, in this regard, to hold in mind the contrasts between the operations of race in the Caribbean and in the United States.

In Jamaica whites constituted a small minority, greatly outnumbered by the black enslaved and freed slaves. In most of the North American slave states whites outnumbered blacks, who consequently – as Brodber and others have argued – were attempting to make a space for themselves inside a dominant white world. In Jamaica, by contrast, and in the Caribbean more generally, ideas of freedom increasingly turned to forging a space elsewhere or outside, as exemplified in the growing imaginative identification with Africa.

In the US the racial gradients were much steeper and supposedly scientifically based on the exact proportions of white and black blood in each person's veins: quadroon, octoroon and so on. Racial differences were thus both more sharply defined legally and more heavily enforced socially in the Deep South than they ever were in the Caribbean. The Civil War, for all its promise, only weakly and temporarily loosened these racial divisions. Reconstruction, an ambiguous attempt by the North to introduce a new social regime in the South, was speedily compromised by the wave of hucksters and carpetbaggers who led the way. States acquired the right to draft their own legislation on the liberties and limits of freed blacks. Organized opposition to racial emancipation soon came to be evident in the efforts to introduce Jim Crow legislation, which hardened and formalized the lines of racial discrimination, creating, in effect, a new colour-line. An extremist section – the Klan – reached for its white hoods and ropes. In effect, the social apartheid of the plantation era was recreated in post-Abolition conditions.

In Jamaica no such racial edifice existed and the colour-line was less strictly institutionalized, working not by law but by custom and habit. One need only think, in the Caribbean situation, of the exclusive white enclaves represented by the yacht clubs, where no prohibitions reign. But where, also, there is no need for them. They simply *are*, habitually, white. In practice, race was a sliding signifier in Jamaica. The social slippage – the sliding of the signifier – was extensive, constitutive of social life itself. There were wide skin colour variations even within the same family, as was the case in my own. Jamaican society gossiped, monitored intensely and speculated riotously about this perpetual, confusing fluidity of the body. When I was a child it's what Jamaica *was*.

Such a social system requires that we think not only about the relations which sustain it but also how, day by day, it is reproduced. This in turn takes us to questions of gendered bodies, of sexualities, and of the manifold transactions between variant 'epidermal schemas' on the one hand, and erotic desire on the other. It brings us to the conjunction of race and sexuality. I've alluded to this when I've discussed my family situation: my fate as a (dark) brown-skinned, middle-class boy, and the powerful presence of my mother. Gail Lewis draws on the psychoanalyst Wilfred Bion to speculate about the nature of 'maternal reveries' and goes on to propose that skin itself can act as the mysterious carrier of 'secrets and desire and knowledge'.

The disavowal of those deemed the most socially abject is not exclusively a racial, or a colour, matter. It runs through the social relations of class, gender, sexuality and intimacy. In contemporary Jamaica the weight of the historical past, in this respect, is immediate. The violence meted out to queer men, to take the most prominent example, bears this out. In earlier times, among the respectable, the circumlocution was pronounced. It wasn't as if respectable society didn't talk about homosexuality; it was a constant refrain, even while it could never be spoken 'as it was'. It was ever present as a dark undercurrent. Today race, sex and power make a dynamic erotic cocktail. The nightmare for white men seems to be that black men might outdo them in sexual size or performance and displace them in the eyes of white women. The fears of being overmastered by an insurgent sexual 'below' provided the ingredients for a powerful white fantasy. In *Black Skin, White Masks* Frantz Fanon observes that whites often imagine that black men have penises 'the size of cathedrals'. In reaction to such prevalent fantasies, an exaggerated black masculinity has become one of the terrains where stolen freedoms are contested and compensated for, where historic struggles are symbolically played out. This deep, troubled vein of male chauvinism in Jamaican society, matched by a correlative homophobia, is a disfiguring contemporary legacy of the racial past. The casual violence to women is another. Sexual prowess is one way for black men to affirm the masculine self in a world of dependencies, one of the few spheres of freedom and power that have not been abrogated.

For significant numbers of black women in contemporary popular culture sexuality, too, has become a highly charged theatre in which to claim and perform their independence, especially with regard to sexual pleasure. These elements figure strongly in the 'slackness' urban culture today, in which both men and women play active and heavily sexualized roles. The way in which young black British men in the diaspora are prototypically described as having irresponsibly fathered children with different 'baby mothers' is another distant relation of the same ideological trope. However, always, at the other end of this chain of phantasmatic desires are those who are the objects and victims of the process – especially women and gay men.

This is to say that race/colour really does work as the principle of articulation across the society as a whole: as the means by which multiple forms of oppression interconnect and take on meaning. Race, whatever it may signify, cannot be seen except through its appearances, while skin colour is only too visible. So it is tempting to use one to stand in for – *to represent* – the other.

Of the two terms – race and colour – race was and is the primordial category. It used to be assumed that racial difference was transmitted biologically and genetically. Indeed, Skip Gates long ago argued that race became 'a trope of irreducible difference between cultures, linguistic groups or adherents of specific belief systems which – more often than not – also have fundamentally opposed economic interests'. The problem which follows is that racial transmission is not visible to the naked eye. It's thus difficult to build a common-sense distinction – an everyday social language – around genetic differences if they don't have visible, obvious and easily available referents. Skin colour, on the other hand, is only too immediately visible. Its visibility was, and is, its greatest discursive value. It facilitates instant recognition. Visibility thus becomes the synonym for truth. To borrow from Jacqueline Rose's wonderful book *Sexuality in the Field of Vision*, these manoeuvres locate race in 'the field of vision'. Thus the substitution of colour for race provided a readable *code* within which one term could be substituted for the other. Ernesto Laclau and Chantal Mouffe call this structure of thinking a 'system of equivalence'.

In this discursive system, biological race was the primary category of difference. But colour was the most obvious visual boundary marker. It enabled us to apprehend processes that could not be seen with the naked eye, but which we knew were at work invisibly within the body. These equivalences are of the first importance: not, as its critics put it, because it's 'just a matter of language', but because such discursive systems shape and govern social practices and vice versa.

The process of social mapping included the stereotyping not just of blood, but also of cultural characteristics. In colonial discourse, non-white peoples were regularly categorized as congenitally lazy, unreliable, aggressive, over-emotional, over-sexed, irrational, not well endowed intellectually and thus destined by nature to be for ever low down on the scale of civilized societies. When the trade in slaves was under way, and when eventually the slaves' basic humanity came grudgingly to be acknowledged, they were most commonly perceived as belonging to the Negro race, understood as an altogether separate and lower order of human beings permanently confined to an inferior stage of social development. Cultural stereotypes could then be thought of as *like colour*: fixed and immovable because – apparently – derived not from history, but from nature. Another way of putting this was that racial cultural characteristics change, if at all, only at the glacial speed of natural evolution. In everyday life they are experienced as permanent, secured and eternal, and thus not subject to reform or change.

The effect of this was to fix, naturalize and normalize racial difference, translating physical appearance into social meaning. In

Mythologies Roland Barthes mobilized such an argument in his discussion of the image of the black soldier saluting the French flag on the cover of *Paris Match*. He called the ideological process involved 'naturalization', the practice of reducing history to nature. In so doing, Barthes was following an observation by Marx about the means by which bourgeois ideology normalizes the workings of the capitalist market, making it appear to be an economic system authorized by nature itself.

The term naturalization also brings to mind Fanon, who calls a system of racialized social distinction organized around skin colour an 'epidermal schema'. From this perspective, the body becomes a thing to 'think difference with', as well as something which immediately triggers anxiety and fear. '*Tiens, Mama! Un nègre!*', the child exclaims in Fanon's famous rendition. In these few words, much of the menace of race is condensed. And as Fanon demonstrated through such seemingly inconsequential practices, white fear of black itself becomes normalized.

It was teasing out this 'system of articulation' which led me to pose the question, in my opening lecture for the DuBois Center for African-American Studies at Harvard, 'Is Race Nothing but a Floating Signifier?' My short answer was that race is *both* a socio-economic 'fact' *and* a social construct or a discursive 'event' – although never, of course, the sign of a fixed, proven, objective scientific law operating outside discourse and as such a warrant for its own validity.

The importance of race/colour as a discursive signifier in the organization of social meaning didn't imply (as the sceptics supposed) that discourse didn't matter in (as they say) 'the real world' because it was 'only language'. Discourse and practice are not fundamentally opposed. Practices always have a meaning, and meanings organize practice and produce real effects. Within a system of representation of this kind, I argued, explaining racism doesn't require that we make a principled, analytic choice between physical and cultural factors. Rather, the two became, as I put it then, 'racism's two registers'.

The process of decolonization in Jamaica had to engage with the home culture on many different fronts. It was crucial to bring to the forefront of conscious thought and language what had been perpetually disavowed. This offers one way of understanding the recurring dynamic of the cultural revolutions of the late 1960s and the 1970s, which promised to liberate us from the social habits of disavowal that had underwritten the workings of modern Jamaica.

When I was growing up this was yet to be. No such collective will existed, outside the various undercurrents of that other Jamaica which could barely be known to people of my class and colour. This resulted in an unnerving, debilitating experience: to feel that there was no available language with which to understand what was most urgent and deep inside every one of us. The journey away from Jamaica also had to become the journey to something new, which would allow us to speak what was in us.

PART II
Leaving Jamaica

5. Conscripts of Modernity

I hope that I've conveyed my unease as a child and as a young man growing up in a colonial Jamaica that impelled me, and many of my generation, to leave. I don't intend to discuss the significant numbers for whom migration was principally a matter of economic necessity. I'm concerned here with those who, like me and myriad others, had been well educated and nursed certain hopes that we could live – in some way – the life of the mind, and who believed that in the Caribbean such hopes could not, in these years, be realized.

And yet mine was also the generation of Independence; 1938 had happened, and in the years which followed the entire configuration of Jamaican – and of the larger Caribbean – politics shifted, creating the formal structures of democratic nationhood. By the early 1950s Independence and Caribbean Federation were not so much distant prospects as increasingly practical political possibilities. Inside the claustrophobia of the colonial situation, these hopes for a different social world came to be part of me.

I've explained this before. But in locating the countervailing political and cultural resources available to me, I want to turn slightly the angle of vision: from the private world of my family to the public world of my schooling. It was the colonial education system which, for good or ill, conscripted me into modernity.

School represented a shift from the relatively closed enclave of my family to the more socially open and racially mixed – more typically Jamaican – world which profoundly shaped me, both personally and intellectually. It provided the historical circumstances, the opening up of a horizon, which slowly set me free from the grip of an oppressive cultural colonialism. It's strange, as schools like the one I attended enshrined deep in their very purpose the 'enlightened' elements of the colonial project. Yet I found that it freed me

from the 'little theatre' of impossible colonial and racial imperatives that my family enacted with such intensity.

Following 1938 and the reforms it precipitated, the old class- and
colour-lines were shifting and the inherited social realities and
habits were in the process of being recast. A broader social spectrum
was recruited to secondary schools like Jamaica College (JC, as it
was known), which is where I went, that opened up the opportunities for social advancement. Education had always been conceived
by reformers as the main route to upward mobility and moral
improvement for 'the clever black minority' who took advantage
of it. The growth in black consciousness, the surge in mass politics
in the colony and the various reports on social conditions following
'the troubles' of the late 1930s provided a further stimulus. I don't
suppose schools like mine had been deliberately designed to arouse
more ambitious social expectations, but that was their effect, even
though universal secondary education did not yet exist. School certainly didn't set me free, whatever that could have meant at the
time. But, in the very moment of conscripting me, it loosened the
grip of that colonization of the mind which, for people of my age,
seemed to be enshrined primarily in the formal education system.

Even the elite schools, typical colonial institutions modelled on the English public school, could not resist the tide of historical change. I think it was in my first term at Jamaica College that Michael Manley, a member of the sixth form (the top class), was involved in an altercation with a teacher and accused of an act of insubordination. Michael subsequently led the PNP, became Prime Minister, was a courageous critic of Washington's role in the Caribbean, a great admirer of Fidel Castro, and in the 1970s established himself as a leading figure in the radicalization of Third World politics. In the school it was said that he had thrown a book at a particularly patrician English master of history who, I presumed, had offered some outrageous colonialist interpretation during one of his classes. Michael was forthwith suspended. His father, Norman Manley – outstanding Queen's Counsel, established member of the Legislative Council and in effect Prime Minister – roared up in his official car to collect Michael and negotiate a solution. Such events propelled the increasingly vibrant anti-imperialist politics simmering outside right into the heart of the classroom. We began, in typical Jamaican fashion, to argue in an animated way about politics. What little my family knew of these occurrences didn't endear me to them. My father rarely expressed a political opinion at home, although I suspected he was more divided in his loyalties than he let on. But he was closely monitored by my mother, to whom so much seemed like the end of the world. However, by the 1940s young Jamaicans like me simply imbibed from the general ethos the ambition to bring about the end of colonial rule, even without necessarily being very politically involved.

Subsequently this generation was to become the new elite during and after Independence. They were to be the ministers and senior civil servants of the independent government, important figures in business and the professions, leading academics at the newly established University College of the West Indies and in the colleges and teacher-training institutions, the poets, writers, journalists and historians of the new nation. Subsequently, in a further twist, the next political generation became the radicals of the 1970s student movement. From a later perspective, one can see that this was one step in the long-term, highly contradictory ascent of the brown and minority black middle classes to socio-economic, political and cultural power, and their assimilation into a certain version of the nation. But at the time, to small boys like me, these clever, ambitious, increasingly self-confident, athletic young men occupying the forbidden veranda outside the prefects' room, many with radical political views about colonialism and Independence, were the 'lords of creation'. I got to know a number of them well as I became older.

One whom I particularly respected from afar was Neville Dawes, a fine poet (his son Kwame became an outstanding one) and a radical academic who taught in Africa, but whom, as an aspiring musician, I especially admired because he was an accomplished jazz pianist. The volume of his papers, edited by Kwame, which has recently been published is a revelation in the way it weaves together the aesthetic and the political. There were many other such figures. These senior JC boys seemed to know that they were destined to inherit power from the colonizers, to become the new political and business class and to form the leading social cadre of post-Independence Jamaica. And so they did.

Anyone who has read C. L. R. James's *Beyond a Boundary* will know what formative institutions these big, single-sex secondary schools were for clever West Indian boys and girls who had come up through the free elementary school system where the majority of children were educated, and beyond which most rarely ventured. Even though James's education took place some thirty years before mine, and in Trinidad not Jamaica, I instantly recognized the social world he evoked. In my time some JC boys were fee-paying, others scholarship-supported. These schools functioned as key engines in the formation and reproduction of the social elite. In the Caribbean and right across the empire, they were decisive in the making of the post-colonial ruling castes. Edward Said describes similar school experiences in Cairo in his eloquent autobiography, *Out Of Place*.

In Jamaica the leading seven or eight boys' schools and the five or six girls' schools at the top of the ladder were intensely academic in ethos, with a developed colonial curriculum, validated through exams externally assessed in Britain. They were fiercely competitive with each other in sport and academic success, and always monop- olized the island scholarships to study abroad. They functioned for the Caribbean elite like the public schools do in England. People still ask, 'Where were you at school?', expecting the reply, 'I went to Jamaica College' or 'I'm a St George's boy'; or in Barbados, 'from Harrison College'; or in Trinidad, 'Queen's Royal College'. Despite Independence, these schools still function as a badge of social iden- tification. The same was true for girls. My mother was educated at the exclusive Hampton's; my sister Pat at St Andrews Girls' School. As I have mentioned, my beloved cousin Sister Maureen Clare went to school at (and subsequently became an outstanding headmis- tress of) the Catholic Immaculate Conception High School, the pre-eminent girls' school of its time, although she comprehensively transformed its ethos and vision.

The curriculum was overwhelmingly Anglo-centric in content and emphasis, with a continuing Victorian bias: formal grammar, punctuation and précis skills, English literature, British (actually English) history, the classics (Latin but not Greek), French (not Spanish, although Jamaica neighbours Spanish-speaking Carib- bean peoples), maths, the sciences, the geography of the developed world. I remember colouring in endless maps of the wheat-growing prairies of western Canada: Alberta, Saskatchewan and Manitoba. These subjects were at the heart of the Cambridge Ordinary and Higher Level syllabuses.

However, by my middle years at the school the hint of change was in the air. I received the early, modest introduction of some Caribbean elements into the formal curriculum, a process which only really took off after Independence. A small booklet published by Jamaica's pre-eminent daily paper, the *Gleaner* (whose crossword puzzle my father completed each day), offered a brief introduction to the geography and history of Jamaica. This was, to say the least, a chequered history, which – properly told – would have captured the attention of young Jamaicans: Columbus's 'discovery' of the New World; the struggles between the European powers played out in the Caribbean; the English pirates raiding the silver-bearing Spanish galleons on their way home and racing to shelter in Port Royal; the British driving off the Spanish, seizing the island, transferring the seat of government from Spanish Town to Kingston, expanding the region as slave plantations, and inaugurating a sustained period of British colonial rule. But much of the salient material and critical aspects of this story were barely acknowledged. The book did say something about each of the various British governors the Colonial Office appointed, one of whom – Sir Anthony Musgrave – had connections with the founding of my school, and after whom my 'house' in school was named. It didn't say much, as I recall, about Governor Eyre and the horrific repression he exercised following the rising in Morant Bay.

My headmaster, Hugo Chambers, a geographer, introduced the *Gleaner* booklet into our classes – I can still recall its flimsy cardboard cover and squashed layout – although it wasn't formally examined. We still knew nothing about many other parts of the empire, or about the role of European conquests in shaping the New World, or about slavery as a system. I remember in 1947 watching Indians marching past our house with drums and flags to celebrate Indian Independence. But I wasn't sure how it connected to us. We read no Caribbean literature. The great flowering of the West Indian novel really took off later, in the 1950s, coinciding with the period when I came to England. Not surprisingly, though, this literary renaissance was produced by writers whose aesthetic aspirations were formed in educational institutions exactly like the ones I have been describing, and who then – it now seems, inevitably – chose to spend time abroad.

Although we were tied to the formal curriculum, other more subversive elements kept creeping in. A current affairs/modern history optional A-Level History paper had been introduced at Cambridge Higher Schools Level and I chose to take it in both my shots at A-Level. I sat the exams twice because I was too young to be eligible for a scholarship to study abroad at the first go. The optional paper required us to learn about 'contemporary historical events': about the rise of fascism, the causes of the Second World

War, Lenin and the Russian Revolution, the scourge of Communism and the origins of the Cold War. We had no texts, but we followed current events in the weekly instalments of *Keesing's Contemporary Archives* and we read, among other things, some British Council current affairs pamphlets, including one about Lenin.

This paper was taught by our history master, an Englishman, who had originally come to Jamaica with the Corinthian footballers' touring side and stayed on as teacher and football coach. I think he regarded our learning about Russia as inoculating the emerging leaders of Jamaican society against the virus of Marxism and anti-imperialist politics. However, we thought it brought history alive. This part of the curriculum stimulated our interest in the contemporary world, illuminated things we wanted to know more about, and provided a respite from Walpole, the two Pitts and the Age of Reform. Such staples of school history were never once connected to Emancipation or to the pressing demand for universal suffrage, then an inescapable, urgent matter in Jamaica; nor to industrialization which, again, no one ever thought to read alongside the question of modern enslavement.

We appropriated the knowledge transmitted by these unexpected sources in unpredictable ways. I remember finding in the library a paperback copy of *The Communist Manifesto*, my first encounter with the captivating prose of Karl Marx. The more the British Council pamphlets thundered at the iniquities of the Russian Revolution and of Lenin on imperialism, the more intrigued I became. Disturbing elements were always penetrating and subverting the protective shell of my colonial education which somehow could no longer insulate itself from them. The Second World War imposed a temporary hiatus on the Independence process. For a time, the struggle for self-government seemed becalmed by a wave of patriotic sentiment, as many Jamaicans volunteered – as they had in the First World War – to serve in the British armed forces and to contribute to the British war effort. At the outset of the war I recall being told that Hitler was a crazed dictator who wanted to dominate the world and threatened the British Empire and 'the democracies', of which, presumably, we were a dependent part! Of fascism or the conditions which gave rise to the war, however, we knew nothing. It wasn't until much later in my schooling that this changed. George Lamming's account of his Barbadian schooling in his extraordinary novel *In The Castle of My Skin*, although a few years before my time, is certainly not far removed from my own memories of the Jamaican situation.

However, I followed the progress of the war avidly and it became a sort of learning process for me, as for many. I tracked the theatres of hostilities in my atlas, inadvertently discovering a great deal about the world as I did so. I knew about Dunkirk, the Blitz, Rommel's and Montgomery's campaigns in North Africa, the invasion of Italy, the Soviet agitation for a Second Front and about the invasion of France on D-Day. It captured my imagination. I wrote stories about landings on strangely named French beaches and played war games with my friends. With a promiscuous disregard for the greater issues of Right and Wrong, we imported these scenarios into our play. We replicated what we imagined were 'sorties' between pilots in Spitfires and Messerschmitts, setting off for our missions ('Chocks away!') and sitting at the steering wheel (our substitute joystick) of the immobile family car, trying not to attract my parents' attention by pressing too intently on the horn or shifting dramatically the gears (our machine-gun triggers and bomb releases).

There were constant rumours of German cruisers and U-boats sighted in the Caribbean. Following the Battle of the River Plate, the memorable scuttling in Montevideo harbour of the mighty German pocket battleship the *Graf Spee* gave them credence. In Jamaica, a few Germans and Italians were very politely interned for the duration in a camp which has since become the campus of the University. But of 'the enemy' in the flesh, not a whisper. We were, of course, pro-Allies, although I also recall a secret passion among us for the buttoned-up uniforms, black thigh-length boots and peaked caps of the Wehrmacht! But we were seeing a lot of Movietone News footage and war films by then . . .

There seemed no guarantee that, after the war, the Independence tide would begin to flow again. But in truth there could be no turning back to the old colonial days. We had entered the final phase of colonization and the war had served as its accelerator. By the time I left Jamaica in 1951, we knew independent Jamaica was only a few years away.

So, paradoxically, the war helped me gradually, and unevenly, to perceive events in Jamaica as part of something larger: in particular, the retreat of colonialism and the advance of the historic wave of post-war decolonization. In Jamaica, this proved to be a different experience from elsewhere in the empire, where decolonization was more ferociously resisted and fiercely contested, being associated with protracted emergencies, a flood of British troops, internment camps, torture and ferocious wars of national liberation. However, the experience of British Guiana in October 1953, when fresh battalions were dispatched from Britain and the constitution was suspended, suggested that such eventualities were not in themselves foreign to the Caribbean.

I don't mean to suggest that my schooling was ever *directly* subversive. It wasn't. But ideas began to circulate which gradually unsettled the solid edifice of colonial knowledge and affective identification codified by English cultural models, to which we were harnessed. Schools were one of the key sites for the production of the colonial subject: of a finely elaborated colonial subjectivity. But they also simultaneously played an unauthorised role in disturbing them.

There can be no question that, quite apart from *what* was taught, schools like Jamaica College were designed to cultivate and conscript a British-oriented, subordinate 'native' elite. Those schooled in such an environment would become 'subjectified' from the inside by having their heads stuffed with a curriculum devoted to an idea of civilization to which, it was hoped, they would be motivated to aspire. This was a sort of 'education of the feelings' as much as of the mind, the aim of which was evident both in the subjects we were taught and in the manner in which we were taught them. These valorized the British imagination, ways of life and habits of authority which the colonial authorities believed to be embedded in the national literature, political institutions, social conventions, manners, values and ideals of 'the mother country'.

The paradoxes and contradictory pulls in such an endeavour were manifest. In the blazing heat, my school planned to get ivy to take root and to cover the chapel walls. Our English headmaster introduced tuck shops. On dress days we sweated in blazers. On buses and trams prefects struggled to make small boys keep their caps lodged somehow on the crown of their woolly heads, and laboured to keep their own caps white and free of the swirling dust. That these 'habits and virtues' really belonged to other people, and could only be practised and instituted properly by them in a place very different from ours, was an unsolved puzzle, a nagging anxiety. To learn what they knew, did one have to become like them?

However, as I've already mentioned, in some ways schools like mine were subversive *socially*. They were certainly elite institutions, dominated (though not exclusive populated) by the coloured middle class, expatriates or local whites who could afford the fees. But they also recruited a majority of clever scholarship boys and girls widely across the social and colour spectrum of Jamaican society, and this made them more representative socially and racially than many other colonial institutions. My school friends were drawn from this wider spectrum, more so than those associated with my home and family circle. Indeed, I was not allowed to bring many of them home.

So school was by this time inevitably mixed, racially and by skin colour, culturally more syncretic, and consequently a site of potential slippage and resistance. It was as well, for me, a place of invisibility and escape, a gateway to another – subterranean – life. After a while I simply cut out, giving my parents no clue as to where I was, or what I was getting up to in this other world. I couldn't bring friends to my home, but I could go to theirs. And I did. I lived in two discrete worlds. Keeping them as far apart as I possibly could was my main survival strategy.

There were, in addition, many impulses in the informal curriculum of the school which introduced us, even if sometimes only obliquely, to different forms of knowing and being. I increasingly came to see these as alternative routes to a different *kind* of knowledge. When I was more senior, my special subjects were literature, history, Latin and Roman history. The latter, I was informed, would give me access to 'the cradle of Western civilization'. What would have been obvious local historical sources for a sixth-form class of history specialists had not, by and large, been worked on by Jamaican researchers or identified as part of an emerging national story. On the other hand, British history was taught without any serious – historical – reference to the empire. It just happened to be there, a matter of faith and providence rather than a historical outcome. It was as if Britain had acquired an empire, as Sir John Seeley famously had it, in 'a fit of absent-mindedness'. Key events in Jamaican history never surfaced, although I had often driven past the statue of Paul Bogle, one of the leaders of the Morant Bay uprising, in the town square.

Much of my private reading was haphazard or distantly shaped by the school curriculum. One of my relations had purchased a special-offer travelling library of classic English nineteenth-century novels, and I read my way through them: Jane Austen's *Emma* and *Pride and Prejudice*, Scott's *Ivanhoe*, Thackeray's *Henry Esmond*, Trollope's *The Way We Live Now*, Hardy's *The Mayor of Casterbridge*, a lot of Dickens. I can't recall any Brontës or George Eliot, but they might have been there. C. L. R. James said he re-read *Vanity Fair* every year. But the rebellious, independent Becky Sharp never put her nose into our family canon.

At night, when the rest of the family had gone to bed and I was still up trying to finish homework for the next day, I could often be found instead alone on the front veranda looking out into the darkness and falling off my chair with laughter at *The Pickwick Papers*. (This makes me think of different times. No sensible Jamaican middle-class person sits on their front veranda alone at night these days without a metal grille, a chained door and a ferocious dog between them and the threatening void outside.) How odd to have a youthful imagination formed in such close relation to the very different fictional worlds of another place, like another planet. I did an interview many years later with Darcus Howe, anti-racist activist and founder editor of *Race Today*, about the formative impact on us both as youngsters of reading *Great Expectations*!

In truth, though, the informal curriculum really came from other sources. Despite the hoops of steel binding the Anglophone Caribbean to Britain, there were already many connections between Jamaica and the US. There had been a significant Caribbean migration to North America after the First World War, especially of intellectuals and writers – Claude McKay, for example, or Eric Walrond, among many, many more – and they were prominent in the political, artistic and religious movements around Harlem in the 1920s. West Indians represented a key echelon in the Garveyite movement. Indirectly, their influence filtered back to the Caribbean, offering a glimpse into what, despite the depth of racism in the US, felt to us like a less hierarchical, more open and demotic society, at least in the North. We became aware of an awakening black consciousness of the post-Civil War world of African-American black life, although I don't think at this stage I had heard of figures associated with the Harlem Renaissance like Langston Hughes, Alain Locke, Countee Cullen, Aaron Douglas or James Van Der Zee. I suppose if I had read the Garveyite press I would have come to know more, but these developments in the US did not penetrate into our social world. Of course, race permeated Jamaican society in the form of endless 'talk' about skin colour; but anti-colonialism remained a more potent force than race at this stage in Jamaica, and until the 1970s this constituted one of the significant differences between the Caribbean and the US.

The Institute of Jamaica, which was the big central reference library in Kingston, opened a junior section and on Saturday mornings I would hang out there and skim-read or borrow all sorts of books. In fact, much later, after he'd returned from Africa, Neville Dawes became director of the Institute for a time. That's where I first encountered, when I was a little older, modern Western literature, painting and contemporary philosophical ideas. I well remember, as an aspiring young poet in the Romantic mode, my first encounter with the recognizably contemporary, vernacular, conversational language and rhythms of T. S. Eliot's *The Waste Land*. Magic! Eliot was greatly favoured by John La Rose, the writer, poet, intellectual and political activist, who founded New Beacon

Books, the Third World Book Fair, the Alliance of Black Parents Movement and the Black Youth Movement, and who was one of the most significant and inspiring migrant political intellectuals of the post-war period. He recalls a similar experience.

The footnotes to *The Waste Land* referred to anthropological rituals and to the literature on myth. In fact, as a result of reading Eliot, James Frazer's *The Golden Bough* was the book I was to ask for when I won an undergraduate prize in my first year at Merton College, Oxford. But who was Frazer, and what did he think? What on earth did poetry have to do with fertility myths? More pertinently, who *were* the crowd that flowed across London Bridge? Why weren't the multitudes who walked up and down King Street, the main shopping thoroughfare of downtown Kingston, worthy subject matter of poetry too? Why did Eliot's crowd seem so depressed? Why was the poem so broken up, so disjointed and fragmented? Why had Eliot allowed Ezra Pound to re-edit it so extensively? And, anyway, who was Pound and what had *he* written? Above all, what had any of it to do with Jamaica and my life?

Every line of this modern poetry seemed wilfully constructed in a radically unhomely idiom. Nevertheless, it opened doors into sensibilities about which I knew nothing. Perversely, perhaps, I wanted to know more, even while – or because – I felt shut out. It was as if, well educated though I was, the knowledge I needed to make sense of the contemporary world had somehow slipped between the cracks.

Modernism, however we choose to understand it, was one of the resources which allowed me to assemble another life, at one remove from the immediate diktats of the colonial order, as I experienced them. Not without contradictions and the occasional cul de sac, of course.

I don't mean by this that I have some exclusive addiction to 'modern' artistic or literary styles, which is far from the truth. Such idioms do, however, have a resonance for me because of when and how I first encountered them.

The idea of modernization as an end in itself does not interest me, although I have discovered that I sort of am, by inadvertence as it were, what Foucault calls a 'historian of the present'. I'm trans-fixed by the question, 'How did we get to where we are *now*?' What did stimulate my interest in modernism was the fact that new currents were clearly emerging which were transforming the intel-lectual world, and that writers, painters, poets, novelists and film-makers were responding to the new situation in experimental and creative ways.

My friend David Scott, in his book on C. L. R. James's *The Black Jacobins*, described Toussaint L'Ouverture, the leader of the slave rebellion in St Domingue, as 'a conscript of modernity' – and it's from David that I borrow the title I've given this chapter. I think he meant that, during the Haitian Revolution, Toussaint could only – or principally – 'think' freedom within the 'problem space' and the limits of concepts drawn from France and the French revolutionary tradition, from which, in another sense, he wanted to liberate St Domingue. This contradiction is personified by black ex-slave lead-ers like Toussaint and Dessalines, who eventually threw the French planters into the sea, adopting the uniforms of *black* Jacobins – in other words, of *Parisians*.

I too wanted to immerse myself, somehow, in the historical time in which I was living. But the route to that was through a sensibility which, by belonging elsewhere, only confirmed my marginaliza-tion. Indeed, modern literary and artistic forms came to seem significant *because* of, not despite, the fact that they spoke to and out of something 'other'. This was colonialism's revenge. Modernity, it affirmed, did not belong to the likes of us. Alienation is a much-used and abused word. But it seems appropriate here.

Modern poetry was not even like the kind of English poetry I had been taught at school, which I could grasp, criticize, recite and above all imitate. I knew Keats's *Odes* by heart and had tried to write poems like them. The modern rhythms I encountered were more urgent, fractured, trying to enunciate a new kind of emotion-ally charged, cognitively challenging contemporary consciousness, mirroring the times of historical crisis which had given birth to them. It wasn't until later that I appreciated that they were speak-ing out of the profound trauma and social crisis of Western society before, during and in the aftermath of the First World War – what the art critic T. J. Clark understands to be the agony that gave rise to modernism 'in the first place'. In retrospect, of course, I can see that one might have guessed this from the distinctly downbeat tone which Eliot adopted. I thought of the First World War – whose iconography is etched into my memory by one of the volumes of an encyclopedia, *The Book of Knowledge*, which I read over and over again – as a war that 'we', 'the democracies', had won. But it was also, so I was to discover, the end of an era, and marked one of the most far-reaching epistemological upheavals in modern history in every field of knowledge – from abstraction and photography in the visual arts and atonality in music, to psychoanalysis, relativity, quantum physics, linguistics and logical positivism.

In fact it was only gradually that I came to understand that much of what I was responding to had to do with something called 'the modern movement' in science, philosophy and the arts (or, even more mysteriously, 'modernism'). We know a great deal about modernism now. But how it looked from the periphery at the time is still not well understood. There was not only poetry and fiction, but painters too: the stylistically protean Picasso, Braque, the translucent colour of Matisse, Miró, Klee and Duchamp. Though if you had added Diego Rivera and Frida Kahlo's names to that list, I would not have been able to make sense of it. I remember thinking that Paul Klee's work, with its distorted lines, caricature figures and comical exaggerations, its sense of the absurd, was absolutely novel and intellectually challenging: an astonishingly wilful departure from the representational function of art I had always taken for granted. I was moved by Klee's willingness, in Philip Hensher's words, to combat oppression and violence 'with laughter'. I'd never seen anything like it. But visual modernism connected with the amelodic music of composers like Stravinsky and Prokofiev and the linguistic experimentation of writers such as James Joyce, Dorothy Richardson and Virginia Woolf.

Predictably, in 1953, on my first summer vacation – a long bicycle tour of northern France, Holland and Germany with my American friend Don Bell – I took only three books: Joyce's *Ulysses*, Homer's

Odyssey and Stuart Gilbert's *James Joyce's Ulysses*, a guide to Joyce's use of Homer.

Encountering these ideas in the steaming midday heat of a tropical colonial city was like experiencing a snowstorm in a Caribbean summer. With what form of life did these strange, unconventional things connect? What circumstances had produced them? Was the way Joyce experimented with language linked to the fact that he was Irish? Or were cosmopolitanism and Irishness mutually exclusive? And, if so, why was *Ulysses* being written in Trieste? Could you compose 'modern poetry' or paint an abstract work of art or write *Ulysses* in Kingston, and what would *that* mean? Actually, as is now clear, Kingston, and many locales like it, are ready-made and waiting for their Homeric reincarnations. We need only think, at this point, of Derek Walcott's *Omeros*. I can see now that the Caribbean is in some ways the prototype *mise en scène* for such an odyssey. But I couldn't see that at the time.

Wasn't it a contradiction in terms to be a modernist in Jamaica? The question, though based on a profound misunderstanding on my part, was not entirely wrong-headed. For the idea of the modern has indeed been extensively hijacked and woven into the teleological and triumphalist Western story, in which everything 'progresses' to its pinnacle of achievement in Western enlightenment and artistic and philosophical achievement. Given this, the idea of modernity has had to be recast, not as a matter of pure disinterested fact but as an exercise in what Foucault, borrowing from Nietzsche, calls 'the will to power'. The emergence of 'the modern' has never been an uncontested or uncontestable narrative: we must also recall the role which what was *not* modern – the so-called 'primitive other' – played in breaking the mould of contemporary thought and representation, releasing the modern from its nineteenth-century confinements into new modes of perception and relationship. Picasso was the *locus classicus* here, although it took another half-century for the idea that 'many modernities' coexist to gain any purchase.

I understood all this better some decades later when I first saw, in the 1970s, the paintings of that great Guyanese abstractionist

Frank Bowling, who lived most of his adult life in Britain and in the US, and whose stunning corpus of work was for a long time – and to some extent still is – without proper recognition in Britain. Bowling once memorably remarked, to the astonishment of many radical young black artists in his audience, that 'The black soul, if there is such a thing, begins in modernism.' What a wonderful way to think! I feel that something of the import of Bowling's insight had touched me as a young person in the Jamaica Institute in the 1940s.

More than this, my identification with modern African-American music was seminal for my rapidly shifting inner sense of who I was. As a young colonial of colour – though not, of course, yet self-consciously black – I could connect directly and emotionally with it, which was not quite so easy with other art forms. In poetry, the complexities of our relationship to Standard English and Received Pronunciation, and the slippages of patois and the varieties of ver-nacular we spoke, proved a difficult linguistic barrier to surmount. Before giving up the poetic vocation altogether, however, I did try to write poetry in a Jamaican idiom – a version of *King Lear*, with a possessively patriarchal Jamaican father and his three daughters at its centre, if you please! We didn't yet have available either Edward Kamau Brathwaite's inspired experiments with the 'mother tongue' or, on the opposite side of the coin, Derek Walcott's mastery of some of the most complex metric forms in European literature. Patois seemed inappropriate as a creative medium, except for the inventive comic verse of someone like Louise Bennett and in ver-sions of popular theatre such as the annual pantomime, which had been hilariously localized and brought popular life into the realm of writing and performance. Jamaican music in the 1940s was very different from the type of music most people associate with Jamaica today. Jamaican mento was principally an Afro-folk music, as in the local patois ballads, or in dance a combination of African rhythms, Latin syncopation and European melody. We knew by heart the words of the mento folk songs, whose content was drawn from daily-life situations laced with sexual double entendres. Their titles often spoke volumes: 'Carry Mi' Donkey Down Dere', 'Come Back,

Liza', 'Brown Skin Girl', the loading-bananas song 'Daylight Come an' Mi Wan' Go Home' and 'Carry Mi Ackee Go-a Linstead Market/ Not a Quattie Wort' Sell' – some of which, in a later period, Harry Belafonte popularized widely, beyond Jamaica.

We danced to this rather innocent music. It certainly had a rhythmic insistence which registered immediately in body movements. We moved to it in what people would now think of as an instinctively 'Caribbean' way: the body hung 'loose', with lots of shoulder-shaking, pelvic gyrations and suggestive, erotic thrusts clearly drawn from Jamaican popular dance – but performed by us teenagers, for our parents' consumption at least, in the best possible taste. The open, confrontational eroticism, sexual simulation and deliberate slackness of contemporary dancehall and other Jamaican musics, which make even reggae seem modest and restrained in retrospect, were still light years away.

However, mento came to be perceived as too familiar, too genteel, too domesticated: despite its apparent worldliness and its clear sexual connotations, too tame in comparison, say, to the explosion of new Jamaican musics like ska, blue beat and then reggae which were to emerge after Independence and which carried a much more powerful political and erotic charge.

Important too were gospel and 'jump blues', which Jamaicans began to listen to at this time on small radio stations playing 'race music', much of it produced by independent record companies exclusively for a black audience.

In the 1940s, only a tiny proportion of the educated Jamaican middle class listened to recorded music of any kind, although there was an intermediary stratum of English sentimental ballads, music-hall songs and Negro spirituals from the old slave South which had found their way into the Jamaican coloured middle-class drawing-room repertoire. I think I must have first heard Paul Robeson's 'Old Man River' at this time. There were some live concerts by a few fine classical musicians. I tried at this time to write my first classical-music review of a performance by a Jamaican pianist. Even so, most of the local musicians keen to follow the classics were obliged to go abroad to undertake professional advanced study.

The other kind of music – modern jazz – being played by sophisticated black musicians from a long way off was a very different kind of summons to the soul of a young, colonial, aspiring intellectual like me. Whereas I couldn't find Ezra Pound's poetry, I could pick up on jazz. Indeed, I played piano in several small amateur jazz bands, from school in Jamaica to the end of my time in Oxford. We could get American stations on the radio, and every Saturday night I listened to early Frank Sinatra – with that perfectly pitched, haunting, stylish, urban-white voice and perfect diction – on the weekly *Hit Parade*, long before he became one of the first white pop-culture heart-throbs. My brother had a lot of jazz records, mainly big-band swing: Artie Shaw, Glenn Miller as well as Count Basie and Duke Ellington. I once staged a sit-down on the pavement on King Street and refused to move because at Christmas he bought a swing record when I wanted something different.

Some of my close friends at school were serious jazz aficionados, and a number of us began to listen to very early modern jazz and to exchange records. First we discovered musicians like Coleman Hawkins, Teddy Wilson, Mary Lou Williams and Louis Armstrong, who belonged to the transition phase between classic and modern jazz. Then a friend (whose first names were Franklin Delano, after FDR) introduced me to the early masters of bebop: Charlie Parker, Dizzy Gillespie, Thelonious Monk, Miles Davis, Kenny Clarke, J. J. Johnson, Max Roach, Horace Silver, Red Garland, Django Reinhardt and so on. I can still remember the first time I heard Bird play 'I Can't Get Started' and 'Lover Man' and Monk's rendition of 'Round Midnight'. I thought the way Parker disassembled the standard melody lines and reassembled them in a wonderfully lyrical flight of audacious improvisation simply startling. I listened to a great deal of jazz through the 1950s, and have continued to do so ever since.

I liked its formal complexity. I fell in love with the audacity and technical mastery of the musicians, the fluidity, the speed and brilliance of melodic movement, the adventurous chord progressions, the freely improvised, intricate fretwork which was woven around standard ballads and show tunes by mainstream composers like

Cole Porter, Rodgers and Hart and Johnny Mercer, translating them from a sentimental idiom into a sophisticated urban one. I relished the cryptic, 'bop' musical phrases which were elaborated into whole tracks. How any player knew where they were was a complete mystery to me. Once I sat in on piano with a much more experienced electric-guitar player, and when he felt I was losing my way he shouted, 'Count!' But I didn't know what he was talking about.

Even as a small boy I was a good dancer and had a sense of rhythm. But I could feel something different and deeply satisfying about the way my body responded to modern jazz's cooler beat. 'Relaxing into the groove' is the only way I can describe it. It was very different from the directions taken by the rhythm-dominated or African-American-influenced Jamaican music, which was up-tempo and heavily rhythmic on the beat. I was caught by modern jazz's laid-back, cool pacing; and by the perfectly controlled speed of faster numbers with a superb free-floating solo. I felt that improvisation had set the music free, but at the same time it was grounded and held in place by the drive of the rhythm section (drums, bass, piano in one of its modes), which underwrote and tethered everything.

Musically, the buoyant, upbeat rhythms characteristic of traditional forms seemed to have been more evenly redistributed across modern jazz, which we heard as equally accented across the beats of a bar. The black, conservative jazz critic Stanley Crouch says that in modern jazz, 'the steady beat . . . so essential to swing is spontaneously replaced by the demarcations of the form . . . Phrases replace meters'. Nonetheless, I felt that despite this basic architecture, the music managed to be freely exploratory.

Modern jazz was an excellent example of the articulation of structure and freedom. I was to learn later that Ferdinand de Saussure, the structural linguist who has been so influential for structuralist and post-structuralist theory, had defined in this way the relation between *langue*, that is the language system, and *parole*, the individual usage.

If you were virtually illiterate in terms of music, as I was, you never knew where the chord sequences in modern jazz would go next or what governed their inner logic. But you were set free to be creative because you knew there was always an underlying structure. I loved this tension between structure and freedom. I responded to the contrapuntal way, as Edward Said would put it, in which these elements played with and against one another.

I tried to replicate the deep structure of diminished and expanded chords, the enjambment and the slurred or delayed phrasing which bent straight musical lines into a more supple, groovy, bluesy modern idiom. But I was also gripped by something else with which modern jazz is not normally associated and which has not been widely discussed by the critics: namely, the almost unbearable emotional depths the music seemed able to plumb without yielding an inch to sentimentality. Take, for example, Miles Davis's 'I Waited For You'. I relished the hard, polished surfaces *and* the 'soul'.

People today who find this music too cerebral would be surprised to know that it was, in large part, its emotional intensity which appealed to my reserved, rather repressed, bottled-up self. I remember saying in my BBC *Desert Island Discs* interview that Miles Davis had put his finger on my soul. He had.

The inspired Irish novelist Colm Tóibín quotes from James Baldwin when he says: 'I don't mean to compare myself to a couple of artists I unreservedly admire, Miles Davis and Ray Charles – but I would like to think that some of the people who liked my book [*Another Country*] responded to it in a way similar to the way they respond when Miles and Ray are blowing. These artists in their very different ways, sing a kind of universal blues . . . They are telling us something of what it is like to be alive. It is not self-pity one hears in them but compassion . . . I am aiming at what Henry James called "perception at the pitch of passion".' I think that Baldwin has it right here. I am embarrassed to admit that, perversely, I probably also liked modern jazz because its syntax couldn't easily be unravelled. You had to work at it, though the ultimate reward was in no sense purely cerebral. I'm afraid there was more than a touch of the hubris of the young intellectual in that response!

When I was in Jamaica I had not heard the classic black blues singers like Bessie Smith or Ma Rainey, or gospel singers such as Mahalia Jackson. I had never heard Buddy Bolden or Jelly Roll Morton, who are often cited as the 'inventors' of jazz. For me they came later, out of sequence, when I started to listen to rhythm and blues, and to the soul and blues revival of the 1960s and 1970s. Nevertheless – in part because of modern jazz, paradoxical as that may sound – I gradually became aware of a new reservoir of feeling and identification opening up. I felt in touch with the slow-burn emergence of a new sort of black consciousness, which might one day enable us Jamaicans to speak our experience – after all the evasions, euphemisms, double-talk, disavowals and self-deceptions – in a conscious language of *race*.

I liked some white musicians: Chet Baker, Gerry Mulligan, Lee Konitz, Dave Brubeck, Paul Desmond. But I always knew that modern jazz was essentially a black voice. What this consists of is difficult to define, and I don't have the musical expertise to do so. It has something to do with prising the music away from the purity of line, the precision of hitting the right note straight and true, or scrupulously respecting the intervals, all of which were typical of great Western classical musical performance. Black popular music deliberately discards or renounces – bends or dirties up, you might say – that purity. The voice of the black female singer especially slides around the note, as if searching along the scale for it; stretching it, sketching in many alternatives on the way; or inferring in the melodic line other notes in the supporting chord which, as it were, it uses in passing. The emotion is generated in these spaces. Black does not have to be taken literally here. It is also the difference, stylistically, between Ella Fitzgerald in full lyrical mode – a beautiful sound in its own terms – and later Billie Holiday, when her voice was ravaged by drink and drugs.

It wasn't only that jazz's leading exponents were black Americans. This was, for me, a voice in which one could hear a whole historical experience of oppression and suffering being resumed and coming through into sound. Despite its modern intonation and sensibility, modern jazz helped me rediscover jazz's strong historical connections back to the sacred and secular blues, gospel music, slave chant and the call-and-response work-song traditions. As James Baldwin said, the blues is not just a type of music: it is really the name for a basic musical form, hiding within – and essential to – many kinds of black music which are far removed from the classic blues tradition. It is a structure of feeling. It has loss and sorrow, suffering and complaint, the cry of trouble and tribulation. But it also carries the promise of freedom and the celebratory shout of 'jubilee' embedded in its cadences. It often takes us to a dark place, but in some mysterious way and without easy consolation, it never leaves us there. It helped me to find my way, by an alternative route, to a different way of experiencing what Fanon in *Black Skin, White Masks* calls 'the fact of blackness'.

Actually my tastes in music are eclectic and inclusive, lacking the rigorous sensitivity and 'good taste' of the jazz scholar. I like rhythm and blues, soul, funk, Motown, reggae, lover's rock, some rap. I enjoy what people might think are unlikely figures like James Brown, Grace Jones, Gladys Knight, Ray Charles, Stevie Wonder, George Benson, The Supremes, Dione Warwick. I'm a fan of cross-over high-life merchants like Gilberto Gil, Hugh Masekela, Fela Kuti; Marley, of course, Jimmy Cliff and the Skatalites; also some hip-hop, drum-and-bass, occasionally house, to choose a revealingly random sample. I greatly enjoyed (though I'm not sure I often identified with) classic white pop and rock, including The Beatles, The Stones, The Clash. Only some contemporary white rock really tests my musical patience to breaking or tuning-off point. My musical loves also include classical music: Beethoven and Brahms, but pre-eminently Vivaldi, Bach, Mozart, Handel. I appreciate the fugal and the baroque, plainsong, some modern music (Bartók and Stravinsky, and even Boulez, rather than Stockhausen and Glass). And, surprisingly, quite a lot of English music, including some of the less chauvinistic Elgar, and – a late discovery – opera: Mozart, Verdi, Puccini and Britten.

However, habits formed early persist because of the resonances they trigger and the depth of the memories they evoke. I went on listening to modern jazz in the 1960s and 1970s – a high point embracing Miles Davis, Freddie Hubbard, John Coltrane, Cannonball

Adderley, J. J. Johnson, Milt Jackson, Eric Dolphy, Wes Montgomery, Paul Chambers, Herbie Hancock, Sonny Rollins and many more. And I have gone on doing so ever since, with this moment of awakening always buried somewhere deep in the experience of listening.

I suppose that these early engagements, in music and in literature among other things, spoke to an urgent desire to encounter new worlds, of a kind beyond the restricted ethos of a provincial colonial metropole. I suppose they appealed to an unspoken desire for wider horizons, though what that actually meant I'm sure I didn't know. The modern artists and musicians I liked seemed connected with their time in a way I wasn't. More particularly, I also wanted to know what life was *really* like 'over there', for those who had for so long mastered us, but whose days seemed at last to be numbered. I guess I was after a sort of final reckoning, a showdown.

My own wish to leave the Caribbean also stemmed from a desire to find a framework in which I could place my existence at the periphery in the context of a wider frame which irrevocably *placed* it. As Michelle Stephens remarks, 'the journey to the metropole was also a journey towards seeing and mapping the bigger picture within which you are articulated, naming the structures to which your experience as a colonial subject were articulated'.

When, in London in the early 1960s, I seriously considered returning home to live, I revisited these contradictory feelings. They had acquired a touchstone status in my reflections on my life. I had by then given up the project to become a creative writer and I didn't know enough music or play well enough to be a musician. Out of such 'failures' are critics and theorists made!

The tragedy is that, for us in the 1940s, these ambitions still unmistakably signified somewhere unreachable. They therefore became the unrequited object of a displaced yearning, an alienated desire. It took the actual encounter with this other scene to shatter the illusion. At the time, I didn't want to be English or British or European or white. But I felt that the difference between here and there was a more complicated matter for me than I had supposed; and this had something to do with *both* the resistance to colonization's closures *and* the opening of windows to other worlds. The enigma was how to connect them.

The immediate circumstances of my departure from Jamaica were these. At school, I was clever enough to have the opportunity for further education. I could either get a scholarship to study abroad, which was the traditional route, as my parents certainly couldn't have afforded such an expense. Or I could have gone to the new University College of the West Indies which, although its largest faculty was the Medical School, had small but expanding faculties in arts, social sciences and the humanities. Very early on I decided I would try to go abroad. By the time I left school I was converted to the Independence cause. I was anti-colonial in my sentiments, although not politically conscious much beyond that. I didn't connect that with the person I was being called to be by my family's aspirations for me. Neither of my parents had been to university, but they hoped that I would go to England to study as it were on their behalf, to fulfil their ambitions by proxy.

At my second go at A-Levels, I was awarded a Jamaica Scholarship and later was selected as the Rhodes Scholar of the year. Between winning my scholarships and going to England, I taught in a small experimental rural school at Knox College, near Spalding in Clarendon, in the mountainous, red-earthed centre of the island. Knox was modelled on a progressive philosophy and pioneered by a charismatic, visionary Presbyterian educationist called Lewis Davison. I enjoyed the school and the whole experience, and felt very much at home there. Away from 'home', at last. The school's vision was to design an appropriate education for local boys and girls from the rural areas: clever, bright as buttons and full of tricks, life and humour, but not sophisticated and from the socially lower colour and family backgrounds. I learned to move easily in that environment, once I was outside my family context. This was a critical moment in my disengagement from my familial culture: the first time I had lived in a rural area, the first time I truly fell in love. I think that was the moment when I knew that what I really wanted to be was a teacher.

I never felt exiled from Jamaica. This may sound odd, since I've spent more than sixty years in England and, although I've often visited, I've never lived for a long period in Jamaica since I left. However, I can honestly say that I never seriously contemplated my life in terms of a permanent exile. 'Strategic exile' is a different matter, as is the notion of self-exile. Thinking again of James Baldwin, who as readers will have guessed has been an important figure for me, Kevin Gaines has noted that 'it was often from the distance of self-exile that Baldwin elucidated the "private life" of the American racial imagination', which I find an interesting take on things.

My decision not to return to Jamaica was made in the 1960s, although actually it had probably already been taken years before, though I didn't know it. I'll explain this in more detail later. But I can say here that the main reason was, in a funny sense, 'private' too, although it encompassed much more than that. I knew instinctively that, had I returned to the close proximity and enveloping embrace of my family, I would have been emotionally destroyed by the experience. This came to me with startling clarity in the middle of my sister's illness. I had vowed, then, to get away if ever I was so lucky. There was no turning back. In ways which are profound, you can never go home again.

But it didn't feel like exile at the time and, I must add, it doesn't feel like that now. I would say, rather, that I chose to live my relation to where I was born, to my past, to my conditions of existence and to the dilemmas associated with them, *in and through the diaspora*: to track them through their various transformations and displacements, which are the forms in which they became – and are still – active and alive for me.

Naturally, I can't help thinking of C. L. R. James at moments like this. His decision to emigrate in 1932; his creative work as a novelist and short-story writer; his journalistic career as a cricket correspondent with the *Manchester Guardian*. Then his engagement with the anti-colonial struggle in Britain; his work with the Independent Labour Party; his conversion to Marxism and, as part of his critique of the Soviet form of Communism, to Trotskyism; his visit to Trotsky in Coyoacán in order to debate the race issue, and quizzing the Old Man about his views on sport. Then came the period in the US, captured in one of the most compelling but in the UK least quoted of his books, *American Civilization*; the formation of the Johnson-Forest Tendency, during which the matter of political organization came to preoccupy him; his analysis of the Hungarian Revolution; his deportation from the US and that most eloquent of protests – written as a homage to Herman Melville – *Mariners, Renegades and Castaways*. Then his return to Trinidad, his involvement with the labour unions, with Eric Williams and with the People's National Movement; the disaster of Chaguaramas and the American bases, dramatizing his political break with Williams. Finally, his return to London, living out his last days as a revered figure in his Brixton flat. It is certainly apposite to recall, in relation to the question of exile, his provocative observation in the appendix to *The Black Jacobins* that 'The first step to freedom was to go abroad.' Despite the fact that he has been retrospectively constructed as a black nationalist, the great Anglophone West Indian historian (of Haiti!) and a 'race man', his relationship to 'home' and 'abroad' was always more complex than any of that suggests. In this respect he stands as a kind of paradigmatic Caribbean thinker of the twentieth century.

For many Caribbean artists and intellectuals, going abroad after the war also seemed to have been part and parcel of the process of becoming independent persons and creative artists in their own right. It became, for the last generation of colonials, a sort of *rite de passage*, a coming of age or growing up. And it was a trans-Caribbean, indeed a transnational, phenomenon. Many of the key figures in the post-war Independence and national liberation movements spent time in Paris or London. The great Antillean poet and 'father' of the *négritude* movement, Aimé Césaire, and Frantz Fanon, both from Martinique, found themselves writing and debating in Paris, alongside important figures from francophone Africa such as Leopold Senghor and Alioune Diop. The founding of *Présence africaine* after the war marked a key moment not only in the makings of *Paris noir*, but in the recasting of phenomenological or existential philosophical traditions along the axes of blackness. This is the intellectual world with which Édouard Glissant engaged. Through the 1930s to the 1950s it generated a sensibility very different from the characteristic Pan-Africanism of black London.

Interestingly, the two traditions were to converge at the 1956 Congress of Negro Writers and Artists in Paris, where the two youngest delegates were Frantz Fanon and George Lamming, and where the presiding influence was the North American writer Richard Wright. The presence of such figures reordered the dispositions of the metropole. In the final decades of the European empires much of the work of decolonization took place in the metropoles themselves.

In an interview for *Redemption Song*, the television series I made for the BBC at the end of the 1980s, Césaire gently reminded me that politically he was, and had remained, a child of the French Revolution, still holding to the watchwords of *Liberté*, *égalité*, *fraternité*.

Fanon, too, belonged to at least three worlds. He was born in Martinique into the 'new' French Empire and schooled at the local *lycée*, where Césaire was one of his teachers. He volunteered to join the Free French forces during the war, was educated in psychiatric medicine in Paris and exchanged ideas about race with Jean-Paul Sartre and Simone de Beauvoir. He thought his way through the contradictions of 'black skin, white masks', giving a vivid description of being constituted from the outside by the glance of the other and wrote a searing indictment of the forces which had created 'the wretched of the earth'. Working as a psychiatrist in a mental hospital in Algeria, listening to French soldiers' troubled confessions of torture, he contemplated the 'cleansing power' of anti-colonial violence and passionately identified with the struggles of the Algerian people against their French masters. This was an astonishing life, which at each moment paid testament to the shifting axes of colonial power.

In Britain, these historical shifts were perhaps more pronounced in a different department of intellectual life: in the organization of imaginative literature. George Lamming, referring to that generation of Anglophone West Indian writers, the creators of the West Indian novel – Edgar Mittelholzer, Vic Reid, Roger Mais, Sam

Selvon, John Hearne, Wilson Harris, Jan Carew, Sylvia Wynter, V. S. Naipaul and of course Lamming himself – declared that we 'all made the same decision [to emigrate] independent of discussion among themselves'. 'Everyone', he went on, 'felt the need *to get out*.' He explained it in this way: 'The proximity of our lives to the major issues of our time has demanded of us all some kind of involvement . . . [However] we are made to feel a sense of exile by our inadequacy and our irrelevance of function in a society whose past we can't alter, and whose future is always beyond us . . . sooner or later, in silence or in rhetoric, we sign a contract whose epitaph reads: "To be an exile is to be alive".' 'However,' he added, 'when the exile is a man of colonial orientation and his chosen residence is the country which colonized his own history, then there are certain complications.' There certainly are!

Of the West Indian writers who migrated in the 1950s, some developed the extraordinarily bold ambition to create a new indigenous kind of literature by rewriting the English novel, or English literature more generally, from a Caribbean perspective. Lamming himself, for example, radically re-read Shakespeare's *The Tempest*. Consider the *inwardness to* and, simultaneously, the *estrangement from* an alien culture which that ambition signified: the passion for translation, for finding another language, the rage to appropriate, to turn a colonial inheritance inside out, to make it reverberate with other stories and histories which made that great creolizing project possible, or even conceivable. Consider the complexity of the relationship of this generation to its own colonized formation which this ambition represented. Note the sheer audacity implied by the diasporic strategies of reading Shakespeare against the grain of history which this implied for the project of 'decolonizing the mind'.

What's so striking is the confidence with which, in the decolonizing moment, these 'children of empire' confronted and engaged 'the mother country' *on the home territory of the colonizers themselves*. They came not to beg, or to be grateful or to be informed, but to look it in the face and, if possible, to overcome it! I am reminded here of Lord Beginner, the Trinidadian calypsonian who led the celebrations after the defeat of the English Test cricket team at Lord's in 1950, singing 'Cricket, Lovely Cricket'. There was no missing the payback moment of triumph this represented. Projects such as these required extraordinary intellectual boldness – indeed sheer, deliberate, bloody-minded effrontery. This was at the extreme opposite end of the spectrum from the mindset of 'exile'. Lord Kitchener, another calypsonian whose name alone was an affront to England's hallowed past, in full occupation announced wryly, in his most lilting, beguiling Trinidadian accent, that 'London is the Place for Me'!

The ambition to write, and to sing and to make art, then, turned out to be itself subversive. It came, not just from the desire to construct an alternative culture out of more indigenous, vernacular or African sources – that came powerfully to the fore later – but from the drive to subvert from within the very colonial cultural inheritance which had shaped and mis-shaped us; and in that way to lay claim as fully modern black subjects to a future which we were coming to regard as rightfully our own. This response was what the art critic Kobena Mercer subsequently identified as a quintessentially 'diasporic' strategy. 'Across a whole range of cultural forms there is a "syncretic" dynamic which critically appropriates elements from the master codes of the dominant culture and "creolizes" them, disarticulating given signs and rearticulating their symbolic meaning otherwise. The subversive form of this hybridizing tendency is most apparent at the level of language itself.'

In an essay on 'Three Moments in the Black Diaspora Arts' I argued that these writers and artists did not feel that their anti-colonial sensibilities were compromised by a universalist commitment to replace the enforced backwardness of colonialism and its institutions with a politics in hock to the ideals of development, progress and modernity. The nationally oriented 'indigenous' trends in art and culture were dead-centre, in consciousness, spirit and practice, to the anti-colonial and Independence movement, not – as it might be assumed today – their opposite. It was possible at one and the same time to be international and passionate nationalists in outlook: this was a generation which saw no contradiction between these two attitudes. Their modern commitment to finding and making new artistic forms 'more appropriate to the sense and sensibility of the new age' – as that very English champion of modern art, Herbert Read, once put it – was, in their minds, an active ingredient in their anti-colonialism. This moment of recognition has since come to be understood as an operative element in the makings of a wider, diasporic, black transnationalism.

There was a great political promise in this cultural ferment which I think is in danger of being forgotten.

At this time there existed in the Caribbean anti-colonial movements radical, politico-cultural impulses of this sort – 'emergent', in Raymond Williams's terms – which later, after Independence, were marginalized, or broken, or cancelled out by the triumph of what later came to be called the nationalist project. Within that project, the primary focus fell on state-building and on a given institutional politics, driven 'from above', whose political horizons were determined by the mobilization of the state at the expense of collective popular energies, of the citizenry of the new nation.

An essential condition for post-colonial societies is what has been called the endeavour to 'provincialize Europe'. And not before time. The discovery of indigenous cultural roots was immensely liberating for the nation and national self-esteem. Nationalism has tremendous creative power and decolonization could not have happened without it. But we have become more aware of its limits and foreshortenings, one of which is the temptation to create a Manichaean world, by inverting without transforming what went before. Where the European colonizer once stood, there shall we stand in his place.

But global capitalism does not leave new nations to trot along as best they can. At certain critical turning points – especially given contemporary forms of globalization – new modalities of power, new forms of subjectification, new interdependencies, new modes of governmentality and new contradictions came into play. As David Scott observed in his essay on 'colonial governmentality', the problem is not the decentring of Europe as such, important as that is, but 'a critical interrogation of the practices, modalities and projects through which Europe's insertion into the lives of the colonized was constructed and organized'.

This serves as a reminder of the paradoxical truth that, preserved in the 'backwardness' of the plantation economy, the West Indies had, in fact, long been conscripted to the modern world. This enforced coupling was especially true of the Caribbean because, as C. L. R. James noted, the slave plantation, based on the exploitation of a pre-capitalist mode of forced labour, was directly harnessed into the most advanced forms of (so-called) 'free labour' created by an agrarian and industrializing capitalism in the metropolitan nations. And so it was, in fact, that 'modernity' was never as far away as we had imagined. These histories need to be disinterred, for the present. A past which is forgotten, or rendered inconsequential, will take its historic revenge.

The diasporic experience, I'm saying, can be marshalled as a privileged, fruitful means for explaining the complex inner relations of this late phase of colonialism, and indeed also of our own post-colonial moment. I find it helpful in opening out to me the dynamics of my own historical formation, of my own life.

The modern idea of the diasporic, with its contemporary reference points, was not yet in use when I made the journey from Jamaica to England. Of course, diaspora formation itself is an age-old process. Diasporas have been created whenever – and for whatever reasons – settled societies have established significantly sized communities of their own people elsewhere which have survived for a considerable period of time, maintain a close connection with the place and cultures of their ancestry, and shaped their practices according to what they imagine are the social codes, customs and beliefs of their ancestors.

At the core of the diasporic experience is a variant of what W. E. B. DuBois called 'double consciousness': that of belonging to more than one world, of being both 'here' and 'there', of thinking about 'there' from 'here' and vice versa; of being 'at home' – but never wholly – in both places; neither fundamentally the same, nor totally different. It thus entails a very different conception of identity's relation to cultural traditions from that of conventional notions, which tend to emphasize remaining true to one's primordial origins and imply continuity, fixity and an unchanging rootedness. Here, 'routes' (change, movement, transformations, adaptation, being always 'in process') are just as important as 'roots', if not more so: an example of what Paul Gilroy calls culture as 'the changing same'.

In recent history the term diaspora is most closely associated with the dispersal of the Jews, their captivity in foreign lands and the genocidal suffering inflicted on them over many centuries, especially in Europe, through a history of anti-Semitism and pogroms, culminating in the Holocaust. Hatred of Jews is deeply embedded in many European cultures and has been in evidence since at least the Crusades. This catastrophic historical Jewish experience has summoned up, in response, a conception of diaspora, the essence of which is that the suffering of the Jewish people will only end when the Jews are unified with their original homeland. The dispersal is never final, the umbilical cord with their sacred home and cultural and religious traditions can never be totally severed. There will always be a redemptive restitution. One day the dream of a long-delayed return will be fulfilled, the broken thread of history seamlessly repaired, God's promise retrieved, the Temple rebuilt and the chosen people reunited with their homeland.

This is a powerful and historically significant idea in its own right, and as such has had deep consequences. It is hard to think of instances of violent capture, forced transplantation, enslavement or mass expulsions of peoples in which aspects of this consolatory dream – freedom as return – have not been present. For Jews, the return to the Promised Land secures the fulfilment of the long-delayed promise. Among enslaved Africans of the New World the idea was certainly vividly present in their dream of freedom. Later it provided the leading inspiration in the black Independence and 'Back to Africa' movements in the Americas, conspicuously so in Garveyism. But it can also be discerned in some versions of Pan-Africanism, and it's forcefully recuperated in the language of 'suffering in Babylon' in Rastafarianism. For all of these beliefs, the encoded message of the Old Testament provided a fertile source.

They are all instances of old diasporas which have persisted into, and acquired particular new resonance in, the contemporary world.

Still troublesome, however, are the ahistorical, mythological, eschatological elements in this version of the diaspora narrative, a variant which acquired its most intense political form in Zionism. There, God's metaphorical language has been translated literally, as is common in many fundamentalisms. In its name, the right of all Jews everywhere to return to 'the land of Israel' was put into effect. It was under the spell of this rubric that the new state of Israel was created – with British connivance, in the wake of the 1917 Balfour Declaration – as an exclusive ethnic and religious nation state. It provided the legitimating framework within which Palestine was recolonized, Palestinians were made second-class citizens, displaced to other places, or confined to two physically separate and divided enclaves, their land expropriated and generations obliged to spend their lives as a refugee population. The state of Israel has pursued extreme violence – war, occupation, invasion, the forced subjugation of civilian populations, collective punishments – as the legitimate means of undoing a historic wrong, and in the process has made itself a willing partner of the West.

In truth, this disfigured conception of diaspora has become the source of one of the most horrendous of historical ironies: the elaborate self-deceptions which have enabled Israel to legitimate its actions, for example in shamelessly occupying Palestinian territory, claiming sole ownership of Jerusalem, so manifestly the 'home' of several religious traditions, deploying its armed forces in violent, aggressive and indefensible acts against West Bank and Gaza protesters, strangling their economies and impoverishing their populations by naval blockade. Such actions legitimate not only a justified sense of the historic suffering and sacrifice of the Jewish people, but an all-encompassing claim to a victimhood which knows no bounds. Europe has assuaged its guilt over its own long practice of anti-Semitism by colluding with the state of Israel in exacting revenge – not on Western anti-Semitism, which caused such a catalogue of horrors in the first place, but on the Palestinian people themselves, who had shared the land with the Jews for centuries. Thus the current political climate has arisen in which anyone who questions this state of affairs is immediately labelled anti-Semitic! It is a re-enactment of the primal crime scene, with a brutal twist.

The concept of diaspora, evidently, is not theoretically innocent! But it has to be excavated from this philosophical terrain and reimagined. The word is used now mainly to connote the specific structure of displacements which have gained historical specificity in post-war global migration. Avtar Brah argues that it has become one of the principal interpretive frames for analysing the economic, political and cultural modalities of contemporary forms and sites of migrancy.

Contemporary diasporas take shape, not 'after' in a simple chronological sense, but in the *aftermath of* – that is, 'post-' – colonization. Their contemporary forms arise from the transformations of the power relations between 'the West' and 'the rest', which for so long stabilized the shape of the global system. The term diaspora references the process by which societies and communities in the poor two-thirds of the world have been exposed to the power and subordinated to the interests of the rich one-third. Many have consequently continued to be devastated by poverty, hunger, disease, worklessness, environmental disaster, civil war and unresolved ethnic enmities, resulting in the militarization of children and youth, the corruption and venality of some of their leading elites, the degeneration of the state into the single-party model, the predations of transnational corporations, global inequality, the systemic inequalities of so-called 'free trade' and underdevelopment: just as the poor nations were once 'dispersed' by conquest, enslavement, the plantation system, the exploitation of rich resources and cheap labour – in a word, by colonization. This is the terrain on which contemporary diasporas are situated.

But diaspora can also be an emergent space of inquiry. In current critical thinking, the modern idea of diaspora seeks to reproduce in thought the contemporary dynamic by which cultural formations coexist and interconnect, drawing one from another, which is one of the consequences when peoples with very varied histories, cultures, languages, religions, resources, access to power and wealth are obliged by migration to occupy the same space as those very different from themselves and, sometimes, to make a common life together.

To think of yourself as diasporic, as I now do, has therefore become a sort of substitute for 'identity'. But the term diasporic both responds to, and goes beyond, the reductive boundaries of what has come to be known as 'identity politics'. Identities are in this process indeed reconstructed, transformed, problematized, pluralized, mobilized, set in antagonistic positions towards one another. The diasporic challenges the idea of whole, integral, traditionally unchanging cultural identities. No identities survive the diasporic process intact and unchanged, or maintain their connections with their past undisturbed. The search for, and even more, the so-called 'discovery' of, an essential identity is often, in any case, the result of what Eric Hobsbawm calls 'the invention' of tradition: not the product of past time but of the day before yesterday. The unification of identities promises to condense all the diasporic lines of dissemination and antagonism, and provide a transhistorical authenticity. But in the modern world it seems doomed to failure. It was as an attempt to capture this reality that I once said that we had come to 'the end of the essential black subject'.

The diasporic is the moment of the double inscription, of creolization and multiple belongings. The new conceptions of diaspora provided the contexts in which it became clear that no single social division is able to explain or account for all the structures and power relations in a social totality. The diasporic proved to be the moment when the politics of class, race and gender came together, but in a new, unstable, unstoppable, explosive articulation, displacing and at the same time complicating each other. It has transformed our understanding of the nature of social forces and of social movements. Accordingly, it does not provide us with ready-made answers or programmes but sets us new questions, which proliferate across and disturb older frames of thought, social engagements and political practices: a new 'problem space' indeed.

This reasoning becomes the vantage point from which I can

understand my own 'relocation' from the Caribbean to Britain. It allows me to unearth and give meaning to my own experiences and sensibilities, which I was unable to articulate as a younger man. To draw for a moment from Gramsci, it provides a way for me to make sense of my own 'philosophies'.

In his *The Pleasures of Exile* George Lamming recalls James Baldwin's comment, in *Notes of a Native Son*, that 'I was a kind of bastard of the West', and yet the heights of European culture 'were not my creations, they did not contain my history'. This is also the point of C. L. R James's observation that black migrants were 'in but not of Europe'. These sentiments register an ambivalence which, Lamming notes, besets 'not just the colonial *vis-à-vis* England but American and Negro up against the monolithic authority of European culture'. In the Caribbean our knowledge of the wider world was narrow, distorted and often misguided. For us in the British Caribbean the lines of identification ran inexorably to the imperial metropole. But going abroad was as if one had the chance – at last – to unmask the phantasmatic dimensions of the colonial relation.

PART III

Journey to an Illusion

6. Encountering Oxford: The Makings of a Diasporic Self

It is uncannily disconcerting to look back at my younger self, arriving in the port of Avonmouth in 1951, ready for a new life but absolutely unsure how it would happen, or what it would look like if it did. I was indeed elsewhere! I can say, however, that the colonial experience prepared me for England. Far from being an untroubled, innocent opportunity for me to step out into something new, this was an encounter which was mightily overdetermined.

My arrival preceded by some three months the general election in October in which the Conservatives ousted Labour and Winston Churchill regained the office of Prime Minister. After a short while I headed for Oxford University, into the very cultural heartland of England.

But this was an encounter which has not yet come to an end. It continues. It was, as Donald Hinds termed it a long while ago, 'a journey to an illusion' – or rather, a journey to the shattering of illusions, inaugurating a process of protracted disenchantment. I didn't really know what I would find or what I would do with 'it' if I found 'it'. I knew I didn't want to be 'it', whatever that was. But I did want to encounter in the flesh, as it were, this phantasm of 'other worlds', swollen with – as it happened – false promise. What I really knew about Britain turned out to be a bewildering farrago of reality and fantasy. However, such illusions as I may have taken with me were unrealized because, fortunately, they were unrealizable. The episode was painful as well as exciting. It changed me irrevocably, almost none of it in ways I had remotely anticipated.

The whole experience was eerily familiar and disconcertingly strange at the same time. One can attribute this to the sense of déjà-vu which assails colonial travellers on first encountering face-to-face the imperial metropole, which they actually know only in its translated form through a colonial haze, but which has always functioned as their 'constitutive outside': constituting them, or us, by its absence, because it is what they – we – are *not*. This is a manner of being defined from the beyond!

On the boat train to London, I kept feeling I'd seen this place somewhere before, as in a screen memory. It provoked a deep psychic recognition, an illusory after-effect. Had I been here before? Yes and no. I hadn't anticipated what the English countryside would look like but, once I saw it whizzing past the train windows, I knew that this was how it *should* look: those proper, well-fed, black-and-white cows munching away contentedly in their neatly divided, hedgerowed fields surrounded by enormous, spreading sycamore trees. Everything I had read had prepared me for that. I knew, after all, the novels of Thomas Hardy. On the other hand, nothing had prepared me for the stark contrast between the sombre brick-and-cement hues and the well-disciplined dark, monotone character of London streets and the chaotic bustle of Kingston street life, with people shoving past one another on the crowded pavements, the handcarts and ice barrows with their rows of syrup bottles, the raucous hubbub and teeming vitality, provincial as it was.

London, when we got there, felt unwelcoming and forbidding. I guess my memories must have been infiltrated by what happened later, for what immediately comes to mind is the heavy, leaden autumn sky, the light permanently stuck halfway to dusk, the constant fine drizzle (where was the proper rain, the tropical downpour?), the blank windows of the square black cabs, the anonymity of the faces in the red double-decker buses, the yellow headlights glistening off the wet tarmac along the Bayswater Road. A dark, shuttered, anonymous city; high blocks of mansion flats, turning up their noses at the life of the streets below. Everyone was buttoned up in dark suits, overcoats and hats, many carrying the proverbial umbrellas, scurrying with downcast eyes through the gathering gloom to unknown destinations. This was post-war austerity London, with its bombed-out sites, rubble and gaping spaces like missing teeth. A faint mist permanently shrouded Hyde Park, where ladies in jodhpurs and hard riding hats cantered their horses in the early mornings; the lights blazed in the Oxford Street department stores by three in the afternoon. There must have been bright and sunny days, for it was only the end of summer. But I don't remember them.

We had some time first, in limbo, in London; then the full impact of Oxford and the beginning of another phase of my life. My mother accompanied me, together with an enormous steamer trunk, a felt hat and a chequered overcoat. We were the second-class passengers on a banana boat courtesy of Elders and Fyffes, the British firm linked to my father's company. It went around the island, stopping at different places to load bananas, and on its last day we drove across to meet it in Port Antonio, its last Jamaican call, for the final leg of its journey 'home'. I remember the boat slipping out in the fading sunset light along the narrow channel of Port Antonio harbour between Navy Island and Titchfield Hill, where the old hotel once stood. We were so close to land on either side that I could clearly make out the faces of my family standing on the promontory, watching the late-afternoon departure and waving farewell.

We had a tumultuous journey. At sea we encountered the

ferocious hurricane which, we learned later, had ravaged Jamaica. I have photographs showing how far down into the ocean the boat descended, burying its prow in the channel hollowed out in the turbulent water. We looked into the chasm, convinced that we would never struggle up again out of the depths. But within minutes, as the vessel righted itself, the sea reared up above us like a wall, so high above the deck railings that it entirely blotted out the sky. The tables and crockery in the dining room were sliding freely to and fro across the floor with each tilt of the decks. It was scarily exciting. But we didn't yet know of the wreckage the hurricane had left in its wake at home. In the spirit of what literary critics call 'the fallacy of imitative form', where the natural world appears to mirror the mood of the narrative, nature seemed to be carrying some ominous latent message about the journey to my destination, although I didn't choose to anticipate what it could mean.

We arrived in August, and since the Oxford term didn't start until October we spent a few weeks in London as tourists. We stayed at Methodist International House, a kind of refuge for overseas students in Bayswater. Among the first people I met there were A. N. R. Robinson, subsequently both Prime Minister and President of Trinidad and Tobago, who was studying law at the Inns of Court and was soon to be a founding member of the People's National Movement; and Doris Wellcome from British Guiana, who became the first wife of the celebrated Barbadian poet Edward Kamau Brathwaite. The house was full of African, Asian and Caribbean students. It was self-consciously international in ethos: 'native dress' (whatever that was) at weekends, food from different regions, many languages. There was a more religious atmosphere than either I or my mother was accustomed to: grace at meals, hymns around the piano of an evening, chapel on Sunday morning. However, it did give me the chance to acclimatize slowly to London in a place which was not impenetrably English.

And then one day I came to see that 'impenetrable England' wasn't impenetrable at all. Passing Paddington Station, which was only around the corner from Bayswater Terrace, I saw a stream of black people spilling out into the London afternoon. They were too poorly dressed to be tourists. Who were they and what were they doing here? In fact, this was my first encounter with an advance guard of what became black Caribbean, post-war, post-*Windrush* migration, which over the years has transformed Britain. One world intruded on another. This was a game-changing moment for me. Suddenly everything looked different.

It is hard to reconstruct the effect of seeing these black West Indian working men and women in London, with their strapped-up suitcases and bulging straw baskets, looking for all the world as if they planned a long stay. They had made extraordinary efforts within their means to dress up to the nines for the journey, as West Indians always did in those days when travelling or going to church: the men in soft-brim felt hats, cocked at a rakish angle, the women in flimsy, colourful cotton dresses, stepping uncertainly into the cold wind, or waiting for relatives or friends to rescue them from the enveloping strangeness. They hesitated in front of ticket windows, trying to figure out how to take another train to some equally unfamiliar place, to find people they knew who had preceded them. Their minds seemed fixed, not on some mythic 'romance of travel' or on the equally unpersuasive notion of an 'unfolding adventure', but on the immediate practicalities: a place to sleep, a room to rent, work.

For them and for me, this was a fateful moment of transition, frozen in time.

The sight of all these black people in the centre of London was astonishing. What I thought I had left behind as an unresolved dilemma – the difficulties my family background had bequeathed to me of neither wanting any identification with my own social stratum, nor being able to feel present in my own homeland, conscious of the chasm that separated me from the multitude – had turned up to meet me on the other side of the Atlantic. This made me feel like I was travelling forwards towards the past!

These were still early days, and migration carried the promise that it would level the colonial playing field. Here, at last, we *all* were what Sheila Patterson, in her early study of post-war migration, called 'dark strangers': travellers in unfamiliar territory, puzzled about what the future held, fearful about whether we would survive, unsettled by how different everything seemed and worried by how much the experience would change us.

I had anticipated all sorts of new beginnings, but I never imagined London would secrete this explosive little time bomb from the past. Of course, any idea of making an absolutely new start had been a fantasy, and I don't think I ever succumbed to it. I was convinced my leaving Jamaica was a temporary break and I fully intended to return and to spend my adult life there. In any case, as I subsequently discovered, the hope of making an absolutely new start – Year One – is often the first of the illusions to go. Besides, it wasn't really a beginning, only another chapter in a long-running story which had begun centuries before.

We did the tourist thing – Westminster Abbey, St Paul's, the Houses of Parliament, Buckingham Palace, the Changing of

the Guard, the Festival of Britain site on the South Bank. I remember catching one of the first performances of *The Mousetrap*, but that must have been a little later. Anticipating the start of term, my mother delivered me, complete with the steamer trunk, to Merton College, Oxford. By some mysterious serendipity our house in Kingston had been called Merton, but I couldn't trace any actual connection. My mother, however, in fine form insisted it must have been Destiny.

We went on a preparatory visit to my College. On arrival at my rooms we were greeted by a College servant who 'looks after the students on your staircase, sir'. My 'scout', Bert, had been injured in the First World War and walked with a limp. A nervous soul, he stared at the impossibly heavy trunk as if it were a drowned body that had floated to the surface in a Ruth Rendell novel and, disconcertingly, manifested its presence. What were we to do with it, this baggage from the past? The three of us couldn't lift it upstairs, so it was settled that it would go down to the basement. I did eventually bring some clothes and other effects up to my room on the first floor, which looked out on the magnificent medieval structure of the College chapel. But after that I never opened the trunk again, and I consigned it back to the past.

I sometimes wonder what became of it. With its rounded top and steel hoops, it was a relic of all I was leaving behind. It belonged with the imported things my mother always insisted on using as a token of her abiding loyalty to the colonial version of modernity and sophistication. It connoted the kind of swanky luggage which glamorous film stars in 1940s movies took on fast, transatlantic steamers from New York to Europe 'to see Paris'. As was fitting for an object so loaded with ambiguous significance, weighted down with pretentiousness and aspiring to what it could never be, it was for me a token of that other life. Newly purchased though it was, it was already an anachronism, out of time and out of place. I abandoned it with relief. For all I know it's still there.

Oxford was my first close encounter with the British governing classes 'at home', and with the institutions by which a hegemonic culture is manufactured. Merton, founded in the fourteenth century, is one of the oldest Oxford colleges, resplendent in its classic Oxford architecture, a place of medieval seriousness, solidity and gloom. I read Chaucer in the Old Library sitting beside books still chained to the wooden desks. College was a plunge into the icy depths and arcane complexities of Englishness, unexpected even by someone who thought they knew England well. A quarter of my course was in languages like Anglo-Saxon and Middle English, which I couldn't understand. High German and Old Norse, other early roots of the English language, seemed impossibly foreign. Actually, I loved some of the poetry – *Beowulf, Sir Gawain and the Green Knight, The Wanderer, The Seafarer* – and at one point I planned to do graduate work on Langland's *Piers Plowman*. But when I tried to apply contemporary literary criticism to these texts, my ascetic South African language professor told me in a pained tone that this was not the point of the exercise. Having given up Latin, I had sworn I would never traffic with an ancient language again. But here I was in another translation class.

There was 'College life', too, to contend with. I remember my first dinner in Hall: white fish on a white plate with boiled potatoes and cauliflower in a white sauce! Survival chances did not look good. I had to give in my ration book at the start of term – post-war austerity was still in command – and, in return, the College gave me a quarter of a pound of butter on a tin tray and a daily jug of milk, which I could take to my room and have for tea with the crumpets I learned to toast on the gas fire. This, by the way, was the only trace of heating in my otherwise splendid two-room quarters.

Merton is actually a seductively beautiful place. The gardens and lawns were meticulously tended, manicured oases of calm, no matter how busy other parts of the College were. The raised walkway running along the back wall looked over the whole expanse of Christ Church Meadow. But the College was also full of dark corners. I had to walk from my rooms in the building opposite the medieval chapel, with the chill mists rolling across the Meadow and up over the stone walls from the river, to get to the freezing, white-tiled caverns that were 'the baths'. Unaccountably, some people on my staircase seemed never to pay them a visit. But those of us who went regularly were a select company. No one went on his own. It was a communal activity. And nobody would dream of venturing out into the freezing darkness without a paperback with which to while away the time until everything had steamed up to a human temperature.

The day I arrived Bert had told my mother reassuringly it was his job to look after me. But he seemed to need quite a lot of looking after himself. He explained a number of College rules and customs. For instance, if you wanted to be private you could secure the outer door to your rooms and no one was supposed to enter. This quaint Oxford custom for young gentlemen was called 'sporting the oak', the double entendre no doubt intended. The trouble was that the sight of the closed door sent Bert into such a frenzy of anxiety that he regarded it as a positive obligation to retrieve his master key, hammer on the door and come blundering in, expecting to see the student at the very least in flagrante with a lady friend prostrate before the gas fire, if not actually swinging on a rope from the ceiling. I had read *Tom Brown's Schooldays* and *Brideshead Revisited* but this was, to put it mildly, something else. The first time Bert woke me on a winter morning, icicles had formed on the inside of the bedroom window. The whole Oxford spectacle unrolled in front of me like a movie, knowing all the time it was a facsimile caricature of itself.

Oxford may seem an unexpected site for coming to terms with being 'other'. But I still remember going some afternoons to a cavernous tea room in Oxford, the Cardena, and hearing again the sound of those raised voices, with their braying pitch and stifled Oxford vowel sounds, addressing themselves to the world at large, as if what concerned them could not fail to be of breathtaking interest to the rest of the universe.

Yet I sometimes wonder now how much of my reaction was a colonial hang-up: the response of the 'illegitimate' colonial 'son', reared in the shadow of empire, confronting his own estrangement from what had been fantasized for him as his true – 'parental' – people and home.

Oxford itself – as place, institution and above all as signifier – came to symbolize for me its centrality to the English sense of always being 'in place', especially among the dominant classes, because it was not only the summit of the higher education system but also a distillation of the hierarchical English class system itself.

I was often the only black person in the room. I tried to ignore this. I'd walk into a pub or a café with friends without apparently batting an eyelid, which itself betrayed a certain class confidence. However, my body was always tensed, as if bracing itself for the covert glances cast in my direction, even when they weren't intentionally hostile. I knew the reason people were looking at me was the awkward presence of *difference*. But I tried to practise the disappearing skill of looking straight back through them. It didn't dispel, though, my sense of always being on show.

Yet, overtly, Oxford was very polite to us black students – there were so few of us we were regarded as oddities, quaint, rather than embodying any kind of threat. Besides, they thought we'd complete our courses and then be off back home. 'And when are you going home?', they'd ask. My tutor, to whom I poured out my finest thoughts in face-to-face tutorials every week for three years, had so little idea of who I was or where I came from that he used to say, 'Of course, Stuart, when you're finished, you'll go back to Jamaica and become a governor or something'! As he said this, he'd twiddle his fingers in sheer delight at the utterly improbable prospect he'd dreamed up.

This wasn't overt racism. I didn't really experience that kind of racism much at Oxford as an undergraduate student: not until I was a graduate student, when West Indians in significant numbers came to work on the buses in Oxford, and after I left university and started to live and work in London. But I was conscious all the time that I was very, very *different* because of my race and colour. And in the discourses of Englishness, race and colour remained unspeakable silences.

For the majority of English undergraduates, the men returning from war service or having recently completed their national service before 'going up', it must all have seemed perfectly natural: a heightened simulacrum of their familial cultures and a reprise of those quaint old customs for which their public-school education, with its fake Oxbridge imitations, had well prepared them.

I was the only black student in my College, although there were some South Asians. The largest non-English contingent in Merton comprised Americans and, as a fellow outsider, I teamed up with them. They too disengaged from – when not completely bewildered and bemused by it – the English boat-club ethos of the College. Many were reading English Literature, although in fact I had tutorials with a brilliantly clever working-class Geordie, Tom Coulson. The American Don Bell I've already mentioned. The extraordinarily smart Walt Litz, born in Tennessee and like me a Rhodes Scholar, was preparing his DPhil on Joyce's *Finnegans Wake*. What Oxford gave him I have no idea, but after he left Oxford, and after his military service, he joined the Princeton faculty and stayed there for forty years as one of its most distinguished modernists.

I remember our whole tutorial group being sent by my tutor, as a special privilege, to Helen Gardner's seminar on the Metaphysical Poets. One American innocent kept asking earnest but naïve questions about the sexual puns in John Donne. She first pointed him to a copy of Ovid on her top shelf, which he retrieved, but he couldn't understand the Latin. When the session was over she wrote a steely but exasperated note to us which arrived in College before we had had time to make our way back, explaining that 'When you find the word "quainte" in Shakespeare or Donne, I think you will find that it is a sexual pun or double entendre, meaning . . .' Later I got to know her quite well. She wasn't at all forbidding and a fine, early critic of 'Mr Eliot's poetry'. In fact, I went to a Merton May Ball in a group with her friend Dorothy Bednarowska, who would later teach a galaxy of renowned intellectuals and public figures.

Most of the other Rhodes Scholars were older, had already graduated from elite American universities and were taking second degrees at Oxford. At the end of my first year I chose to move out of College with some of them into a North Oxford boarding house, in itself a memorable experience. Most of the residents were ageing or retired Oxfordians, whom we, this bunch of interlopers (myself, Walt Litz, Charles Forker, the future US Shakespeare scholar, and others) must have bewildered as much as they did us. Our landlady kept a strict watch over the meter we had to feed coins into to get hot water. We befriended an old lady who regularly took a helping of marmalade from the breakfast room back to her quarters by surreptitiously syphoning some from the communal supply into a jar concealed in the handbag she kept open for the purpose in her lap. I gather this is a well-known boarding-house speciality. I say 'surreptitiously', but in fact everyone knew what was going on and watched closely to see whether or not the mission had been accomplished. I'm sure she thought it had passed unnoticed.

With this American group in my first two years, I read very widely and argued mainly about literature and literary criticism. I read for the first time, under their guidance, a great tranche of American classics: Hawthorne, Melville, Whitman, Thoreau and modern writers including Hemingway, Faulkner and Fitzgerald, as well as representatives of the New Criticism, particularly Cleanth Brooks, Allen Tate, Yvor Winters and Lionel Trilling. The Americans had more money than I did, but within these limitations we lived an entertaining social life for a year or two. They took to the idiosyncrasies of English life more readily than I did. They didn't have the same baggage from the past to deal with. But we occasionally took my tutor – an eighteenth-century scholar called Hugo Dyson Dyson, no less – to the pub or out for Sunday lunch to nearby villages such as Thame.

There were also a small number of West Indian undergraduates like myself, including V. S. Naipaul, who was at Christ Church at the same time, although he wasn't much interested in knowing any of us. Like me, he read English Literature. Most of the others were doing PPE – Philosophy, Politics and Economics.

I knew Naipaul, but not well. Even then I didn't find him friendly or engaging. He didn't want anything to do with other West Indians, especially black ones. He never came to West Indian Society meetings. I'm sure he wouldn't have approved of our nationalist ambitions or anti-colonial political attitudes. I knew that he wanted to be a novelist; and later I discussed literature with him on one or two not very memorable public occasions. I still think the earlier novels and stories – *Miguel Street, The Mystic Masseur, The Suffrage of Elvira, A House for Mister Biswas* – with their sympathetic, comic feel for Trinidad's Indian community, just at the moment when the rural Hindu customs were collapsing, represent his greatest literary achievements. But *A Bend in The River* is, to put it moderately, one of my least favourite of his novels. I suppose his deep ambivalence and sneering attitude towards the Caribbean – coupled with his hostility to nationalism, his irritating and uncritical Anglocentrism and what Derek Walcott has called 'his genteel abhorrence of Negroes', which so disfigures his later work and his great literary gifts – were already a well-entrenched part of his persona, even in his Oxford days. He seems to have been driven by an ambivalent aggression: self-loathing, even, despite his studied self-regard, superiority and sometimes woundingly insulting jibes. I once heard him at a public lecture at the South Bank refer to C. L. R. James as 'that vain, old, black man'. If I'd been able, I'd have left there and then.

His later so-called travel writings on India, Pakistan, Islam and Africa are frankly disgraceful productions, full of an almost uncontrolled bile and wilfully offensive, although no doubt well written; I found his – feigned? – inability to acknowledge that they were turned largely against himself and his origins in some ways the most unforgivable thing about them. There was, for all of us, an 'enigma of arrival' (which was certainly a great title he gave to one of his later books). But his version of it seemed to be the fact that England had such difficulty recognizing him as the great English novelist and an authentic English country gentleman. Whatever his enigma was, it certainly wasn't mine.

At Oxford, I got to know a number of other Trinidadians whom I found considerably more congenial. They were the largest minority of Caribbean students there and they became my closest friends and principal reference group. I even picked up a faint Trinidadian lilt and was often mistaken for one. A group of very bright young civil servants had been sent by their government to Oxford to work on development economics, in preparation for the coming of Independence. They included J. O'Neil (Scottie) Lewis, who later became head of the Industrial Court, and Doddridge Alleyne, with whom I played squash and who was to work closely with Eric Williams, the first political leader of independent Trinidad and Tobago, in his new government as one of his most senior and trusted civil servants. It was with him that I celebrated in a Chinese restaurant the fall of Dien Bien Phu and the subsequent expulsion of the French from Vietnam. There was also Willie Demas, a brilliant student who came to live in Oxford but was completing his Cambridge PhD, and who took on many important responsibilities for economic reconstruction in the new government. Max Ifil later became an independent economic commentator; and Eldon Warner, a master of the carnival arts, subsequently had a senior position in British West Indian Airways. Eric Williams, one-time protégé of C. L. R. James, with whom James subsequently broke, was later to face a stern critic and political opponent in the widely read, scholarly, politically sophisticated, expansive and imaginatively creative Lloyd Best, who was studying at Cambridge. I met him travelling back to England on my first visit home. These were all figures of the Independence generation, poised to play significant roles in the organization of Caribbean politics.

The debates among this group about politics and the future of the region of independent states were wide-ranging, fierce, endlessly stimulating and conducted in typically Caribbean high spirits. Most of the group were to become the luminaries of Eric Williams's administrations: graduates of the elite secondary schools and of the popular rallies of the University of Woodford Square, the open-air space in Port of Spain where Williams's public lectures first galvanized audiences and signalled his intention to enter Caribbean politics.

Together in Oxford we formed a deeply committed West Indian grouping, looking forwards and slightly intoxicated with anticipation of the coming of Independence and the excitement of planning for self-government, impatient with what seemed to us the glacial pace of decolonization, vigilantly critical of the manoeuvrings of the Colonial Office, often in despair at the state of formal politics in the islands and keeping very close track of events.

This group also included Noel Henwood, a Trinidadian wild card who sweet-talked his way into St Catherine's College on the basis of his questionable academic qualifications. He said he was both a member of the Communist Party and a priest in a strange African sect, about both of which he could be very amusing, although as ever with him the reality proved hard to pin down. He had been dismissed in dubious circumstances from the Colonial Civil Service and many years later, probably in the belief that revenge is a dish which must be eaten cold, he masterminded the takeover of the Russell and Palmerston, an Oxford political dining club and the heart of Oxford Liberalism, which a group of us West Indians, always impeccably kitted out in evening dress, of course, subverted for ulterior purposes. Noel invited the former Labour Colonial Secretary, Arthur Creech Jones, to be our guest speaker. He did so specifically for the pleasure of being able to greet him at Oxford station with the statement, 'I believe you are the person who signed my letter of dismissal from the Colonial Civil Service.' We dined thereafter in silence in an upper private room in Balliol.

Henwood was a practical joker and provocateur. He used to turn up below my window late at night and shout 'Nigger!' to attract my attention. This was two decades before the term gained a certain currency as a term of affectionate greeting among the black brothers. The lights of respectable, working-class Jericho would flicker into life. He once told us he had been censured for this racist practice by the Communist Party, but I don't think he took it very seriously. Certainly it never stopped him doing it. He later married the relative of a rich banker, lived in Switzerland and, through his friendship with a Nigerian in Oxford, got involved on the wrong side of the Biafran War.

This 'tightly knit group of politically motivated men' (as Prime Minister Harold Wilson later referred to striking seamen) constituted the backbone of the very active Oxford West Indian Society. When we went to London we stayed, with the other 'bearded radicals' my parents had warned me against, at the West Indian student residence at Hans Crescent and spent much of our time at the West Indian Students' Centre, a radical organization representing West Indian students in the UK. Through its activities we kept the fires of Independence lit and debated with many visiting Caribbean political figures as well as the group of West Indian writers that included Edgar Mittelholzer, George Lamming, Sam Selvon, V. S. Naipaul, Andrew Salkey, Jan Carew and, in later years, Wilson

Harris. They all wrote and broadcast for the BBC's *Caribbean Voices*, pioneered by that brilliant, dedicated producer, Henry Swanzy. The programme, beamed to the Caribbean, served as the midwife to West Indian writing in these crucial years.

I was still residually an aspiring poet and novelist, as well as a critic, so I started doing some work for the programme. Later on I participated in the Caribbean Artists' Movement, founded by Kamau Brathwaite, Andrew Salkey and John La Rose, whose important intervention Anne Walmsley has described in her generous and illuminating book. In these different ways I kept in contact with Caribbean writing and thought, current developments and politics, reading and occasionally contributing to small literary periodicals like *Bim* and *Savacou*. I was also reading Caribbean academics: the historians (Elsa Goveia, Douglas Hall, Roy Augier and Brathwaite), anthropologists (M. G. Smith), economists of the new generation (Lloyd Best), and veterans such as W. Arthur Lewis, the St Lucian Nobel Prize winner. It was in this milieu that I both kept alive my commitment to the Caribbean and first began to practise a diasporic West Indian identity, of which more in a moment.

This is strange. Not only did many of us first become *West Indian* in the metropole, as opposed to Jamaican, or Barbadian, or St Lucian. But also I had never been to the other Caribbean islands and I didn't know about them in detail. Colonization had done its divide-and-rule work. Places with similar histories were separated from each other by virtue of patterns of settlement, ethnic composition, the different national origins of the European colonizers, language and culture. This distance meant that all the lines of connection inevitably flowed through London and the Colonial Office – especially for Jamaica, which was relatively far away from the main cluster of Anglophone islands in the southern Caribbean. So my lack of familiarity with the rest of the Caribbean was an effect of power as well as of space. The result was that I didn't really know the Caribbean at all.

In the southern Caribbean there was a great deal of inter-island migration. People who lived in Trinidad, Barbados, St Lucia, Grenada or Antigua might have had relatives or known people who had migrated or regularly moved between the islands. But Jamaica, located at the top of the island chain, was an exception in this regard. It is closer geographically to Cuba, Haiti, the Dominican Republic and of course to Florida. At that time, relatively few Jamaicans had travelled in the region, although many, including an uncle of mine whom no one ever saw again, had made the historic journey at the start of the twentieth century to work on building the Panama Canal. Others spent time in Cuba and later, because of its US connections, some intellectuals gravitated towards Puerto Rico. Few Jamaicans were aware that in St Lucia the local patois is a French-based creole language or were conscious that we were surrounded by the remnants of a Spanish Empire which had once governed Jamaica. Nor for my generation was there much knowledge of the struggle against Spanish rule by Jamaica's neighbours, the Dominican Republic and Cuba. No Jamaican I knew at the time could speak a word of Spanish.

So when I arrived in England, I had no West Indian consciousness to speak of. But whenever, in the years immediately following my arrival, I went to Brixton or Notting Hill, or to Tottenham or the area by Marble Arch, I found places were populated with recently arrived migrants from all over the Caribbean – who, to their great irritation, were simply called Jamaicans by the British. This was just one instance of the misrecognitions in play. Mike and Trevor Philips say that this was the moment when, for the first time, West Indians came to understand that they were seen by the British as all having the same racial/ethnic identity. Now we were 'elsewhere', the differences seemed to matter less. But, these misrecognitions notwithstanding, the creolization of the English cities continued apace. North Kensington, for example – the site of the white riots at the end of the summer of 1958, and later home to carnival, the Trinidadian-Catholic Mardi Gras restaged for the London Caribbean community as a whole – came to be a byword for the new kind of mixed Caribbean 'colony' settlement in Britain, creating new centres for an emergent diasporic West Indian identity.

We all read Lamming's *In the Castle of My Skin* and Sam Selvon's *The Lonely Londoners* as soon as they appeared. These novels were about *us*. I wrote a Selvonesque short story, entitled 'Crossroads Nowhere', about my chance encounter with a young Trinidadian liming his way down the Edgware Road. Andrew Salkey generously published it in his *West Indian Stories* collection, which came out in 1960 and indeed marked a properly *Caribbean* moment in the diaspora.

Aside from Jamaica, Barbados was to be my first Caribbean port of call on the occasion, in 1965, when Catherine and I made our first summer vacation visit home by boat after we were married. This was a wonderful journey, mainly memorable for thirteen days' sailing into the sun in a haze of rum punch, deck quoits, swimming in the canvas pool, cards, four-course meals and making love in the afternoons as we steamed south parallel to the coast of Africa before swerving sharp west across the Atlantic to the Caribbean.

Barbados was more Anglicized than I was accustomed to. It used to be known as Little England. Bajans were thought to be very proper, socially conservative and loyal to the Crown. They were rightly proud of their many accomplishments. Barbados has one of the highest literacy rates in the world. It remains a favourite (and one of the safest) Caribbean holiday destination for foreign tourists and still has a significant expat population, as well as a sizeable poor white minority, deriving from the unfree whites who were sent to the island in the earliest moments of colonization. When I visited the Bridgetown Yacht Club years later even then, late in the day and a good while after Independence, it reminded me of nothing more than a redoubtable colonial encampment. There is a story that when Britain declared war on Germany it received a reassuring message of support from the Barbadian people saying, 'Carry on, Britain! Barbados is behind you!'

In fact Barbados had experienced one of the highest densities of white settlement in the Anglophone Caribbean, as you could see from the topography. If you stand on high ground – which is not all that easy, since the island is flat – you can see the chimneys of the different plantation sugar refineries sprouting from every corner of the landscape, testifying to the extent to which the old plantocracy had penetrated the land. Every corner of the island had been colonized, whereas in Jamaica large tracts of the mountainous interior, where runaway slaves took refuge, remained unclaimed. There must have been many runaway slaves in Barbados, but it is hard to tell where they took refuge.

The first Barbadian I remember meeting was Carl Jackman, who came to my school from Codrington College in Barbados to teach Latin. Codrington had been established (in a fit of absent-mindedness, surely?) as a teachers' college by All Souls, the most prestigious and exclusive of Oxford colleges, which took no undergraduates and numbered very eminent scholars, former prime ministers, front-bench parliamentarians, senior judges, generals and distinguished civil servants among its fellows. In Jamaica I had been taught by English, Scottish, Welsh and Irish teachers, alongside local Jamaicans. I remember our class being lined up outside the entrance to the impeccably English headmaster's residence and made to repeat in unison French vowel sounds, which I found unpronounceable: 'ai', 'é' with an acute accent, and the impossible 'eu'. 'Try saying "i" with the tongue behind the teeth', the headmaster insisted. *What*? But to be taught Latin by a Barbadian was a new experience! We'd never seen – or in particular, heard – anything like it. We imitated his accent, pretended we couldn't find Barbados on the map, said the place was so small that cricketers had to use the whole island as the cricket pitch, and insisted that Bajan rules required the batsmen to hit the ball into the sea in order to score a four. Actually, they were magnificent cricketers. We teased him mercilessly. It's obvious that we were scandalously provincial and out of order in our small island mentality.

Thus it was that in the first years of the 1950s London was, paradoxically, an essential staging post in my transition to becoming a West Indian. My experience matches George Lamming's famous observation in *The Pleasures of Exile* that 'most West Indians of my generation were born in England'. The category 'West Indian', he adds, 'formerly understood as a geographical term, now assume[d] cultural significance'. Indeed so. And to compound the irony, not only London provided the location for this transformation. So too did the University of Oxford! Strange times.

Through the 1950s there was strong support among Caribbean peoples in Britain for the Federation of the West Indies, which was established in 1958. The idea for the Federation had not originated in the diaspora, but it was positively nurtured throughout it. In the beginning it was still a novel and unformulated idea, more a hope, a dream of the future, than a plan. But it was certainly the case that at Oxford support for the Federation was the product of a less island-driven, more inter-regional outlook which prevailed in our group. Basically, many of us came to believe that, economically, each island on its own was not strong enough to stand up to the US and UK and to other foreign interests; that political independence would stand a better chance if resources were pooled; and that our common historical backgrounds made integration easier, despite the distances between us. It seemed to us better to use our strong regional association to confront the challenges of building independent nations, overcoming colonial dependency, diversifying our economies, developing a national consciousness, fashioning political and administrative institutions, addressing the scourges of unemployment, racism and poverty and constructing more egalitarian, more democratic, less class-and colour-divided, post-colonial societies. On this, there was little dividing those who were already destined for official posts back home and those who hankered after positions further to their Left, and who already espoused reservations about the political terms on which Independence was being mapped out. We were aware that many people in the group would before too long actually be in charge of making Independence a reality and that they could therefore influence the course and shape of events. This was the soil in which the idea of a West Indian Federation took root among us.

There were other, less tangible and instrumental reasons for the formation of the Federation. Immigration itself had thrown us together, making us convinced that the similarities of our history and background mattered more than our differences. We shared a strong West Indian sense of common belonging and identification. We were less attached than many to our island mentalities. Being in Britain, we had developed a more inclusive concept of the Caribbean. Some of us even dreamed of connecting with the French, Spanish and Dutch territories and perhaps even with the Central American nations which bordered the Caribbean basin, in a wider, multilingual post-colonial confederation, creating a broader entity which could confront our powerful neighbours to the north. At the time, these were all straws in the wind of an incipient trans-Caribbean consciousness.

Federation was an important and noble dream. But after a short while it succumbed to island nationalism. We had radically under-estimated the strength of island particularism and inter-island rivalries. Its ultimate collapse had a major impact, long-term, on my political outlook and blunted my hopes for the region. Despite efforts to revive cross-Caribbean institutions the idea remains a largely unturned page in the post-colonial history of the region.

I'll hold the story there. In the previous chapter I focused on that phase of my life in which I determined to leave the Caribbean for Britain, as many of my generation felt compelled to do. Once in England, my emotional and political ties to the Caribbean remained strong. In some respects, I think, they deepened, while in other respects of course they attenuated. The Caribbean diaspora repre-sented a powerful intellectual formation. As I've been describing, an enormous amount of my intellectual activity was devoted to Caribbean issues, both aesthetic and political. To identify myself as diasporic is another way of demonstrating the degree to which the Caribbean was still inside me and shaped my approach to the world. Some of my critics believe that I wasn't concerned about the Carib-bean, or about black culture and politics, until the 1970s. It's true, perhaps, that my publications weren't centrally preoccupied with Caribbean or black matters. But they nonetheless formed an indis-pensable, active seam in my intellectual inquiries, from the 1950s up to the present. Looking through my papers the other day, I was taken aback at how much material exists on the Caribbean which I never sought to publish, or which appeared only in marginal, little-known magazines. My diasporic identifications depended on keeping this dimension of my intellectual world alive. And in this I wasn't alone. Whether West Indians stayed or returned, these intellectual commitments kept us going. They kept us alive. As part of Jamaica necessarily diminished inside me, there were strong counter-currents at work, for which I remain very grateful.

From the very moment I watched the shoreline of Port Antonio receding into the distance, I was shadowed by the question of whether I would return. I think I knew from the beginning that there could be no return, in the sense of regaining what had once been. That delusion never entered my soul, in part, I suspect, because I had no desire to relive my earlier life. But the complex amalgam of these questions about the self impressed itself sharply, both in my inner life and gradually, later, in my more academic theoretical investigations. The line dividing the two was never great; I hope that this book will explain why this is so.

The core of the conceptual problem we are dealing with here is this. Are the positions we take regarding the general problem of return to one's origin best understood as the product of our psychic formation and the way inner conflicts are 'resolved'? Does psychic formation, in other words, ultimately determine where we stand in relation to such a discourse of restitution? Or, alternatively, are we positioned by discourse and power, as Foucault suggests? This is the theoretical dilemma I'm left with, turning on the explanatory weight we accord to the psychic, on the one hand, and the discursive, on the other: the 'subjective' and the 'objective'.

The question of whether to return or not certainly possessed me at the time. Although I didn't have the vocabulary that I have now, I don't doubt that I was conscious of both registers at work inside me. In that sense, my experience of migration, and then being confronted by all the imponderables of whether to return, has indeed fed into my later attempts to theorize the dynamics of subjective life. But on the other hand (of course!) I am as interested in the social-discursive as I am in the psychic dynamics of the inner life. As I was growing up in Jamaica I couldn't remain unaware of the way the psychic and the discursive combined. It was only too clear to me that the social system of colonial rule carried within it its material, psychic conditions of existence. That's what I was endeavouring to explain when I talked of the response inside my family to the labour insurrections of 1938, and the consequent fashioning of the colonial family romance.

It's no doubt true that the dilemma of whether to return home distilled all these dilemmas in peculiarly concentrated form. But I'm making no larger claim than that. It wasn't an experience that was exceptional. So the problem I was confronted with is, I think, not explained by, but can be illuminated with reference to, both these levels: the psychic and the discursive.

One last point. Although I find it productive to think in terms of a diaspora, the concept of diaspora can surely be used for exactly the opposite end: not to confront but to disguise, evade or repress these sorts of inner emotional dynamics and the resulting traumas involved.

The great value of diasporic thought, as I conceive it, is that far from abolishing everything that refuses to fit neatly into a narrative – the displacements – it places the dysfunctions at the forefront. In the imaginary it is possible to condense different persons in a single figure, to alter places, to substitute different time frames, or to slip 'irrationally' between them, as dreams frequently do. Montage is its lifeblood. We have to work *with* such ways of telling and speaking, with no attempt to iron out the disruptions. There are no alternative, direct routes. In historical reality, we cannot turn back the ever-onward flight path of time's arrow. We can never go home again, and we need to fashion narrative forms able to catch the full complexities – the displacements, again – of this collective predicament.

Through the years I have come to see this point in time – when I struggled face to face with the civilization of the metropole, first in Oxford, then in London – as my first diasporic moment. My 'rebirth', perhaps, as a diasporic subject.

I was caught between my colonial formation, from which I was in flight, and my anti-colonial sentiments, which I had not yet learned to put into practice. At the time, I found them impossible to reconcile. But I was already an uneasy traveller between conflicting symbolic homes. What became clear was that leaving Jamaica had not resolved the ambivalences I had about belongingness. This is no doubt why I've come to think and write so much, not only about the similarities, the continuities, the many reprises of 'there' one finds 'here', but also the distances, the differences, the gaps between these two diasporas; and why I characterize my particular brand of being 'out of place' as the product of a 'diasporic' displacement. This is the insider/outsider perspective of Georg Simmel's 'stranger', the terrain of Homi Bhabha's 'in-between', the controlled doubling of Ashis Nandy's 'intimate enemies', W. E. B. DuBois's 'double consciousness' and Edward Said's 'out of place'. I think the form of belonging known now as black British, which expresses these complicated double attachments in more contemporary form, makes perfect sense for younger generations born in Britain, but of Caribbean descent and background. But I cannot own it. I am of a different generation.

The diasporic perspective offered a new vantage point, since by definition diasporas imply more than one positioning. Diasporas are inevitably creole or 'mongrel' contact zones, and impure. Immediately, this offered me not a solution but some distance from the raw emotional impact of the renunciation of my colonial family formation, and from the inevitable sense of rupture, refusal and loss which that entailed. On another level it provided what new 'problem spaces' always do: an opportunity, as David Scott puts it, to change not the answers but the questions. It provided not only a home from home, but a new site of knowledge. Watching mass migration close up, from a diasporic position, I was privileged to see a past I knew well in the process of unravelling, and a future emerging whose shape I could not foresee but in which I would be a participant. I could at last put these issues in a wider historical and personal context.

7. Caribbean Migration: The Windrush Generation

'*Suddenly everything looked different.*' That's how I earlier described the effect of my seeing West Indians, dispossessed folk most of them, spilling out of Paddington Station days after I myself had arrived in London. It turned around every preconception which lived inside me. The prerequisites of the colonial order had placed us *here* and them *there*. That was the preordained state of things. And yet now – in London, in front of my eyes – I could see in that instant the world turning inside out. I was mesmerized. It was as if the 'real' Caribbean which at home had remained beyond my reach had come to meet me in, of all places, England. Although I didn't have the mental means to explain what I'd witnessed, I somehow knew that what I'd seen changed everything. It marked my instinctive, unworked-through commitment to what later came to be called a diasporic conception of the world. I felt as if that scene had literally imprinted itself on my mental retina. I still remember every detail. It altered the possibilities I possessed for understanding who I was and who I might become.

At home we have in the hallway a huge reproduction of a news photo taken on the *Windrush* of three Jamaican migrants – two older men, carpenters, and one younger, an aspiring boxer – in their formal, sharp gear ready to step off the boat and make their entrance to the mother country. The older ones are wearing double-breasted pin-striped suits and felt hats, at a rakish angle. The younger man is in heavy salt-and-pepper trousers – drapes, the height of fashion at the time – which were baggy at the knees, tapered to exaggerated turn-ups, and sports a hat with the brim upturned all around. This was *style*. They were on a mission, determined to be recognized as participants in the modern world and to make it theirs. I look at this photograph every morning as I myself head out for that world.

A while ago, at the opening of an exhibition of *Windrush* photos at the Pitshanger Gallery, Mark Sealy, the director of the charity Autograph ABP, invited me to say a few words of introduction. I was overcome by the emotional weight of the images which surrounded me and by the memories of the varied fortunes of my migrant generation. We'd all undertaken the journey to our many illusions. Embarrassingly, I found myself in tears.

The experience of seeing difference played out in front of me was formative: I understood that difference was not to be evaded. I have continued thinking about this ever since. Standing at the juncture between a Jamaica to which I wasn't sure how to belong and an England to which I knew I didn't belong, the diasporic scene and its lived incongruities provided me with a space in which to think, a place on which to stand.

Looking back at these years I'm struck by the prominence of *sight* in the operations and theorizations of race. For me the visual components of these memories are potent. I've written before about the emotional valence carried in the archive of photographs in which these memories are now fixed and are given form. Yet

I am sure I'm not alone in this regard. This has something to do with the fact that we, the migrants, had traversed the colonial world. I've explained how racial classification in Jamaica organized a highly calibrated system of thought which enabled everyone to navigate the social world and to impose order on the chaos of the random, disconnected perceptions of those who passed before our eyes. That's how others became 'others'. It generated a particular social way of seeing, with powerful effects.

But in the transition from colony to metropole this racialized manner of looking – binding see-er and seen in a mutual but acutely unequal relation – existed in new circumstances and couldn't function as it once had. For a start we were all uniformly designated as 'black', which was itself a misrecognition of Caribbean realities. And secondly, because in the metropole the black other was now *here*, close by and intimately present, the inherited racial hierarchies required renovation if they were to remain serviceable. The field of vision shifted. In the metropole the underlying syntax was reassembled and the disposition of the racial other was thrown more sharply into relief. New modes of looking emerged – had done from the time we boarded the boat out. They did so day by day in our new lives: in the street, at work and in the neighbourhood. And they entered the feelings we took home with us at night to our rooms, free from the immediate gaze which – intentionally or not – worked to position us as outside the shared habitus of England.

Think of Frantz Fanon on a cold Lyons street overhearing the small white child cry out, '*Tiens, Mama! Un nègre!*', and of the consequent rent in his selfhood. This was a *metropolitan*, diasporic moment. Fanon's white mask – his accustomed Frenchness and the sophistication of his French learning – was torn asunder from his black skin. In the wake of this episode Fanon was obliged to re-evaluate his own racial being. That's how *Black Skin, White Masks* came to be conceived. The encounter between Fanon and the little child occurred at the time of *Windrush*. This preoccupation with the racialized look also runs through the literature of the Anglophone diaspora. Similar experiences to Fanon's appear in

Sam Selvon's *The Lonely Londoners*. The idea recurs, too, in George Lamming's novel *The Emigrants*; and it's accorded a separate chapter – under the title 'Ways of Seeing' – in Lamming's essays, *The Pleasures of Exile*.

The centrality of the metropole in these encounters reminds us of the philosophical influence of phenomenology or, in a less technical vocabulary, of existentialism, which in these years claimed significant intellectual currency. Yet we need also to recall that the historical experience of being black in Europe itself worked to revive the phenomenological inheritance, recreating (in David Macey's words) 'philosophy in the first person'. It transpired that existentialism, by an unexpected detour, offered a philosophical resource to recover the abjected black self that had been bequeathed by colonialism and slavery. In this the role of the racial *look* proved a significant vector through which competing, disparate histories coalesced and entered collective consciousness.

These have now become historical matters. It's part of the phenomenon of my having become history! There exists a growing historical literature on Caribbean migration to Britain in the middle decades of the last century. We're learning more all the time. But we're only just beginning to grasp the deeper connections between these structures of migration and the great historical transformations which were occurring in the period: the breaking of fascism; the seismic geopolitical effects of the Second World War, followed by the speedy onset of the Cold War; the weakening of the European colonial powers, and the rapid upsurge in the struggles for decolonization; and the installation of social-democratic regimes, symbolized in Britain by Labour's victory in 1945 and the dispatching of Winston Churchill. When I read C. L. R. James I find myself, like him, struggling to understand how these historical connections worked.

The migration to the metropole of the 1940s and 1950s reversed the tides of the colonial era, and presaged the post-war movements of peoples from periphery to centre. The formation of the black British diaspora itself was a component in the contested process of decolonization. For a time Caribbeans, and others from the colonized world, were viewed as the exemplars of the modern migrant experience. As the British journalist Gary Younge once pointed out, in this period there still existed a degree of equivalence between 'race' and 'place'. This was to be closely followed by the accelerating contraflows of globalization. In effect, the migration of my generation brought two historical eras – the post-colonial and the global – explosively together. Yet as this happened, the older colonial mentalities refused to vanish. Inside the new, the older forms persisted.

The history of migration can't be comprehended without the imperial connection. Jamaicans came as colonials, drawn by an invisible gravitational pull to the 'absent centre' which had defined life in the colony for centuries. They came, as Ashis Nandy felicitously put it, as 'intimate enemies'. The unequal relations of power, wealth and authority separated the colonized from the British. But colonizers and colonized were locked in struggle with each other in a re-enactment of Hegel's master/slave dialectic. This was a relationship, in other words, which could not be transcended. It could only be fought to the death.

Those who had made the journey from the Caribbean could be understood as symbolically enacting the third, long-postponed and final leg of the historic process of unequal exchange known as 'the triangular trade'. This had originally taken British traders and trinkets to Africa; followed by the transportation of the enslaved to the Caribbean; and then lastly the shipment of rum, sugar and profits produced by forced labour back to England's seaports. The new generation of Caribbean migrants, on the *Windrush* and on the many vessels which followed, were 'completing' that shattering Middle Passage, bringing it all back 'home' where it belonged. History was turning back against itself.

I was intrigued to read Andrea Levy's novel *Small Island*, where these historical themes – the sharpening tempo of Caribbean migration to England; the war; and the end of India's 'subaltern empire' in 1947 – are located in a single frame. At the same time *Small Island* tells a story of the integration of black West Indians into domestic, feminine England, in a way that the earlier generation of writers, the Selvons and Lammings, were never able to imagine. Levy's is also a tale steeped in ambiguity, in which the metropolitan consequences of race remain dramatically uncertain. Promise and defeat are intertwined. In the same conjuncture, contrary, dissimilar and unresolved histories coexist.

To understand the entanglements between Britain and the Caribbean at the moment of post-war migration we need to grasp the Second World War itself as a global, imperial nexus of historical events. It's too easy to fall back on a stock set of images depicting a beleaguered England confronting single-handedly the ferocious might of a militarized Germany. This I think of as the *Dad's Army* version of the national story. Seen from this viewpoint, the history of Caribbean migration makes no sense. From beginning to end the war was an imperial affair, drawing into the cataclysm one colonial region after the other. The rivalry between the British and the German Empires governed the outbreak of hostilities, continuing the unfinished business of the First World War. For the duration, imperial interests informed every significant strategic decision. In the immediate post-war years few, if any, British politicians were able to see that the vast global conflict had transformed the structural conditions on which the British Empire, and British power more generally, had thrived. Much grief was to follow from this serious, although widespread, misapprehension about the movements of history.

There's no doubt that, up to a point, the heightened self-consciousness of national unity engendered by the Second World War ideologically cemented the British nation. This was the effect of confronting the spectacle of possible defeat, the dangers posed by the strength of the rival German war machine, the victory-snatched-from-the-jaws-of-defeat of Dunkirk and the threat of imminent invasion. Churchill's political rhetoric – 'we stand alone' . . . 'we are all in this together' . . . 'we shall never be defeated' . . . 'their finest hour' – crystallized a national climacteric, responding to the historical realities of a nation a hair's breadth away from destruction. While one can appreciate the political determination and a popular vein of heroism, it was nevertheless the big battalions which prevailed. In the final reckoning, it was less plucky England that counted than the overpowering resources of America, of the Soviet Union and, significantly, of Britain's colonial Empire.

The war is still primarily remembered as the achievement of the common people all mucking in together: the people's war; the home front; the egalitarian experiences of the Blitz; the Land Army; women in the munitions factories; families sleeping in Tube stations; shared air-raid shelters; blackout wardens; evacuation; rationing and the cheerily tolerated hardships of daily life. The war remains the resonant dividing line, the hiatus, in the British imaginary around which ideas of then-and-now are still mobilized, certainly for my generation. It has become riveted in the historical memory of Britain, triumphant as a unified community. While much of this version of the national history may be untrue and in need of qualification, it does have the merit of articulating the shift in social power that the war carried in its wake.

The war was, after all, the principal factor in the social-democratic remaking of the nation. Labour's victory delivered a redistributive programme; Keynesian dedication to full employment; a publicly funded, universalist benefits system and egalitarian experiments such as comprehensive education and that proud British institution, the National Health Service. Together they represented a social revolution. One only has to think of the social difference between Churchill – with his immovable imperialist sensibilities and persona as the British bulldog, revered as the war leader – and Clement Attlee, the understated, pipe-smoking, respectable, middle-class, middle-of-the-road social democrat.

Experiences of the war also did much to loosen the hierarchies of class and gender, a social transformation which gathered pace in the 1950s and 1960s, and which came most deeply to be felt in terms of generation. This socially inclusive encoding of the nation, both in the formal legislative programme of the Labour governments as well as in the lived relations of the everyday, ran contrary to the dominant tendencies in inherited colonial habits of thought. But these conflicting conceptions of the world were never harmoniously resolved in the post-war years, particularly in matters of race.

Though vigorously disavowed, race has played a historically determining role in the self-definition of Britain as a nation. There's a long history to, and many discursive slippages between, race and nation in imperial discourse. Liberal imperialism thrives on these contradictions. There was, in the one register, the endless invocation of the civilizing mission and of the duty to advance the empire at a moderate, gentlemanly pace towards its own transcendent abolition. And in a separate register the colonial masters repeated their conviction that it was their duty to administer their unbridled authority wherever they deemed it necessary. Seemingly opposites, over time each voice combined with and came to exist inside the other.

These were elements in an unrolling dynamic seeking to codify the nation-empire. In each historical phase the discursive elements fused in different and perpetually contradictory combinations. Race operated as the silent partner. Whenever the British began to imagine themselves as lovers of liberty they also conceived of themselves, at one and the same time, as the imperial lords of humankind.

During the war the many black colonials who had volunteered to enlist, or who ended up contributing to the war effort on the home front, presented the British with an unwelcome dilemma. The colonials had, after all, loyally joined up and offered their lives to defend 'the mother country' – a remarkable fact in itself, if one thinks about it. On the other hand, these black 'comrades in arms' were perceived to be foreign to 'our' ways. Throughout the war, formal and informal colour-bars operated in every department of British life; they were haphazard rather than uniform, and seldom the consequence of an explicit central directive. The institutional colour-lines were simultaneously both pervasive and -- due to the degree of circumlocution which governed their installation -- open to official denial. Blacks, both colonials and the GIs serving with the American forces, were regularly refused service in cafés, hotels and restaurants. There existed a free-floating hostility and sporadic, racially inspired clashes between whites and black. Brawls in the street, and in the pubs and clubs, were sparked most of all by the sight of white women fraternizing with black men.

The dangers perceived in relations between black men and white women go to the heart of race in Britain in the 1940s and 1950s. The erotic element proved the combustible factor in the racial imaginary. Blackness was commonly felt to be violating the feminine, the domestic and the sexual, jeopardizing the inner private sanctum of the Englishman. Racial and sexual fears conjoined, each feeding off the other, positioning the fantasized figure of the white *man* as the redoubtable bastion against the subterranean, menacing currents of disorder. As Sonya Rose shows in *Which People's War?*, public opprobrium regularly fell as heavily on the 'loose morals' of the white women who were willing to be so involved – the so-called 'good-time girls' – as it did on black men. Women were advised that, if in the darkness of a cinema they found themselves sitting next to a coloured man, they should move to another seat; if a coloured man came into a shop, the woman should 'make her purchase and depart immediately'; if she met 'one' coming towards her on the pavement, she should cross to the other side. When such infractions of the social taboo came into view they marked the moment when the official force of the state and the outburst of popular violence 'from below', were unleashed and met, representing a vital if spontaneous and unspoken compact between state and people.

Sensibilities such as these possessed a kind of pathological extremity, fuelled by a raft of perceived injustices. They were driven by the presentiment that identity itself was on the point of being stolen from the indigenous whites, who in the process were transmogrifying into unlikely 'victims'. The annihilation of the self – of the white self – was just around the corner. This was evident in the anxieties in the racist imaginary which accrued around miscegenation. Such ways of thinking incubated the sensation that those who were mixed-race faced the prospect that their identity, *as such*, was in danger of obliteration.

The consequences were profound. White England, of course, had been blessed with history, tradition and civilization in abundance: from such resources identities naturally flowed. But within the racial logic the non-white migrants, out of place in the metropole, could only ever maintain a precarious hold on identity.

Miscegenation came to be the overdetermined element in this pattern of thought, invoking older structures of feeling in which the racial taint worked as a kind of contagion, as 'bad blood'. Within this farrago of fantasies it was easy to imagine that whites were in danger of being dispossessed – not of this or that identity, but of their very claim to be human subjects. They were in danger, in a curious paradoxical twist, of being reduced to the state of the colonized.

It was in these circumstances, in the immediate post-war years, that the *Windrush* arrived from Kingston, carrying some 500 Caribbean migrants in June 1948. It marked a symbolic turning point in black diasporic history yet it was not, as is often imagined today, the original moment of the black presence in Britain. Black people had lived here for centuries, washed up by the currents of empire, as Peter Fryer shows with verve and sympathy in his *Staying Power*. The black presence was both more varied and more involved in British social and political life than the subsequent histories of black settlement have allowed. For long, London particularly had functioned as a migratory junction for all manner of colonial peoples. The significance of *Windrush* resided in the public recognition that the incoming migrants were coming to Britain not as temporary visitors, but to stay. It carried the alarming prospect of a permanent presence of blacks in Britain.

Many of the West Indians who'd served in the war and returned to the Caribbean found the economic and social conditions back home so desperate that they determined to make the return journey to Britain. Whatever the hardships they'd confronted in the metropole the first time around, they reckoned that at least they had a better chance to make good if they returned. Some third of those on the *Windrush* had served in the forces and were embarking on their second voyage to the 'mother country'.

When I arrived I hadn't expected to see large numbers of ordinary black people looking for jobs, carrying with them their worldly possessions and their dreams of a better future for their children. Many were from the countryside, although their unskilled status has been exaggerated. Peter Fryer reckons that one in four were non-manual workers. By one means or another they had scrabbled together enough money to buy a one-way ticket in order to find work which, as many had discovered, was impossible at home. They found jobs in places the like of which they had never known before: in factories, steel and iron foundries and on assembly lines; on building sites; in hospitals; and on the buses and the railways.

Many of the sites of the new publicly owned economy, particularly the NHS and transport, were staffed by Caribbean migrants, reproducing inside the welfare state familiar colonial hierarchies. This becomes a matter of historical irony when later generations of migrants find themselves regularly condemned for exploiting indigenous Britons. Where would the welfare state have been without its migrant workers?

My strongest memory is of the survival spirit of the new arrivals. I kept thinking of the years of back-breaking labour, poverty and colonial humiliation which had impelled them to up sticks and leave. The questions came tumbling in. What dreams and ambitions had fuelled this momentous break with their roots? What were their prospects? Would life in the metropole transform them into different sorts of people? How would *their* presence transform Britain? Where did they stand in relation to empire, given that the long-settled relationships of subordination and dependency in which they had been schooled were being radically interrupted? What of Jamaican or Caribbean culture would be retained or reproduced, and how much lost? Could they resist new modes of subjectification? Did they ever anticipate how *different* they would seem? Would they adapt or resist, or both? What new patterns of life would they produce? These questions were to preoccupy me. They were directed at *me* as much as at *them*. Even so, they opened up for me a new 'problem space'.

The newspapers were full of reports on the migrant 'crisis', and from the late 1940s the figure of the black migrant assumed an instantly recognizable social disposition. The broadsheets viewed the situation with faint distaste. The statesmen and moral guardians muttered their 'expressions of concern'. The tabloids gave voice to a populist brand of outrage. The photographs hit the page like cold water thrown in the face. The metaphors began to unroll, the moral panic to unfold. An unstoppable tide of black migrants, the public commentators prophesied, is headed in this direction! The British way of life would never survive the influx! The British would become a khaki-coloured, mongrel race! You could feel the air becoming thick with casual racism, prejudicial talk, hostile looks, insulting innuendoes, shouted insults and *sotto voce* name-calling. As if to ward off trouble, the 'No Coloureds' signs sprouted in the windows of houses advertising rooms to let. England was retreating behind its net curtains.

I had the impression in the early days that many of the newly arrived Caribbeans shunned public visibility and held back an accustomed gregariousness, trying to keep themselves to themselves. But this couldn't hold for long. Whether they liked it or not they were in and about the world. And they were, in any case, highly visible. They lived in white areas, had white neighbours and white workmates, and they used the same streets, pubs and shops. It was just not a situation made for the organization of an informal apartheid.

These were the years when the colour-bar came to be a more openly acknowledged facet of domestic life, both for its advocates and its critics. The invisibilities and the 'unspeakability' of the existence of such a racial barrier were slowly fading. This isn't to claim, though, that the prohibitions imposed on the non-white population lessened. In some respects they did; and in some respects they categorically didn't, with the invention of violent new colour-lines disfiguring the social landscape. The situation was one composed of paradoxes. With the tide of international opinion turning against colonial rule, gradually and unevenly the colour-bar in Britain's overseas possessions began to be dismantled, with varying degrees of resistance. As this was happening, in the 'mother country' itself the colour-bar emerged as a more visible feature of the urban landscape.

The seeds of white, working-class racialized resentment were sown in the antagonism between two sections of the same disadvantaged underclass who, because of racial difference, grew to misrecognize each other as the main cause of their misfortune. Many of the white underprivileged came to believe that what they experienced was not because they were poor and exploited but 'because the blacks are here'.

These new configurations of racism are also part of the *Windrush* story. In the 1940s reassertions of a social attachment to racial whiteness assumed a renewed hold on public life. In the longer historical duration they were to exert a sharper social gravity, in the white riots of 1958, for example, and in the popular upsurge in Powellism at the end of the 1960s and in the early 1970s. To say this, of course, doesn't tell the whole story. The reason why, for example, the prohibitions against cross-racial erotic encounters redoubled was, well, because they were happening – or about to happen – wherever one looked. But nor is it right to take the arrival of *Windrush* as indicating the beginning of the nation's accession to a triumphant multiculturalism in which the injuries of race were dispatched to the darkness of a bygone age, like children up chimneys.

As I've been suggesting, the backstory to this racial encounter turns on historical forgetfulness. This did much to organize indigenous responses to the dark-skinned migrants. Their histories, and their long historical entanglements with Britain, disappeared from daily consciousness. Who are these people? Where are they from? What language do they speak? And, above all, what on earth are they doing here? This constituted the dominant, repetitive refrain among white Britons. It represented a disavowal of collective force. It was this that impelled George Lamming in 1960 to coin his pithy provocation: 'We have met before.' His insistent plea for the British to remember who *they* were, and where *they* had come from, articulated a defining objective in the struggle for decolonization in the diaspora.

Moreover, from the 1950s the idea of empire was beginning to conjure up the shadows of decline rather than the high noon of triumph. The sooner one ditched the worn imperial associations, it was often felt, the better. For many the empire was a past from which people wanted to run. This isn't to say, however, that the imperial past fell into oblivion: that never happened. Rather the memory formations became ever more selective, such that the stories of the empire which most easily survived worked to conceal, or to screen, the most troubling dimensions. The British still possessed a reflex, residual image of their former imperial splendour. Perhaps it was Stanley and Livingstone shaking hands in a nonchalant, English and civilized manner, watched by their black 'bearers' somewhere in 'the dark continent'. Or it could have been a royal durbar in 'exotic India', the jewel in the crown. But it all became more mystifying when the 'bearers' and the 'jewels' unaccountably turned up in the streets of Brixton or Toxteth or Southall. That was never in the script!

In 1978 I delivered a lecture entitled 'Racism and Reaction'. This was some while before the media had confronted the full force of black despair and anger on the streets, though there was enough evidence there for anyone to see. For some years I'd been working with my co-authors on *Policing the Crisis*, where we'd identified the emergence of a new political authoritarianism, organized through the prism of race – or, more precisely, through the prism of *blackness*. It was this research which allowed me, the following year, to grasp what was historically new in the politics of Thatcherism. In 'Racism and Reaction' I was at pains to explore the idea that post-war racism in Britain 'begins with the profound forgetfulness' about the conjoining of race and empire that has overtaken British life since the 1950s. George Lamming raises the possibility that misremembering of this order is connected, by some means, to the matter of racial violence. The connections between forgetfulness, disavowal and violence are not contingent. *The Pleasures of Exile* stands as a reflection on the state of England after the white riots of 1958, which I'll come to in a moment. But – scandalously – Lamming turned his attention away from the white 'hooligan' or Teddy Boy patrolling the colour-line in the crumbling, impoverished inner city and focused instead on the higher reaches of the national culture. The forgetfulness of Britain's imperial past incubated in *these* locales must also be acknowledged, Lamming maintained, as an active, morally consequent agent in the violence which erupted.

Why this forgetfulness? How can we understand it to be a social fact? The spatial organization of empire was an important factor in the process of forgetting. It was one thing to be deeply mired, as Britain was, in exchanging trinkets for captives in West Africa, shipping them across the Atlantic in the genocidal Middle Passage, selling their bodies into plantation slavery, exploiting their forced labour, consuming the commodities they produced and repatriating the profits of an activity they could safely conduct hundreds of miles away, without compromising the nation's self-image as a 'sceptered isle' or a 'green and pleasant land'. It was quite another – an abrogation of a law of nature – to have the natives' descendants next door, renting a room in your house, clipping your ticket on the bus and touching your body in hospital.

Disavowal is a complicated psychic manoeuvre. It allows people to 'know' and 'not know' at the same time. It suppresses and conceals. But it also releases and sets in motion all manner of morbid symptoms, dangerous and aggressive feelings, and the return of the repressed. Yet it is exactly at this point that the collective mind convinces itself it has been cleansed for other, higher purposes.

What whites in the 1950s really wanted to know was how the 'primitive' and the 'civilized' would be played out. What roles can these blacks possibly have in modern British life? What sorts of people will they become? Can white and black, at different civilizational stages, live together on equal and peaceful terms in the same communities? Can we fraternize, cross-breed and prosper? Whom will *they* marry or have children with? Whose daughters will *they* sleep with? Whose black sons will come knocking at the door? Could someone ever be black and British? When will 'the good old days' return, when white authority prevailed? And when will they be going back to the places to which they properly belonged? The purchase of these questions may be slowly dwindling. But they have not disappeared. Nor has their efficacy wholly diminished.

Yet in British eyes the differences embodied in the black migrants were pronounced and appeared to be everywhere one turned. For a start, to the British the migrants *looked* different. They dressed in inappropriate, outrageous clothes. You could hear, as intended, the disapproving stage whispers: 'too *loud*'. They cooked and ate different food, with notoriously different smells. They didn't speak properly tutored English. They walked 'differently'. The men were defiantly priapic, while their women were complicit in shameless, overt canoodling. Here, though, you could *feel* the quiver of ambivalence! Even, it was said, they smelled differently. They were voluble, excitable, high-spirited, quarrelsome, truculent and aggressive. Not like 'us' at all.

Black people had easily aroused tempers, whereas the British (actually, the English) were practised in the refined art of managing themselves. The migrants didn't understand the virtue of reserve. They were stronger in the emotional department than in rational calculation. Besides, they were too inclined to show off, lacking moderation and restraint. Ostentatiously, they drove flashy, souped-up cars even when they couldn't afford them. They were not habituated to 'hard graft' – an old canard from the plantation, this. They, of course, played their music loud, loved to dance and inveigled 'our' women to party with them, leading to goodness knows what.

One could go on. And on, in an endless self-confirming spiral. Where was difference located? In all departments of human life, with any – or every – human trait open to racialization.

In these ways the black newcomers represented an affront to the careful modulations of the Englishness of the late 1940s and 1950s. They appeared resentful, although why this should be confounded the English sense of themselves. Sometimes, it appeared, migrants looked at the British as if they thought they'd perpetrated some deep but unidentifiable wrong against them.

This rich reservoir of stereotypes will not surprise anyone familiar with plantation depictions of the true nature of 'the lazy Negro', or with the language of the eighteenth-century cartoons of 'the African', or with the tirades of anti-Abolition pamphlets. How widely such sentiments circulated in popular speech we can only guess. But they were applied to *all* blacks, as a category. They represented an extreme, demeaning form of social reductionism whose traces provide a continuing, underlying dimension to race talk today.

Numbers of British people convinced themselves that, since West Indians were black, they must also be – literally – dirty. This was particularly wounding. And ironic too, since we prided ourselves on being scrupulously clean even when, as they say, we were 'dirt-poor'. Indeed, we were entertained to discover that some of the English only rarely took a bath. Besides, we couldn't fathom how in winter one could keep clean if one had to feed money into a meter in order to get hot water. The calypsonians were comically eloquent about this mysterious, very English practice. We encountered the potentially explosive hot-water tanks with their cash meters perched ominously above the bath and exuding the faint aroma of leaking gas – which lit with a ferocious *thump* – as threatening, anxiogenic objects. Almost as dangerous as the fabled paraffin heater.

Generically, of course, West Indians were not dirty. However, we were seen, metaphorically, to be *'like dirt'*, in Mary Douglas's more profound sense of 'matter out of place'.

Such were our experiences, as I recall them. But how were these investments in racial difference assembled? How did they work? British racialized discourse was founded on a biological/civilizational classificatory system in which nature and culture are read off against one another. In this scenario race and skin colour played the familiar game of hide-and-seek with each other. But once a system of equivalences had been forged between race and culture, civilizational status was marked and indexed by something more *visible*. By skin colour. The putative, invisible but ineradicable operations of genetic and biological racial inheritance, long at work in the plantation societies of the New World, with its mysteries and hidden scandals, were made socially readable through the 'floating signifier' of skin colour.

Contrary to scholarly common sense, race and cultural difference don't produce two separate racist discourses. They constitute racism's two discursive registers, interpenetrating and substituting as equivalents for one another. Converting cultural differences into racial categories, and physical markers into civilizational ones, turns out to be a key mechanism in the discourse of difference. Nor is it limited to the so-called Negro races. It is to be found everywhere in the colonial world. And in the post-colonial world too.

The persistence of colonial mentalities continues into the post-colonial years as well as into the organization of race in the metropole. This was conspicuously evident, for our generation, in the white riots of 1958 which erupted in Notting Hill and Nottingham.

The riots marked a sharp caesura in the lives of Caribbean migrants to Britain. Both Ladbroke Grove in Notting Hill and the St Ann's district in Nottingham were areas of dense migrant, black settlement. They were the forerunners of what came to be known as black 'colony areas' occupying run-down areas of the inner city, even though they never were exclusively black ghettos. In the 1950s, such concentration of non-white peoples was relatively new outside the seaports. Each was fast becoming a significant area of colonial settlement: Brixton, North Kensington, Tottenham and Peckham in London; St Paul's in Bristol; Handsworth and Balsall Heath in Birmingham; Moss Side in Manchester; Toxteth in Liverpool; as well as the old metal-manufacturing areas in the West Midlands and the equally old textile towns in the Bradford area. These were locations which indelibly came to be associated with race, particularly in the late 1970s and 1980s when they were gripped by revolt. In the 1950s these inner-city, bombed-out or abandoned sites, with their multiple-occupation houses and their palpable deprivation, generated distinctive ways of life. They were the sites of the transition from the first generation of migrant life to the second, in which a new black subject emerged.

By the later 1950s the immediate post-*Windrush* shock of arrival was tapering off, and the slow-burn trauma of racial discrimination had begun to take hold. In Notting Hill and in Nottingham the initial unrest was triggered by the sight of white women accompanying black men, instigated by aggrieved whites. These were white riots, invoking in London the unrestrained racial violence associated with the segregated states in the American South, and bringing to British streets the invocation of the Klan and giving renewed life to dark memories of lynchings. An organized fascist presence was active. Notting Hill had been the location of calculated, violent nocturnal assaults on lone black men.

The riots themselves proved a shock for the governing classes, unsure how it was that such things had come to pass in England. Not that any public figure demonstrated any commitment to visit Notting Hill and to listen to those who had suffered the violent attacks. While the politicians dallied in making the journey from Westminster, all of a couple of miles away, Norman Manley – Jamaica's Chief Minister at the time – flew in from Kingston, in an act recognized at the time as a show of public solidarity. Initially the media indicted white working-class youth – the 'hooligans' and Teddy Boys – seeking to condense two of the pressing dysfunctional social figures of the day, the white Teddy Boy and the black migrant. But as the crisis unfolded, unobtrusively the black migrant, the unwitting victim of violence, moved to the fore as the principal agent of disorder. In a perverse logic, the victim transmuted into the perpetrator.

These were menacing times. They bequeathed two long-term, significant consequences. First, they inaugurated the moment when race in the inner city properly became a police matter. Second, the events of Notting Hill and Nottingham did much to convince significant numbers of Caribbean migrants that assimilation in English society was no longer a matter to be considered.

Early in 1959 the Antiguan Kelso Cochrane was knifed to death on the border between White City and Notting Hill. This was a terrible moment. The *Daily Mail* called it 'the first fatality in the "war" that flares intermittently in the seamy side of the Royal Borough of Kensington'. The reluctance of the police to identify the murderers was there for all to see, a phenomenon we've witnessed repeatedly in the intervening years. It's taken fifty years for the story to reach the light of day. In 2011 Mark Olden's meticulously researched *Murder in Notting Hill* unravelled the dense web of racism in which for many years the entire event – the assault and its long aftermath – had been enveloped.

Kelso Cochrane's funeral, held in St Michael's in Ladbroke Grove, demonstrated the presence of an alternative, multicultural sentiment. A great crowd of mourners gathered, both black and white, and followed the coffin to Kensal Green Cemetery. In itself this was a modest enough response. Yet at the time – after the public displays of racial violence and fascist intervention – it betokened the possibility that within civil society the future was not entirely closed.

The riots also spurred on new possibilities for political and cultural activity from within the migrant population. A dazzling figure was the Trinidadian Claudia Jones. She had recently been deported to Britain from the US on account of her Communist commitments, even though she had never previously set foot in Britain. She was a tireless, energetic organizer, full of irrepressible charm and, whatever the state of her finances, from top to toe as chic as anyone around. She founded and edited the *West Indian Gazette*. This had first hit the streets a few months before the riots broke out. She wrote much of the copy and, when that was done, she hawked the paper wherever there was a likely spot for sales. The *Gazette* operated as an inspired medium for the organization of the Caribbean population in Britain, although not for West Indians alone. After the riots migrant London needed to be remade emotionally and politically, from the inside. Claudia Jones and her co-workers realized that there was no point in endeavouring to pursue a politics of assimilation. Migrants had to create for themselves what they might claim as their own, coming out of the life of the Caribbean. And so a group of activists arrived at the idea of transplanting Carnival to London. As a consequence, in the February following the riots Carnival was launched, a momentous step in the creolization of the old imperial capital.

This was a matter of political intervention. Other responses were less calculated, emerging as a means to navigate the hostile landscapes which pressed in. One such initiative was to create a common bond with fellow migrants, reinventing the lives that had been left behind in the Caribbean. Shops began selling West Indian produce; one or two adventurous entrepreneurs opened improvised clubs where migrants could drink in a free space and play their own music; and also where single men could take those white women willing to go out with them. These were more akin to community centres than drinking dens. The stunning photographs of black life in Hackney taken by Dennis Morris, although from a later period, capture the dynamics of these tentative bids for fraternization across the colour-line. They show mixed-race couples dancing, and also the occasional mixed-race wedding. They tell an eloquent story.

In the aftermath of the riots West Indians had no choice but to rely on their own resources when they rented property or needed to raise the deposit for the purchase of a place to live. Small-scale, improvised businesses catering for the migrant population began slowly to evolve. As migrant families settled, the ingenuity of diasporic adaptation was everywhere to be found. For example, the emerging creolized domestic interiors condensed an entire collective life experience. The contrasting, vibrant colours of the wallpaper, sofa covers, curtains and mats dominated the West Indian living room. Anything less would have signalled a lack, a social collapse in the private domain. The cabinets displayed the 'family treasure', prized but seldom used gifts such as florally decorated crockery, long-stemmed wine glasses, cake stands and Coronation mugs. Things didn't have to match. That wasn't the point. They captured the sensibilities of the busy round of family life and were testament to an affirmation of the future.

The question of belongingness takes time to touch the habits of the everyday and only properly surfaced as a fully politicized issue in the cultural politics of the 1960s and 1970s, with the coming of age of second-generation black youth. Many of this new generation had been born in Britain and schooled here. Others had remained in the Caribbean with relatives while the adults came to Britain to test the water, their sons and daughters joining them later. It's been estimated that between 1955 and 1960, migrants from Jamaica to Britain brought with them 6,500 children. But they had left behind with relatives many, many more, substantial numbers of whom were later to make the journey for themselves. For this generation, both the road *back* to a Caribbean identification and the road ahead *to*

English belongingness appeared to have been closed to them. Yet when they transmuted into 'black Britons' they did so as an act of intransigence, with fire in their bellies.

By the 1970s a long, complex and troubled route had been travelled from the 'black migrants' in my *Windrush* photo to 'Afro-Caribbeans', to 'Rastas and Rude Boys', to 'black British' and to the 'black posse'. The Britain of the 1950s – 'Keep Britain White' and 'No Coloureds' – is barely recognizable today in the era of the globalized players who compose the Premier League football teams, the many varieties of skin colour which make up the British and English sporting teams, the casts of the TV soaps, those who present the TV programmes, or model the couture, or perform the music listened to across the nation. This much is true, and it's a sign that the world still turns. But the journey to where we are was long, contested and often bitterly divisive. Its final destination remains still undecided. The historical entanglement between Britain and the Caribbean proves a difficult lesson for the British to learn. But it is an issue to which I need to keep returning. Through the imperial connection Britain and its colonies were intertwined – as dominant and subjugated subjects, not as partners in a shared enterprise – in their very inequities, differences and fates. This thought is not always welcome and British historians particularly are prone to resist such 'speculation'. And indeed, to a degree the same was true of Caribbean historians in the high nationalist moment, when the urgent task seemed to be to rewrite the national narrative and decentre what were commonly perceived as the demeaning dependencies on European history and thought. However, the Caribbean cannot be understood on either side of the Atlantic without taking into account the moment of colonialism and imperialism, and the capacity of both for conscripting those who lived under their authority.

This highlights imperialism's contradictory, double inscriptions: of the reciprocal but uneven relations between metropole and colony, and the converging and diverging lines of connection between 'the West' and societies with histories long predating 'the rise and rise of Europe'. It alerts us to the conflicting patterns of encounter

and conquest, of the 'wonder' and greed which drove the colonizers on; to the diverging mechanisms which harnessed the two
worlds – together but different – into a single economic system; to
the mirror images of free labour here, and forced labour or enslavement there; to the implantations in language, culture and
institutions across the imperial world which followed the viola-
tions of conquest, and the antagonistic cultures of 'respect' and
'resentment' which these contradictions fuelled.

Conquest, colonization, plantation slavery, colonial government
and liberal imperialism were significant phases in British history.
The colonial relationships were essential ingredients of Britishness –
as much a part of daily life and the national imaginary as the sugar
at the bottom of the emblematically English cup of tea, or the ache
at the root of the proverbial British sweet tooth. I deliberately con-
flate English and British here to show how the former sometimes
does, and sometimes does not, include the latter. It's one of the
trickiest of ambiguities underwriting the discourse of British
national identity.

Today people might wonder what all this has to do with us now.
Why should the sins of the fathers be visited on us? Haven't we paid
our dues? Didn't Wilberforce give 'them' 'their' freedom? Isn't that
why he deserved to be buried in Westminster Abbey? And didn't
that bring closure to that whole episode? Isn't that a sign of our
benevolent nature? Didn't Abolition redeem the British soul? The
great liberal virtues seem to have wiped the slate clean. The Whig
interpretation of history, which reveres moderate and uninterrupted progress, lives on in our post-imperial times. It represents a
tricky, self-deceiving but powerfully persuasive discourse.

The history of empire really does seem, in any strategic sense, to
have fallen out of mind. It is judged impolite and faintly anachronistic
even to mention it. Post-imperial scholars and historians, who have
been remapping these contradictory interdependencies, still encounter a wall of scepticism and incomprehension from – particularly –
scholars of empire. Was empire, they ask, really so significant in
shaping British society? In fact, the civilizational discourses of
empire, and what Catherine calls 'the rule of difference', left their

ineradicable imprint and did their corrosive work inside the continuing vicissitudes of British culture. Unpurged, the imperial moment remains the discursive shadow of the nation's self-image. These matters still have a long, unfinished history. Let me recount a recent episode to explain what I mean.

When in 1998 I served on the Runnymede Trust's Commission on the *Future of Multi-Ethnic Britain*, chaired by Bhikhu Parekh, 'diversity' (a polite word for 'difference') was still much in vogue. Early on in our deliberations the Macpherson Report was published. This was the official inquiry into the 1993 murder of Stephen Lawrence by five white youths in Eltham in south London. Much like the murder of Kelso Cochrane a generation before, the police at the time signally failed to apprehend any of those responsible. Macpherson drew a distinction between direct and 'institutional' racism, and he indicted the Metropolitan Police for its 'institutional racism': that is, for its uninspected racist assumptions that shaped everyday interactions and underpinned the casual attitudes of the 'canteen culture'. In the evidence I submitted on behalf of Stephen Lawrence's companion, Duwayne Brooks, who was with him on the dreadful night of the murder, I drew a similar distinction between 'formal' and 'informal', or 'unwitting', variants of British racism. That an official inquiry could suppose that there existed such a thing in the everyday culture of British life was, for leading public figures, the cause of deep unease, and Macpherson came in for sustained personal attack. I should add that it was only in 2012 that two of the white youths were finally charged with Stephen Lawrence's murder and that the truth of Macpherson's interpretation, and its wider implications, came grudgingly to be acknowledged.

This was the intellectual climate when the Labour Home Secretary, Jack Straw, gave his blessing to the establishment of the Runnymede Commission. However, once our Report was published it met with lurid publicity and comprehensive outrage. When Straw could see which way the wind was blowing, he joined the chorus of dissent and publicly rubbished our work. The unexceptional observation that Britain remained in many ways a racist society, blown up by the tabloid press, set his sensitivities on edge.

In response, he went scurrying back to the writings of George Orwell – containing a sort of love letter to a certain version of Englishness – in order to establish the virtues of English nationalism so as to counter our arguments. The only parts of our Report which interested him were the passages on 'social cohesion', which became – for a time – a defensive mantra in government circles, before disappearing down Mr Cameron's 'multiculturalism is dead' plughole.

These are depressing reflections. Things may have changed since the 1950s, but not necessarily for the better. Racism and racial injustice still prevail, although maybe not in the unapologetic forms I encountered when I first arrived. The violence among black youths, perpetrated on local black rivals, remains a serious problem. Repatriation continues to offer to some on the 'respectable', populist Right a covert fantasy solution to all our troubles.

The old reflexes are hard to dislodge. From the *Windrush* moment of 1948 onwards West Indian migrants came to be perceived not just as black, different and perhaps less civilized, but as essentially *not part of us*: a foreign element in the body politic, a permanent excluded minority. This has engendered an entrenched and defensive understanding of Englishness. 'We' – the English – are, by definition, not just white. Whiteness remains the signifier of a particular, unique and uninterrupted progressive history, an 'advanced' civilization crowned by a worldwide imperium. 'We' are this *because* 'they' are not. Binary oppositions like this create meaning. What is absent – excluded, in this instance – becomes manifest by its very absence. 'They', the blacks in our midst, become the constitutive *outside* of this national story.

This absent/present works in dialectical mode, such that the dynamic which binds the two elements together – white and black – also ensures that each exists inside the other. Indeed, they can only exist in relation to the other. The other is always, necessarily, inside us.

Which takes me back to where I started the chapter: to my own proto-diasporic moment by Paddington Station all those years ago. I set out for England with many unresolved ambivalences about belonging. I identified with the aspirations of black Jamaicans and the emergent indigenous culture which, I believed, only the end of colonialism could fully release. But I had been formed in a distanced and troubled relationship to my own nation. I was also shaped in relation to the culture of the colonizer 'elsewhere' but, for very different reasons, I found it impossible to identify with *that*. This seemed to leave me only with a binary choice between impossible alternatives. Then, unexpectedly, a 'third space' opened up. The route to it was via a detour, by means of a knight's move. 'By indirections find directions out.' This, I realized subsequently, was the space of the diasporic.

Diasporas always maintain an open horizon towards the future. They are in that sense spaces of emergence. Because they are finally unpredictable, they are necessarily contingent. The long-term consequences of the formation of a black diaspora in Britain were never transparent. They constituted an intellectual enigma. They presented themselves to me as a matter for analysis, investigation and interpretation, as well as of engagement, involvement and commitment. I was not contemplating something already decided but something 'in process'. And I had become, not entirely through my own choosing or intention, part of it.

The idea of diaspora raised by the post-war black migrations was therefore the reverse of the classic Jewish or Zionist conception. Of course memories, connections, traditions, continuities with the past are powerful, even at times compelling. They persist, well beyond conscious retrieval. They summon us into place and win our identification. They have real effects for diasporic subjects, shaping our material and cultural conditions of existence, our experiences, our social memories and symbolic worlds, our commitments and loyalties, our hopes and fears. For this reason, the creativity of a 'scattering' is inevitably accompanied by a sense of loss, a mourning for what was left behind and cannot fully be recovered. One of the consequences of diaspora seems, strangely, to be an attenuation of historical memory and the haunting afterlife of an impossible object of desire. But that alone can't bring it back to life. We are beyond circular journeys which end where they began. We are beyond the era of the mythic 'now'. We live in a historical world, not a mythological one. We have entered the era of what Edward Said called 'the worldly'. So the diasporic 'dissemination' is, in any realistic or literal sense, irreversible. This fantasy of a return to a reconstituted 'one-ness' and to the elimination of difference tends not to unify, heal and resolve but, on the contrary, it releases deadly pathological impulses.

In these circumstances, the inherited narrative paradigms we depend on cease to work. They are becoming obsolete. Difference will out. The interesting thing is that the disturbance introduced by difference forces its way into even the classic myth-narrative itself, despite the strategies adopted to circumvent it. Ambivalence in classic myths, Lévi-Strauss proposed in an early essay, is often captured in the figure of 'the trickster': the transitional figure who belongs to two worlds and thus to neither, but who negotiates – who 'migrates' in both the literal and figurative sense – between them. In 'The Structural Study of Myth' Lévi-Strauss was drawn to the analysis of stable, synchronic and repeating narrative structures. However, he found himself obliged to recognize the importance of the transformational trickster figure, who seems to be necessary in order to take account of the passage of time and change across history.

The leading trickster in Jamaican folk tales is the Yoruba-derived figure of Anancy, 'The Spider', the supreme conman, hustler, fixer and double-dealer, who exploits the ambiguities of belonging-ness. He is a genius at manoeuvring between irreconcilable tasks. He is the one who disrupts and disturbs the choreographed stability of the synchronic narrative sequence. The trickster has the capacity to move through time and across the narrative order.

Migration is a Humpty Dumpty phenomenon. Once shattered, the past can never be put back together again as it once was, in all its essential identity. This is because the past has not been stranded there all the time, preserved and unchanged, waiting for us to come home. Nothing would be more mistaken, for example, than to imagine that, because black people in the New World are overwhelmingly of African origin and because there are many connections to African cultures, something called Africa – an imaginary construct, in any event – has been frozen in time since its inhabitants were forced into servitude, waiting for us to rediscover it. This is not so.

Here I am, ruminating on the historical moment of post-war Caribbean migration to Britain, and resorting to Anancy and Humpty Dumpty in order to catch something of the properties of diasporic thought. Such are the imperatives of indirection. You can never be sure where you are going, or who you are going to meet on the way.

So my journey to an illusion was a fraught transition: going forwards, as I thought, to what Lamming called the ambiguous 'pleasures of exile', only to be immediately confronted by the return of the repressed. I knew that my sojourn in England was not destined to be a one-way street. Many years later I came to understand this better through something James Baldwin observed about Richard Wright and his idea that for black American writers Paris might be a place of refuge. 'It did not seem worthwhile to me', Baldwin wrote, 'to have fled the native fantasy only to embrace a foreign one.'

PART IV

Transition Zone

8. England at Home

Finding myself in England, I discovered that, like other migrants, in order to survive and to navigate my way through daily life I had to become *a practical reader* of England, of Englishness – particularly in relation to what was unconscious, or disavowed or couldn't be put into words, or where speech itself functioned as a screen. That this was so is corroborated by much of the West Indian writing in the diaspora of these years, in fiction, to some degree, and more explicitly in memoirs and in essays. I'm thinking particularly of C. L. R. James's *Beyond a Boundary* and George Lamming's *The Pleasures of Exile*. I see this practical reading of England, even as it was nurtured as a tactic for survival, as one route which eventually took me to the intellectual motivations of what was becoming Cultural Studies. It was also the means by which my political trajectory took on a defining, central focus.

In retrospect I regard this period of my life as a transition moment. I'd decided 'not yet' to go back, but had made no commitment to stay. I was suspended between two worlds, which were different but at the same time profoundly entangled historically and politically. Perhaps I already knew that I probably could not make a life 'there', but hadn't a clue as to how – or whether – to make a life 'here'.

Immediately, the experiences of departure and arrival were cumulatively shattering. I'm not conscious, even now, when or for what particular reason the decision to stay was finally made. For a time it took the form of a long postponement. By the time I thought I really had to decide, I discovered the decision had already been made.

With the benefit of hindsight I am better able to understand the transition experience as largely about the shattering of false illusions: a disenchantment which, although certainly not pleasurable, was necessary and in the end liberating. This was followed by the slow, uncertain coalescence of another phase of life created out of the debris of the old.

England seemed simultaneously familiar and strange, homely and unhomely, domesticated but at the same time a thoroughly dangerous place for the likes of me. I knew a lot about it; and yet I didn't *really* know it at all. Encountering the metropole at first hand, not through the screen memory of the colonial displacement, it now seemed populated with unquiet graves and ghosts that wouldn't lie down to rest. This unease reminds me of Roshini Kempadoo's photographic series about English country houses. Superimposed on the walls and gates are the faces and bodies of the enslaved from far away. They unaccountably begin to seep into the line of vision. Far from 'coming home' – as I suppose my mother's class and generation must have fondly imagined – I felt altogether more dislocated, literally out of place. Many large questions remained unanswered. Who was I? What kind of person could I become?

I was the subject of an education modelled on an English one. I knew how, formally, to read the script of England. But I hadn't anticipated the actually existing experience of – as Patrick Wright put it – 'living in an old country'. I didn't really *get* the deep structures of Englishness: what governed its styles of social interaction, its reservations, ironies and ambiguities, its silences and evasions. I didn't understand how the place hung together, to use a favourite Henry James phrase, as a 'scene'. I knew about the stereotypical British stiff upper lip. But what impressed me more immediately was the tensed way the English inhabited their bodies: a 'settledness-in-place', a visceral resistance to movement, to fluidity, to letting go. People in the Caribbean simply carry their bodies in a slacker way, which you take for granted until you are in a world which moves to a more self-patrolled, corseted rhythm.

One thing I realized almost at once, and about which I've never changed my mind. The English persuaded me that I could never become English. I found the British label less problematic, despite colonization and all its resonances of the old imperial connections.

I have to admit that the question of a distinction between English and British didn't occur to me at the time as salient so far as matters of identity were concerned. I was, as stipulated by my passport, a colonial 'Subject of the British Crown'. Of course, relations between the English and the other nations of the United Kingdom are very complicated: a set of internal colonizations nestling inside a larger one. I didn't understand those tensions at the time. Even so, my feeling about not being English ran deep and never changed.

At the same time I learned that my chances were not high of being a first-rate scholar of English literature with a potential Oxbridge academic future, remote as that had always been. It's not that I wished for this, or that it was something I was planning or wanted. Not because I wasn't clever enough or hadn't read enough – which may or may not have been true – but because such a vocation seemed to depend on an innate, unreflective belongingness, knowing the social grammar of the place; an ability to feel instinctively the pulse of the culture *behind* a text, to inhabit what, years later, Raymond Williams called in his characteristically oxymoronic phrase its 'structure of feeling'. Most of my English peers seemed to share something of this deep structure of affiliation, irrespective of their different class and regional backgrounds. I had read – and loved – Jane Austen too. But I couldn't seem to get hold of what intricate resonances 'Bath' or 'the parsonage' stirred in the English imaginary. I found it difficult to call on, let alone to claim, an insider's attentiveness to the subtle nuances of feeling and attitude which played across the text. My fellow students seemed to have unconsciously internalized what I would have self-consciously to learn.

By my unfamiliarity with the lived experience which informed the text, I don't mean, literally, being unfamiliar with its location, geography or history. Rather, it meant that I was excluded from sharing a *habitus* – a way of life, forms of customary behaviour, a structure of common sense, taken-for-granted assumptions, affective identifications and presuppositions about the society, and how things work, below the conscious or purely cognitive level. These things were embedded as much in the minutiae of daily life, in facial expression or in body language, in what was left unsaid, as they were in what was spoken. They were evidence of the tacit knowledges which underpin cultural practices, the shared codes of meaning which those who belong unconsciously bring to bear to make sense of the world. This is what enables a culture's members to 'know' and at the same time 'not to know' the unwritten cultural rules as to what can and can't be said, what is and isn't reasonable or appropriate to say or do, when and where things can and can't be done. 'Being English' had everything to do with this deep structure of national cultural identity, an 'imagined community', in Benedict Anderson's phrase; based not only on a set of institutions, but on a 'lived imaginary relation to its real conditions of existence', as Althusser has it: a fantasy of the nation, as well a gift of the gods, a state of *grace*.

The passage from these lived, improvised and halting engagements with England to a more crafted and systematic reading, in the form of Cultural Studies, was long and taxing, and didn't occur easily. Nor when I set out did I have a clue about any particular destination. But once the journey had been accomplished, I then realized that I had known the predominating fault lines instinctively before they'd become conceptually available to me. I think this is why Larry Grossberg calls me a 'contextualist' as well as a 'conjuncturalist'. The French linguist Michel Pêcheux writes of the unspoken foundations of meaning: of what must be taken for granted unconsciously if conscious comprehension is to follow 'naturally'. He calls it the *pre-construit*.

Even more important was Saussure, the founding figure of structural linguistics and the 'father' of what subsequently came to be known as the linguistic turn. Saussure used a similar paradigm with which to think about language, meaning and linguistic communities. To construct a grammatically correct English sentence requires mastery of a set of rules which most of us can't ever remember learning. This is not Freud's unconscious, but it is what one might think of as 'the discursive unconscious'. Meaning, at either the literal or the metaphorical level, depends on the relation between the *langue*, the general linguistic and perceptual rules of a language unconsciously shared within a linguistic community, and the *parole*, the unique, specific things which individuals want to say.

Without these shared underlying codes, the reciprocity between speaker and hearer can't be sustained. Subsequently, drawing on this analogy, I came to think of meaning as operating in much the same surface/deep structure way. In his essay on ideological discourse, Roland Barthes argues that an advertisement which, at the literal perceptual or *denotative* level, simply shows two figures wearing sweaters walking in the woods, comes to be 'read' as – or *connotes* to anyone familiar with the shared cultural codes – a richer set of metaphorical associations: romantic walks in the woods, two attractive young lovers 'wrapped up' in one another, oblivious to the rest of the world, the warmth of their affection symbolized by the sweaters they are wearing. In short, it mobilizes the shared perceptual codes which enable us to decipher the literal, denotative meaning of the scene. But only by accessing the cultural codes can the reader decipher, interpret or tune into the wider metaphorical or connotative meanings which the visual message is designed to convey. All ideological discourse, Barthes argues, operates at this 'connotative' level.

This is the gateway through which ideology invades language.

It's a matter of both cognitive comprehension and what Barthes identified as 'the pleasure of the text'. At the connotable level, Barthes's advertisement organizes a discourse of romantic love and its recognizable scenarios. It arouses pleasure and desire. Needless to say, the desire that the advertisement awakens is also transferred to the commodity – in this instance, the sweater – which, as a commodity, so the advert instructs us, will satisfy desires we never knew possessed us. All we are required to do is buy it.

This is also the case with the *Paris Match* cover which Barthes discusses, showing a black African soldier saluting the French Tricolour. As is well known, he argues that this image is organized, at the connotative level, to signify the loyalty to and love for France felt by her black colonized subjects. Just as a string bag with a packet of spaghetti and a tin of tomatoes connotes – stands for, or represents – Italianness.

Cultural codes provide the contexts of meaning within which individual events or things are classified. Here we return, in more abstract mode, to the points I was making about the structures of interplay between race and colour which drove the classificatory systems in colonial Jamaica when I was growing up. It's the same issue here: how we come to recognize the cultures we inhabit. Connotative contexts of meaning offer pictures of the world, rules of interpretation, a set of unspoken background assumptions, non-rational discursive logics, 'taken-for-granteds', pleasures and sentiments which constitute the semantic *langue* of a culture. They allow us to make sense of particular events, images, texts, utterances or acts. They also provide a route into the study of popular consciousness and of what has become common sense, because our forgetting has made it seem natural. Cultural Studies, I came to understand, deconstructs meaning not only at the level of specific content but also of these connotative frameworks. It is at this structural level that language and ideology, or language *and power*, connect.

For example, I still think the best way to analyse the ideological dimensions of a media statement is not only in terms of the so-called bias of its overt content, or the material interests which it serves, but also in terms of the deep propositional structure, inner logics, structures of inference and interpretive schemas which ground the discourse.

I have argued in 'The "Structured Communication" of Events' that 'all news events, of whatever kind, require to be "set in context" (an event, like a term in a discourse, cannot signify on its own), or presume or entail "an explanation" . . . The whole process of social communication . . . implies an interpretive, contextualizing code . . . The discourses by means of which the broadcasters translate historical events in the "real world" into "communicative events" (messages of one kind or another) are, fundamentally, *indexical* in [Aaron] Cicourel's sense.'

These abstract reflections were rooted in my coming face-to-face with England. Encountering Englishness on home territory – England at home – made it possible for me later to develop within a Cultural Studies framework a critical model of how culture itself worked, although I didn't take it up in these terms until after the fact. Far from settling into this Englishness, however it was conceived, I became increasingly aware of the chasm between me and it. Difficult accounts remained unsettled between us. In these conditions, it is not surprising that I never really attached myself to Oxford, and to what it represented, as the apogee of all that unsettled me.

There's one other current at work here. Unexpectedly, the medley of experience I've been retrieving – the suspended animation, the dislocations, the strangeness within the self – undermined my desire to write creatively. I couldn't do it from within the culture I found myself inhabiting, from within its imaginary geography. Instead I observed everything. Life was like conducting a permanent native ethnography. What a bizarre situation to find oneself in! This strengthened my critical as against my creative instincts, a shift which is difficult to undo. I felt excluded at exactly the deep level where, for me at that moment, creative writing began.

This experience brought the crisis about identity and belongingness roaring back inside me. Since I could never be English, or indeed Jamaican in the version my parents offered me, in what sense could I write about my experiences of home without capitulating to nostalgia? What would I become as a result of having been set apart from the resources of an alternative identity? These questions were troubling. And they excluded certain options. Of the poetry I wrote in those years, the only decent poem was a short, well-disguised, unsent love letter. The narrative poems included the creole version of *King Lear* in the Jamaican nation-language, which I've mentioned before; another was a *Lord Jim*-ish experiment about a man who decides to get away from the past by leaping overboard into the uncharted sea. My longest prose, written in Henry James's most mannered style, told of an exiled Jewish scholar (courtesy of Isaac Babel) who dies when his library falls in on him (an ending borrowed from E. M. Forster). Pretty derivative stuff!

I didn't seem able to find my own voice. It was only years later that I felt at home in language again – when I had managed to lose the Oxford cadences which had crept uninvited into my speech, and somehow unconsciously relearned to speak more conversationally, *with* rather than *at* an audience, in the rhythm of my own feelings, in a more relaxed, vernacular style. Given that I have spoken in public and taught so much during my lifetime, it is startling to track these unconscious modulations. My friend Sophie Watson claims the she can identify a rise in tempo, pitch and speed in my delivery, a sort of shift of gear or take-off point, reminiscent of the register of a Baldwin-esque shopfront preacher, such as you might hear in Jamaican Pentecostal churches, which I never knew was there.

Indeed I feel less English now than when I first arrived. Cultural identity is not fixed. It is a moving feast. But it is at the same time remarkably stubborn. I guess this is why people – politicians especially – keep posing to those of us who weren't born here and don't in their sense properly belong, the question of our loyalty to Britain, or to England, and to their cultures as a form of belongingness. However, the English themselves don't really seem to know what these cultures comprise; I wonder if the politicians do either.

I'm sure the sharpness of my response towards England had something to do with the fact that I arrived at the imperial centre at the moment of the onset of its decline, the beginning of its sunset years, the last days of empire. For the first time, we were not mesmerized or cowed by it because we could, as it were, see around its edges to a time beyond empire. Subjecthood was not the end of history after all. What such a confusing conjuncture required was the will to speak back: confronting England with its own imperial history, a past which had deeply fashioned the nation but which England itself somehow couldn't quite recall and was in the process of trying to forget. My response had to do in particular with my recoil from that absolutely innate, unspoken, taken-for-granted assumption of natural superiority which went along with empire, and seemed still to be fed by the tributaries of an unexamined racism and national chauvinism. Even today you can hear some of this: being English as a 'gift of nature'; the 'burdens' of civilization, suffered with a quiet, resigned but self-assured forbearance. The profound legacies of empire, many decades after decolonization, are still culturally, politically and socially active and somehow still underwrite, or overwrite, everything. In this respect time is not the Great Healer. Things sometimes get worse, moving in the opposite direction from the days of multiculturalism. Englishness can feel more fragile, beleaguered and defensive than it once did.

Now, after more than fifty years, although I feel at home enough in England, where I've lived my entire adult life, and with the English – I've been happily married to Catherine, who happens to be English, for most of those fifty years; my children were born here; and the English are as familiar to me as the back of my hand – I still feel in some profound way not-at-home. And so it shall be.

When I return to Jamaica after sixty years' absence I also feel homeless there. It isn't my daily milieu and hasn't been for almost a lifetime. Nevertheless, I identify emotionally with Jamaica at a depth of intimacy which England can never match, although by now this, too, is skewed by memory. Whenever I am flying back to England after spending time in the Caribbean, and look through the aircraft window at the island below slowly receding into the distance, I'm assailed by a wave of melancholia which always arises in me in relation to Jamaica as the lost object of desire.

I find that these unreliable half-memories are best captured in terms of places, landscapes and tastes rather than of people: the perilous, potholed roads, the roast-corn and shrimp sellers on the road from Sav-la-Mar, the piled-up-high triangles of oranges, grapefruit and tangerines on the stalls on the Junction Road, the taste of fresh coconut water drunk straight from the husk, eating mangoes in the sea and – what even other Caribbean people regard as bizarre – the Jamaican taste for ackees. These aren't eaten, with or without salt-fish, elsewhere in the Caribbean! Do they *know* what they are missing? Now that I am unable to travel, can I believe that I will never see, feel, smell and taste these things again?

This is the emotional imagined or remembered space to which long-term Caribbean migrants return when they finally retire after a long spell away. This return is never as unproblematic as they fondly imagine it should be. Jamaicans nowadays expect relatives who come back from a long sojourn 'in foreign' to bring home trophies – a present for everybody in the family, money to show them a good time, stylish clothes – the fruits of and justification for migration. However, many of them regard the visitors as somehow no longer quite one of them. What is even more surprising is that many of the retirees have a hankering for aspects of England where the pace of life is faster, the atmosphere cooler and the choices in everyday life more open, even if actually negotiating them is difficult and there are many obstacles in their way. This no doubt explains why such a large proportion of retirees choose to live in and around Mandeville, where others like themselves have made a home and the climate is cooler!

It's compelling to track how these lived, subjective, ambivalent ruminations – Where do my inner attachments lie? Where do they take me? – have been hijacked by the highly *unambivalent* imperatives of contemporary British politics. I have in mind the so-called 'Tebbit test', which seems to hang on in the public culture, ever present and ready to be summoned when the times require.

Norman Tebbit is a right-wing politician of decidedly outspoken views who came to fame at the height of the Thatcher period. He stands at a kind of historical juncture between the politics of Enoch Powell and the new manifestations of a right-wing populism evident in the UK Independence Party (UKIP) of today. In 1990 – I can't believe it was so long ago, so embedded in the symbolic landscape it's become – he was perturbed by what he perceived to be the lack of support from the sons (and daughters, though I doubt he had the daughters much in mind) of South Asian and Caribbean migrants for the English cricket team. On occasion he – rightly – feared that their allegiance was to the teams from India, Pakistan, Bangladesh, Sri Lanka or to the West Indies, even though they'd been born and brought up in England or Britain. For Tebbit this was proof that Britain's migrants had insufficiently 'integrated'. His 'test' swept aside all the necessary ambivalence in play, reducing one's allegiance to a sporting team to a catechism of national faith. This has lodged inside the national culture as an immovable feature of the landscape. There have been moments, though, when opposing ways of thinking have been vindicated.

I'm not sure I would, even after forty years, pass the 'Tebbit test'.

Supporting the West Indies cricket team is my default position; although these days Caribbean Test cricket is so diminished, often such a shambles, so shorn of its former glory, that I'm sometimes tempted to desert it. Athletics is different, for here these tiny islands have made a gigantic global impact.

On the other hand, England is so hopelessly hopeful about occasionally winning international sporting contests, so resolute about doing well in the face of overwhelming odds – the Dunkirk spirit, snatching victory from the jaws of defeat – that to support England would require drawing on reservoirs of faith which I don't possess. In cricket, though, England vs Australia is a particularly taxing moment for me, since there is so little room to choose between the masculinist bravado of the Aussies and the manly diffidence of the English. Fortunately there is always India and Sachin Tendulkar.

However, as the 2012 Olympics suggested, these endeavours to mobilize and fix national allegiance are not set in stone. Half of 'Team GB' was non-white and only in the most complex way English. I'm told the people of Somalia think that, despite being draped in a Union Jack, the incomparable Mo Farah, with his hands pointing at his bald head as if to say 'Look what people like me can do!', was running for them, as in a metaphorical sense he was.

The day after Usain Bolt won the Gold in that same Games – he was one of the three Jamaicans competing in the final of the 100 metres, along with a Trinidadian: this out of a starting line-up of nine! – London was full of folk sporting the Jamaican colours, a significant minority of whom appeared to the naked eye in no way to be Jamaican. This worked as a great response to Tebbit.

Despite the astonishing differences in terms of power and wealth between the West and the South, in a globalized, multicultural, transnational capitalist world I think that for Britain there is no long-term historical future in retreating to national character and national culture as defensive redoubts – where difference, and 'the other' can be kept at arm's length in all their inevitable messiness. In the short term it could destroy us all. The 'island story' days are numbered, which is not to say that the destructive possibilities of that imagined narrative are exhausted: its potential to go on skewing everything is far from over. Both Europe and the Third World were, in their different ways, fashioned by nationalism. But in the era of its decline, rather than in its ascendancy, cultural nationalism may yet do for us all in its sunset years.

That was what was so baffling about the English when I first arrived: the contrast between the ordinariness – dreariness, even – of much of everyday life and the certainty possessed by the English of their exalted place in the world.

In the various discussions provoked by the Tebbit intervention I don't think sufficient attention has been paid to the fact that he took the instance of cricket as primary. The historical meaning of cricket in West Indian popular culture is eloquently captured in James's *Beyond a Boundary*, though one needs to think through his recommendation that the West Indies, in their symbolic task of beating the imperial masters at their own game through self-discipline, should learn from – of all institutions – the English public school, the playing field of Imperial Man. James's respect for Thomas Arnold's Rugby and the English public school provides an unexpected twist. But the side of James which made him, as well as everything else, a sort of black Victorian gentleman never fails to catch me off guard.

In any case, James was writing after Caribbean cricket had proved itself. The contrast between England and the West Indies was encapsulated in the radically different cricket styles of, say, Len Hutton and Brian Close as compared to that of the Three Ws: Worrell, Walcott and Weekes. The patient, stubborn, steady advance of the tortoise existed in marked contrast to the fluidity, and sometimes intemperate flashy elegance, of the hare. The West Indies victory in the 1950 series, on the home territory of cricket, showed that the most English of games could be creolized. The match played in the presence of a noisy crowd of black people was a historic fulfilment, properly a 'jubilee', a real bacchanalia. The march through London which followed, led by the calypsonians, was the first, but not by any means the last, occasion when a Caribbean carnival has taken openly to the London streets. It not only anticipated the annual Notting Hill Carnival, but reminded us of the centuries-long practice of colonial mimicry and masquerade through which slavery had been challenged. This was a phenomenon which was triumphantly realized in 1976 with Viv Richards's thrilling affiliation to the protocols of Black Power cricket. It's a fine example of Kobena Mercer's idea of a diasporic aesthetic strategy: the Caribbean appropriating the disciplines of the game engendered by the master to 'turn the world upside down'. It entailed the *carnivalesque* unravelling of the master narrative from within.

At this point, in the spirit of James, I intend to move from cricket to literature, as two different departments of English, or of Anglophone, civilization. In particular I'd like to explain my investments in Henry James, whose fiction I chose to study as a postgraduate at Oxford. On the face of it this was an unlikely conjunction: me, engaging with the upper-class New Englander. Trying to help me escape from the tyranny of Anglo-Saxon translation classes, my US friends had taught me about North American literature, which up to then I hadn't really read. I gravitated to the old masters – Hawthorne, Poe, Melville, Whitman, Thoreau – followed by the moderns – Faulkner, Hemingway, Fitzgerald – whom I read alongside European experimentalists like D. H. Lawrence, James Joyce, Virginia Woolf, Marcel Proust, Thomas Mann and Dorothy Richardson. When I started postgraduate work I really wanted to work on American realism. I was keen to explore the muckraking tradition of the early twentieth century, perhaps, or the social realist novel – Dos Passos, Dreiser, Steinbeck, Sinclair Lewis, Upton Sinclair. But I was strongly advised against it by my potential supervisors, who asked, seemingly in all innocence, (first) 'Are they worth it?' and (second) 'Aren't some of these authors still alive?' They asked me this pointedly, as if their questions signalled an endgame. Which, in fact, they did! So I moved steadily backwards in search of a topic until I finally settled on Henry James, and there I stopped. This was an improbable place to end up; and my choice to work on the international themes in James's novels has puzzled many people. In fact, I'd been specifically introduced to James by my American friend Walt Litz.

But the attraction proved powerful: England and Europe through American eyes; America put to the European test; 'there' from 'here'. For a cultural comparativist, what could be more tempting? I doubt Henry James could have found Jamaica on a map. But he certainly knew the 'unscripted' nature of England!

He had perfected a refined sensibility. However, it was not a question of temperament but of insight. He understood the complexity of cultural translation. I was drawn to him precisely because – not despite the fact that, but precisely *because* – the themes that concerned me he transposed into a different key.

James's life and world were the polar opposites to mine. His family were part of the New England 'Newport set' who moved between lower Manhattan and Boston, and later James himself made Paris, London and Rome part of his life. His father was a sophisticated Transcendentalist who believed that institutions were ultimately corrupt and that only out of the independent individual could true community arise. He cultivated this genial view by taking his family on European grand tours. Henry's brother, William, became the famous psychologist, although his sister Alice, to whom Henry was deeply attached, was a casualty of this familial culture. He lost a brother in the Civil War. Some critics believe Henry himself never recovered from being declared unfit for military service on account of an old injury. Through his life, he seemed incurious about race and slavery, and was drawn to the romance of the affluent New Englanders tutored in Europe's ways and, subsequently, of the English well-to-do, the lesser aristocracy and the country-house set. He busied himself in the social round of the propertied middle class. At one point it seems he dined out every night of the week. The dinner-table anecdotes and gossip provided him with many ideas for his fiction, although he never wanted to know too much in case it overwhelmed his creative imagination.

However, my lifelong attachment to Henry James arose from quite different impulses. It derived primarily from the discovery that in him I could witness elements of my own life, although organized, as I say, in a different register. His work resonated deeply with me, poised as I was between two worlds. And now again, towards the end of my time, as I look back at the consequences of the choices I made he enters my life once again, with a rather different set of presuppositions.

'How can you be interested in Henry James?' Edward Thompson – the historian E. P. Thompson – once admonished me, with exasperation. 'Ah!' I thought to myself. But what about his sensitivity to the little deceptions and evasions of the English which one finds in his works, and the complex dialectic he weaves between innocence and experience, for which America and Europe came to be rich and interchangeable signifers? In *The Portrait of a Lady* he was alive to the tragic depths which accompany such things. He was brilliantly perceptive about how the fine sentiment and the exquisite good taste of his characters mask a crude, vulgar and venal self-interest. He intuitively grasped the moral vacuum at the centre of worldly wealth and aesthetic sophistication, the corruption secreted at the heart of a refined class self-confident in its own ethical superiority. He had an instinct for the fact that individual moral choice is always also cultural and social, and vice versa. He brought to bear on his unpromising material profound insights into the finely tuned distinctions between American and European versions of civilization.

He took the question of cultural and social *difference* as the substantive theme of much of his work, and made it the basis of his ethical judgements. I admired his ability to assemble and condense all the questions of moral action, innocence and experience, good and evil, around these cultural contrasts. And I admired too the scrupulous dedication with which he went over – again and again – these American and European oppositions, as if never satisfied with what he had done with them. Each time he deepened and complicated them, breaking down the transparent but charming binaries of the early work into a more complex set of discriminations. I am thinking of the shift in tone from the brilliant surfaces of *Daisy Miller*, *The Europeans* and *The American* through the deepening shadows of *The Portrait of a Lady*, which is magnificent in the balance it holds, stylistically, between the clarity of perception of the early novels and the hyper-complexity of some of the later work. Then came the splendid three great novels: *The Ambassadors*, *The Golden Bowl* and *The Wings of the Dove*. The latter offers a heartrending portrait of an 'innocent' American heroine, Milly Theale, who becomes all too aware of European duplicity.

The three so-called innocents – the Princess in *The Golden Bowl*, Strether in *The Ambassadors* and Milly Theale in *The Wings of the Dove* – triumph through ethically sublime acts of self-renunciation. The exceedingly wealthy (and terminally ill) Milly discovers that her friend, Kate Croy, and Merton Densher are lovers; she discovers too Kate's plot to engineer Densher's marriage to Milly herself, in order to secure her (Milly's) inheritance for themselves. Milly nevertheless decides to leave the conniving, duplicitous pair what they want most in the world: her money. In this way she exposes their venality by displaying ethical qualities they do not possess: honesty and generosity of spirit.

'The wings of the dove' enclosed them, smothering them with kindness. By giving them what they want in abundance, Milly made it at the same time both possible, materially, and impossible, morally, for them to profit from the fruits of their duplicity. When Milly dies, Kate – upwardly aspirant but without the material means of sustaining her ambition, and a 'moral realist' – ruthlessly goes on trying to persuade Densher that, despite all they have done, they can now simply see the plot through to its conclusion. But as Densher tells her at the end, 'We shall never again be as we were.'

Not satisfied with what he had achieved in these three great novels, James went on to the 'afterwork': the exploratory, unfinished fictions which most critics ignore, particularly *The Sense of the Past* and *The Ivory Tower*. This late work reprises what might have happened when the cultivated, Europeanized American expatriate, having escaped the vulgarities of a materialistic culture, confronts his alter ego, the inordinately wealthy American businessman, the ghost of the person he might once have become had he remained at home. In a beguiling manoeuvre James imagines those 'parallel lives' in fact meeting, as T. S. Eliot projected it in his mind, 'at the first turning of the third stair'. I couldn't help but read my own life in the scenario. How would I have been different had I decided to return to Jamaica? Who might I have become? And what would it be like, now, to encounter this 'other me' – myself as I would have become – coming back in the opposite direction?

As someone who had wanted to be a writer I identified with James's ambition to be 'someone on whom nothing is lost'. I loved his capacity to look, watch and listen; to capture and register in language every subtle shade or shift of feeling and attitude in a dia-logic exchange. In this respect he was a 'dramatist' who was – to his chagrin – not very good at writing plays. He brought self-consciousness to a high pitch. After James, the interior life could only be brought to the surface for inspection by going below the threshold of consciousness, via the break-up of language itself. The next stop was James Joyce's *Ulysses*.

I don't suppose many critics have thought of James as a diasporic novelist. I could have found – and did find – a more direct route to these themes, through Caribbean writers, poets and painters living in England. But I don't regret for a moment the detour I made via Henry James.

In a previous chapter I described how in Jamaica modernism in literature, music and painting had given me access to alternative realities which went unrecognized in the curriculum of colonial life. In this respect, the formal Oxford curriculum wasn't much different from that which I'd been presented with in Jamaica. Modernist works were discussed informally. But modernism as a literary movement was no part of the University's conception of English literature, which ended in the 1850s. Many people chose in finals to do the optional Victorian paper, which allowed you to write about the nineteenth-century novel, and also the Criticism paper where, if you were canny enough, you could deploy the ideas being developed in modern literature and critical thought. But I can't remember ever hearing the word modernism mentioned as part of a serious discussion with my Oxford tutors during my undergraduate tutorials. I have, though, previously mentioned Helen Gardner, one of the earliest and most intelligent critics of Eliot, with whom we had memorable discussions.

And we encountered many writers informally who never surfaced in the official curriculum. Despite the vaunted personal tutorial system, the small band of 'critics' to which I belonged educated ourselves, and each other.

However, as I moved from the strictly literary interests I had brought to Oxford into wider concerns with Caribbean culture, society and politics, my focus became less centred on specific modern writers and more concerned with the very idea of modernity itself. What sort of condition was that? What was it exactly that we so desired? Could the Caribbean, which intellectually was represented as provincial, be a modern place too, generating its own modernities? This became a sort of metaphor for the 'elsewhere' to which I keep referring: for what we could not be or could not have. It was a symptom of our lack, of our marginality. The very idea of modernity puzzled me. It seemed to carry such different, such contradictory meanings. 'The modern' was the name of an actual chronological period, as in 'early modern' Europe and so on. But it also stood for a different attitude of mind, even a new type of civilization, not at all defined in chronological or historical terms.

There were modern movements in art and literature across the world, as I subsequently discovered. But modernism's positive connotations, like those of the Enlightenment before it, had been hijacked by Europe and then extensively renovated and transformed when extended to post-war America, and particularly to post-war American painting. One of the conspicuous things which disappeared in this transatlantic translation was the politics of modernism, which in Europe was notoriously experimental, disruptive and for the most part liberal, free-thinking and (mostly) Left-oriented, whereas in its American form it lost its radical edge. Compare a Corbusier building with the Manhattan skyline which became American modernism's signature. Think of the enormous gulf between, say, Picasso and Jackson Pollock.

The modern came to connote technologically developed, scientifically advanced industrial societies, not the 'backlands' of the colonial peripheries. It was identified with the present – the 'now' – and even more with the future. However, curiously, it also seemed to leave room for the prospect of an end to the 'now', opening the possibility of something else after it. This is, I suppose, what later evolved into the postmodern. 'Now' was always represented as an advance over 'then': not only different but better, more in tune with the *Zeitgeist*, pregnant with future possibilities as yet unrealized. The concept seemed to mark a decisive rupture with tradition, a hectic pace of innovation, a permanent revolution. It was believed to mark a new, higher stage of human development. It drove forwards experimentation, the replacement of old forms and hierarchies, dispelling the last traces of superstition and religious belief with a technical, factual, rational, logical, scientific mode of thinking. This was Max Weber's 'disenchantment of the world'. Its effects ranged across the full span of knowledge: the arts, architecture, design, science, philosophy, economics, linguistics and epistemology. It required jettisoning old forms, styles and paradigms and, as enthusiasts like Clement Greenburg urged, 'making them new'.

'Modern' people were therefore those who thought and behaved in these updated ways; who surrounded themselves with new technological products; who expected in their lifetimes to enjoy the fruits of these 'advances'; people who could model ways of living appropriate to the transformed circumstances, and have rights of access to the capacity to live and realize to the full the possibilities of modern life.

Not many of those kind, I realized, were to be found in Kingston. Clearly, some people and societies were closer to this ideal than others! It was part of a civilizational race in which colonized peoples of the periphery were not likely to be well placed. Was there therefore really only one idea of the modern – that represented by developed Western societies – and only the one pathway to modernity? Caribbean people could read about it; we could mimic it from afar; but it seemed we were destined to experience it second-hand. Yet somewhere in the collective imagination of our generation arrived the thought that the idea of the modern itself had been, like everything else, expropriated and colonized by the West. Could there be many modernities? And was the right for their recognition worth struggling for?

I did want to be able to witness at first-hand, and to experience for myself, that symbolic dimension of the world which I'd always considered to be 'elsewhere' – that world which I had been tutored into believing was unavailable to me, brought up in a provincial colonial city in the tropics where I was a conscript to *their* modernity and who had no claim to be a modern person in my own right.

This object of desire on the part of a young, aspiring colonial student, excited by Joyce or Eliot or Picasso, did not survive the experience of migration untainted. I remained at heart – and remain – a sort of belated modernist in my aesthetic preferences. But I never felt exclusively partisan about it. I have always had eclectic tastes in the visual arts, music and literature, spanning different centuries, cultures and styles. I could see how Western modern art had, at certain points, cultivated *tradition* as a way of renovating an enervated gap at its centre. Just consider Picasso's *Les Demoiselles D'Avignon* or Gaugin's 'native' bodies. However, I do believe that the historic break with the idea of verisimilitude – art as ultimately the mirror to nature – was profound. This marked an epistemological shift in Western thought, more fundamental, dramatic, original and paradigm-breaking than the more recent, and much-vaunted, commitment to postmodernism which, as the word 'post-' presupposes, is a more dependent phenomenon, reproducing much of what it is breaking from in the very moment of the break itself.

One route into this was by my becoming seriously involved in criticism, the literary theory of its day. We were avidly reading the critical journals – *Scrutiny, Partisan Review, The Sewanee Review* – and following too the arguments between the Leavisites, the American New Critics like Cleanth Brooks, R. P. Blackmur, Yvor Winters, and the more socially oriented critics. In the early days we were Leavisites of a kind, although I was never won to Leavis's elitism and to his commitment to fine-tune a minority to resist the advancing tide of mass culture. I was already too mired in popular culture to think this either possible or desirable.

However, although *Scrutiny* was the avowed enemy of the debasement of cultural standards by mass culture, it was writers associated with the journal, or with its larger intellectual axis, who took the broader social perspective seriously and nourished my continuing concern with cultural, rather than exclusively literary, issues. I am thinking here of Q. D. Leavis and her *Fiction and the Reading Public*, Denys Thompson's work on advertising, John Speirs on Chaucer's world, Alfred Harbage's interpretation of Shakespeare and the Elizabethan audience, L. C. Knights's *Drama and Society in the Age of Jonson* and D. W. Harding on Jane Austen's 'regulated hatred'.

Our self-conscious identities as critics already marked us out, in relation to Oxford, as outsiders. Not only because we were seriously committed to critical ideas, but because Oxford literary people hated Leavis for his class background as much as for anything else. They also, given the ethos of literary dilettantism which prevailed at the time, despised his Cambridge 'seriousness', his Puritanism, his belief that literature, language and ideas mattered, his attention to wider cultural questions. My tutor was appalled by the fact that, when Leavis was invited to lecture on Lawrence at Oxford, he began by unbuttoning his shirt in an exaggerated, Lawrentian gesture! He thought him 'vulgar'. Like members of a not-so-secret brotherhood we used to troop off to Blackwell's to buy those uncut issues of *Scrutiny* in a spirit of defiance every time it came out, and we'd studiously thumb the back issues in the Radcliffe Reading Room. This was undoubtedly, for me, the start of a lifelong intellectual disengagement from Oxford and all it stood for.

Another avenue of retreat was music, which I've discussed at length in relation to my time in Jamaica. All I'll say here is that in my graduate days I began to play piano again in a jazz group with a Barbadian bass player and two Jamaicans who worked on the buses, on drums and sax. Fifty years later this friendship still continues. They must have been among the earliest working migrants from the Caribbean in post-war Oxford. We practised around an ancient piano in the basement of the student house where I was living and played publicly whenever anyone would invite us, although for a couple of years we had a regular booking at a local café every Friday night.

Film was already one of my abiding passions. It seemed to me the most innovative of the modern arts. I had always had a passionate addiction to the movies, and as a youth in Kingston I saw on Saturday afternoon matinees at the Carib Theatre everything from Hollywood that found its way to Jamaica: westerns, melodramas, thrillers, musicals and film noir; Bogart and Bacall, Barbara Stanwyck, Joan Crawford, Bette Davis, Gary Cooper, Cary Grant, Henry Fonda, John Garfield, the lot. This passion continued in Oxford. We went to the cinema two or three times a week. My first experiences of Continental cinema included Eisenstein and Pudovkin, Italian neo-realism and the French New Wave. They were a revelation. I realize now that this combination of arguing about literary criticism, reading modern literature, especially with the Americans, following the Caribbean novel and poetry, going to the movies, listening to and playing jazz meant that I began to construct a sort of intellectual counter-life to Oxford, more appropriate to my growing sense of being a radical outsider, a feeling which deepened as I came to the end of my time as an undergraduate.

Such, in outline, reprises my earliest engagements with both modernism and with what is now called theory. Informally, however, the story is more complicated. Many things were happening at the same time, and different avenues were opening up.

As I'll show in the following chapter, politics itself provided a significant theoretical dimension, particularly as I came to understand the social. Not only that, but in the debates about literary criticism the larger cultural questions were never far away, albeit in a highly displaced form. The Leavisites had their own peculiar way of posing the question of the relation of language and the literary text to culture. Think of F. R. Leavis's own *Sketch for an English School*. Though *Scrutiny* is now identified with close textual reading – 'these words, in this order' – critics such as Knights, Speirs and others followed a more militantly historical view. Leavis himself conducted a long debate with the Marxist critics of the 1930s, which Williams picked up in *Culture and Society*. I then reluctantly agreed with Williams that Leavis had 'won'. But this was a time when we didn't yet know Lukács, Adorno or Benjamin. It's true, though, that I, like many of us, began to be increasingly interested in the social and historical context of literary studies.

Moreover, the longer I postponed my return to Jamaica the more I needed to understand better the nature of Caribbean culture itself: its complicated interrelation with Britain and to Africa, the complex negotiations of creolization, how a distinctive culture had arisen, tempered in the blast furnace of slavery and colonialism, and also my relationship to the long, continuing historical consequences of this formation. The black presence in Britain made understanding its complex dynamics of adaptation and resistance increasingly pressing. What followed was my first systematic reading about Caribbean culture, the 'survivals' of African systems through the centuries of slavery and the plantation, and the syncretic character of the cultures of the Caribbean region. I undertook this study, informally but seriously, ensconced in Rhodes House Library in Oxford during my years as a postgraduate student. There's more to say about this later.

I'd also – for the moment – decided to stay in England and I knew that this meant I had to create, somehow, a stake in British society, even though I had no desire to 'assimilate', or to be 'assimilated'. A more active involvement in British politics turned out to be the most appropriate vehicle for this because it required me to understand more about the society and how it worked, while at the same time committing me not to fit in, but to a project to change and transform what British society was, and what it had become.

And there was also Marxism. I've mentioned the fact that I'd read Marx at school in Jamaica. One of the first of these was the two-volume, blue-covered Lawrence and Wishart selection of the writings of Marx and Engels. I continued to read – and to argue with – Marx alongside my other interests. By this time I had got to know many people on the Oxford Left and became more fully engaged in the debates on contemporary capitalism, the Cold War and the theory of socialism and of politics in general. The more disengaged from the whole atmosphere and ethos of Oxford I felt, the more politically involved I became.

The start of my graduate studies in 1954 marked the decisive turning point. I had postponed the difficult question of when or whether I was to go home. Many of my closest West Indian friends had departed. I was no longer imprisoned in the Oxford undergraduate syllabus, but free intellectually to roam further afield. I had also moved out of College and was living in a student house on Richmond Road in the Jericho area, presided over by two American friends, Gerry and Beth Bentley, the former a major scholar of Blake. Richmond Road subsequently became a *foco* for political activity and intellectual argument, a crucible out of which *Universities and Left Review* and the Oxford New Left emerged in the wake of 1956.

Even though I never felt England was mine I was learning to find my way around it, both the formal artefacts of its civilization and its informal, lived aspects. There was, however, much work to do. As there still is.

9. Politics

Freeing myself from the University was good for me, and I discovered that Oxford generated its own rebel enclaves. In an entirely new relation to England, I was able to tunnel through the detritus which I'd internalized from the colonial past. It's not that this dark inheritance simply vanished, just like that. It was not so. But I did find a means of working through the inhibitions and, in the process, remaking my own selfhood.

I was involved in the founding of the *Universities and Left Review* (*ULR*), which first appeared in 1957, a year after the twin cataclysms of the Anglo-French-Israeli invasion of Egypt and the almost simultaneous Soviet invasion of Hungary, whose aim was to dismember the popular democratic – the anti-Stalinist – revolution from below. At the beginning of November 1956 a group of us had travelled to London on the Sunday to join the huge demonstration in Trafalgar Square. It was the first mass political demonstration I'd attended and it was the biggest since before the war. It was the first time, too, that I encountered, face to face as it were, police on horseback, bent on hostile confrontation. It was a good lesson in experiencing the repressive power of the state. The charismatic Labour radical Nye Bevan was the principal speaker, his booming Welsh voice sending the pigeons scattering across the square. Soon after, we realized that history was moving faster than we were. A day or two later the invasion began.

I'd always vowed to steer clear of the Oxford Union, the prestigious student debating forum and the forcing ground for future public careers. But when the Suez debate took place I was invited and spoke, for the first and last time. These two events – Hungary and Suez – combined with Khrushchev's condemnation of Stalin earlier in the year meant for us that the old practices of the Left could no longer be viable. We were stimulated by the news which filtered back from Hungary about the role of workers' councils as the means for furthering democratic life. The fashioning of a new politics had now become, as a matter of survival it seemed, urgent; 1956 fundamentally shaped my political thinking thereafter.

From 1956 until I made the move to Birmingham in 1964, 'normal' life was suspended by my political activity: by my editing *ULR* and, from 1960, *New Left Review* (*NLR*); by the larger attempts to build around these publications social movements, eventually organized by the creation of the New Left Clubs; by the long and arduous struggle to get the ideas we were generating mobilized, and by our attempt to activate them inside the Labour Party. At the same time, as we experienced what felt to us as a thaw in the Cold War, we invested great energies in the Campaign for Nuclear Disarmament (CND), which represented a strategic social movement in its own right. Suez and Hungary had fractured the old politics, and the carapace of the Cold War had been – temporarily, as it turned out – shattered. Out of this emerged our 'between/against both camps' position and the hope for the creation of an independent, popular Left politics.

As far as we were concerned this opening had first been created

in France by Claude Bourdet, the erstwhile Resistance fighter, and by the associated *France-Observateur*, our close institutional allies. On the initiative of G. D. H. Cole I went to Paris for the meeting of the new International Socialist Society, where we first met Bourdet, and also, I remember, Lelio Basso, whose life had long been distinguished by his prominence as an anti-fascist in Italy. Bourdet and the International Socialist Society represented the móvement of ideas which had emerged in order to think across orthodoxies. We were fortunate to persuade him to contribute to the founding issue of *ULR*.

The New Left in this period endeavoured to be a popular movement. In Britain, contemporaneous with the founding of the New Left, there emerged the makings of a mass movement determined to dismantle the UK's political investment in maintaining its role as a nuclear superpower. Relations between the New Left and CND were of the first importance. They were complex and often fraught. But from the first CND Aldermaston March of 1958, this became the principal site of my committed political activities.

After about 1958 or so I also got to know England – geographically, that is – as a result of travelling the country, week after week, night after night, speaking at CND meetings.

It was out of these practical activities that an expansive conception of the domain of 'the political' also began to take root in me. It was this very conception that gave meaning to the work of the New Left and later, in a different social domain, to the founding project of Cultural Studies. Arguably, one might suggest that the social basis for thinking in these terms was founded on the emergence of new strata of intellectual and cultural workers, whom the New Left particularly, but certainly not exclusively, addressed. This is the world we found ourselves facing.

ULR was founded by four of us: Gabriel Pearson, Ralph (later Raphael) Samuel, Chuck (Charles) Taylor and myself. Thanks to the generosity of the Barry Amiel and Norman Melburn Trust, the entire run of the journal is now available online. Those curious about what constituted the 'new' in the New Left can consult the journal in its entirety and make their own judgements. Of course, what was once 'new' is now very old. Nonetheless I think that there are some not entirely unwelcome surprises.

What sticks most immediately in the memory is the collective frenzy in getting each issue to the printers and the domestic conditions of existence of the venture. Gabriel would often not arrive until very late at night, and hold forth about Dickens, or other literary interests, around the kitchen table. That's where Raphael, the moving spirit in *ULR*, and I corrected the proofs of the first issue. Next morning the cat had had kittens on them. In the basement, along with the piano where our jazz band rehearsed, was a spare bed which from time to time was occupied by Peter Sedgwick, a stimulating intellectual of impressive calibre but also at this time, after the disintegration of the Oxford Communists, something of a waif and stray. Then, variously, there were the Trinidadian Willie Demas, completing his Cambridge PhD in economics; two young women from Grimsby, Tessa Lippa and Veronica Bridges, who were studying art at Ruskin College, became close to and much loved by all of us, and who were permanently Caribbeanized by the experience; Scottie O'Neil Lewis, who's appeared before in these pages, also from Trinidad; a figure whom we perceived as the quiet American, Warren Deem, who habitually wore a suit and whom some believed was a CIA agent, but who had a tiny harpsichord and taught me about Bach; Francesca, an Italian running the library at the American air force base at Brize Norton. And Ortwin Bock, an Afrikaner medical student, bewildered by finding himself in this racially mixed intellectual centre of subversion by which, however, he was mesmerized. We expected him to last a week but he stayed and stayed, whether out of fascination or the call of the exotic was never clear. What he told his family about where and with whom he was living remains unknown.

The house was essentially run by us, as a collective. Initially the Bentleys acted as kind of house parents. But after they left it was up to us. Our absentee Dutch landlord lived next door. He happened to be an enthusiast for the paranormal. His main material interest, so far as we were concerned, was in the regularity of our rent. We ate communally, took responsibility for the weekly cooking and tried as best we could to accommodate each other's needs and habits without formality or acrimony.

Thus free and independent at last, in charge of my life for the first time, I felt liberated from the burden of the past. The worlds associated with politics, intellectual debate, the lively networks which clustered around the house in Richmond Road and the friendships on which our various activities were based became the heart of my social world, leaving College life behind. I went in for tutorials, but rarely ate there and never frequented the Junior Common Room. I was much happier living my alternative life. To say such a thing – *my* life! – was new for me. But it was how I felt.

I suppose that these new investments weren't really a surprise. I had come to Britain as a committed, if intellectually unlettered, anti-colonialist. The debate about the future of the West Indies after Independence had been heavily weighted for me by economic and political questions, which for a time ran in parallel to my literary and critical concerns. Gradually, however, they came to overlap. Many of us had been radicalized by the succession of anti-colonial struggles in the Gold Coast (Ghana), Kenya, Cyprus, Malaya and a host of other theatres including, later, Algeria. The consequences of global polarization had already reached deep into the decolonization process itself. The post-war intervention of the US in the affairs of the Caribbean basin – Haiti, Cuba, the Dominican Republic, Grenada, Panama – was, we can see in retrospect, only just beginning.

In Jamaica in 1952 the People's National Party had purged its far Left with the expulsion of four leading Marxist intellectuals – Richard Hart, Ken Hill, Frank Hill and Arthur Henry – with positive encouragement from Washington, in a cloud of unsubstantiated rumours of planned armed uprisings. A year later, we were enraged when the momentous election in British Guiana in April 1953 of Cheddi Jagan's Marxist-oriented People's Progressive Party (the PPP) government was followed, in October, by the British coup, resulting in Jagan's overthrow and the dismantling – in the treacherous deep-freeze circumstances of the Cold War – of the PPP experiment in multi-ethnic Left politics. The intervention was an anticipatory shadow of the subsequent destruction of the Árbenz government in Guatemala in 1954, of the historic breaking of Chile's Popular Unity by Pinochet, and the American intervention in Grenada which put a precipitate end to the New Jewel Movement. In Guiana the British government, in cahoots with the country's major sugar company, Bookers, which virtually owned half the place, used a divide-and-rule strategy to help bring about the disastrous split between the African and Indian communities which Jagan had had considerable success in unifying, and replaced him with his rival, Forbes Burnham. The resulting violence has disfigured Guyanese politics ever since. And as I've mentioned before, in 1954 I celebrated, in a Chinese restaurant with Doddridge Alleyne, the fall of Dien Bien Phu and the defeat of the French in Vietnam. This is a memory I've always held dear, although little did we know what was to follow in its wake. These were pivotal years in the articulation of decolonization with the darker geopolitics of the global Cold War.

It was also the time of the Bandung Conference, which convened in 1955, and of our subsequent hopes that Third World leaders such as Nehru, Nkrumah, Sukarno and Nasser would create the power to constitute a 'third force' in global politics. However, what we'd identified at the time as 'positive neutralism' came to grief on the rocks of the remorseless politics of international polarization, on the nuclear arms race, as well as on the conflicts within the decolonization movements themselves, despite – or because of? – their struggles to build 'one nation, one party'. We didn't foresee at all how the global imperatives of the Cold War would overwhelm the liberatory promise of decolonization.

Indeed, from such engagements the politics of the Cold War ceased for me to be an abstraction, or something which one would only know about through reading the newspaper. This was the high point of the post-war East-West polarization, of the ideological deep freeze which followed the announcement of the presence of the Iron Curtain, the Korean War and the division of the world into rival socio-economic systems and into two opposing nuclear-armed camps. Much of this fed into the politics associated with my subsequent involvement, after 1956, with CND.

I wrote two pamphlets for CND which indicate the drift of my thinking. One was an attempt to broaden CND's anti-nuclear stance into a political critique of NATO and of the NATO Alliance. The other was on the strategy which we espoused, positive neutralism, in which we turned away from the choice between the two nuclear camps. The latter was informed by my anti-colonial commitments, in that it sought to look to the newly independent states as an active, strategic component in global geopolitics.

In this period, the Left in general was shaken by hard-running moral panics identifying fellow-travellers, spies and 'reds' in high places, in a bid to expose those who were subversives, or those who might, according to the highly strung temper of the times, be construed as carriers of subversion. This was the era in the US of the Rosenberg executions, of McCarthyism and of the mobilization of the House Un-American Activities Committee in the front line of the ideological battle to locate and punish those deemed to threaten the nation. In Britain in 1951 two prominent, upper-class Soviet moles, Guy Burgess and Donald Maclean, were unmasked and fled to Moscow. A while later, in 1963, their co-conspirator, Kim Philby, a pillar of the old-school English establishment, followed them to the Soviet Union. These represented dramatic highlights of the Cold War which gave credence to prevailing fears of treachery. But they don't explain the depth of the collective psychosis which underwrote the endeavour by the state to root out subversion. In Britain the reflexes may have been more gentlemanly than in the US, but the ruthlessness with which dissidents, or supposed dissidents, were singled out was serious. It's difficult to convey how such mentalities came to be sedimented in the practices of everyday England.

It was characteristic of the tenor of the times that the most interesting intellectual journal of the liberal Left – *Encounter*, which we all read – turned out to be financed by the CIA by way of its US editor, Melvin Lasky. Its (unstated) purpose was to rescue a broad swathe of intellectuals – Arthur Koestler, George Orwell, Philip Toynbee, Kenneth Tynan, Anthony Crosland and Richard Crossman all come to mind – from drifting unawares into 'enemy territory'.

I followed these domestic events with particular interest. In the deepening atmosphere of suspicion and conspiracy, I could quite properly see myself being scapegoated as a 'fellow-traveller', or as a Communist dupe. It wouldn't have mattered that I had always been critical of the Soviet Union, that I'd never been a supporter of Stalin, and from the beginning – even in my politically most innocent days – had resolved never to join a Communist Party. My anxiety was not far-fetched. When some years later I had trouble getting a US visa, I was affronted by the consular official in London, in his Brooks Brothers shirt, who said I would be allowed entry if I'd be willing to renounce my membership of the Communist Party. He showed me the hieroglyph in my passport which – falsely – attested to the fact that this was indeed 'who I was'.

Thus running alongside my literary and critical interests, which dominated my first years in the UK, there were these other, deepening, historical, social and political questions. The two refused to stay in their separate boxes. I was becoming progressively involved in social analysis and political argument. My anti-imperialism was merging with a broader critical Left, or democratic socialist, outlook. But since I found the ethos of student Labourism, stiffened by the Cold War, deeply antipathetic, and since I was never at any time drawn to Stalinism or starry-eyed about the Soviet Union, I didn't find it easy to identify with any particular political tendency or party of the Left.

Nevertheless, I got to know many people active on the Oxford Left. I met Chuck Taylor, a French-Canadian Rhodes Scholar, at the time a sort of Christian Marxist influenced by Emmanuel Mounier and his journal *Esprit*, and close intellectually to Maurice Merleau-Ponty. He subsequently became a leading Hegelian scholar and a most distinguished philosopher. He'd been a member of the World University Service and had travelled to Vienna to help Hungarian refugees cross the border. I had also met the small Communist group – all twelve of them! – including Ralphael Samuel, Gabriel

Pearson, Peter Sedgwick and Stanley Mitchell. In what must have been 1953, I went on one of the first anti-nuclear marches, organized in Oxford by Raphael and Chuck, anticipating the formation of CND and my later involvement with the anti-nuclear and the peace movement.

For a time I was particularly close to Chuck. He held a grand fellowship at All Souls College and was already recognized as a rising star by Oxford philosophers. His affiliation to a kind of Catholic Marxism was, for all his brilliance, the cause of a degree of uncomprehending mirth from the established dons at the University, who found such a thing difficult to countenance. He proved to be an unofficial intellectual mentor to me, especially on Marx and Hegel and the more abstruse areas of philosophy. I remember the excitement when he brought back from Paris the recently published *Economic and Philosophic Manuscripts* of Marx, not then known in English. It played a significant role in his commitment at the time to a humanist definition of Marxism. He was intelligent, widely read and rigorous in argument. His manner, though, was gentle and unassuming. He refused to play to the Oxford customs, lacking the required hubris and preening self-regard. He was exemplary in his openness and receptiveness to other positions, engaged, humane and generous. I once attended a clever, teasing, patronizing Oxford-style conversation in the All Souls Common Room between him, Isaiah Berlin and Stuart Hampshire. Chuck simply shrugged off their faintly ironic tones with a generous smile and persisted with his argument. I remember thinking it made them look childish.

Shortly after beginning my graduate work in 1954 I came across Alan Hall, a Scottish archaeologist who had come to Balliol College from Aberdeen, and with whom I was to travel to Paris. He had wide intellectual and political interests. He and I became very close friends, companions in arms. Finding ourselves isolated on the non-aligned Left, we began seriously to explore political Oxford: the Labour Club, the student branch of the Labour Party – a nursery for later generations of frighteningly ambitious, front-bench career politicians – and other diverse sorts of groupings.

We even attended, by invitation, a few Communist Party student branch meetings, although this was irregular since technically they were closed affairs. We found this an unnerving, peculiar political sub-world. I think the Communists had high hopes of recruiting us. We had the impression that they thought we would sooner or later fall like ripe apples into their hands, although we were never tempted. As it turned out, however, we – as it were – recruited them, rather than vice versa. In 1956 they all resigned when the Communist Party branch was dissolved in response to the Khrushchev revelations about Stalin, and to the events in Hungary. My friend Rod Prince joined in his first term at Magdalen College, only immediately to resign!

In the autumn of 1954 I took the decision to offer a paper on class in contemporary capitalism, critical of orthodox Marxist class analysis, to a discussion group which Raphael had set up. I later reworked my argument in the article I contributed to *ULR*, 'A Sense of Classlessness'. Both Raphael himself and Edward Thompson vigorously criticized me for, as they saw things, my playing fast and loose with Marx. In this regard, it could be said that I entered Left politics a born revisionist.

The response to the paper when it was eventually published – on Thompson's part for sure – was certainly 'vigorous', suggesting, perhaps, that inherited Communist sensibilities hadn't come to an end when Party cards were torn up or returned. Raphael took me to task for being insufficiently historical, arguing that many of the deeper changes I'd identified in the post-war years in fact stretched back to the mid-Victorian period of industrial capitalism. In itself, this was an important argument, although it signally sidestepped the question which had framed the initial argument: What was particular about the post-war composition of class? Thompson's position represented a more concerted attack on the substance of my politics. Nestling up to the fraternal – and I'm sure sincere – courtesies were a number of harsh judgements. It makes me wonder, in retrospect, about the political virtue of the impending merger of *ULR* with Thompson's *The New Reasoner*, out of which the *NLR* was born.

Looking back, I am struck by the continuity of my position between then, when I was embarking on a political life, and now. I don't mean by this that what I said then is what I would say now. Whenever I happen to return to these earlier writings I'm sharply sensitive to their conceptual shortcomings. Even so, I can't help but feel some sympathy for the gravamen of the arguments emanating from my younger self.

In an earlier *ULR* contribution, for example, I'd presented a reading of the Conservative Party after the destruction, or the self-destruction, of Anthony Eden following the catastrophic war with Egypt in 1956. This was my first properly political essay. It hints at the possibility that I was already attuned to the dysfunctions and displacements of political life, and that I possessed a regard too for the specificity of the domain of politics itself. It suggests as well, perhaps, the degree to which historical events outpace the theories which endeavour to explain them. And it anticipates what would later, in another lifetime, become crucial for me: the primacy of conjunctural analysis. It reads like an earlier, practical incarnation of my 1979 intervention, 'The Great Moving Right Show'. I'm thinking particularly of the critique of the Left; of the invocation of the political salience of the popular; and of the centrality of displacement and disequilibrium. So if not an incarnation, then a kind of anticipation in intellectual sensibility of what was to come in my theorizations, much later, of Thatcherism. The severity of the ripostes I received on each occasion, from the Left, was sharp.

Until recently I haven't thought of these writings for an age. They've been gathering dust in the archives, free for the mice to nibble away at. But the larger issue turns on the collective work of political revision on which our generation, after 1956, felt compelled to embark. There was never for a moment any consensus about the directions which this work of renovation should take, nor what it should entail. The project was built on differing, sometimes contrary, investments. The single shared motivation was that, in our conception of politics, something had to give. After that, everything was open.

In this period there emerged a ferment of critical debate on the margins of Oxford, not only about politics but also about cultural, literary and intellectual matters. I suppose it concerned the role of culture and ideology in political practice – what Lévi-Strauss in his inaugural lecture at the Collège de France called, a little after, 'the neglected problem of the superstructures' – which classical Marxism had accorded a subsidiary and dependent role. I became more engaged in questions of social theory and of the historical shaping of social formations – a sort of resolution, in practice, of my earlier quandaries as to whether to study literature or history at university. These debates pulled together a whole spectrum of people on the Left, from the Labour Left, the Communists – who in the climate of the Cold War were subject to serious bans and proscriptions about taking part formally in Labour Party meetings – and a great array of independent socialists and what were then coming to be known as Third World activists.

We all clustered around the Socialist Club, a shell organization created in the 1930s in the days of the Popular Front by Communists and fellow-travellers. Many had gone on to distinguished careers and a number of them had never remembered, or bothered, to cancel their subscriptions. A tidy sum had accrued which we resurrected. G. D. H. Cole, the independent guild socialist from an earlier political generation who had gravitated to the Socialist Club, proved to be a benign presence, and a number of us attended his Thursday seminars.

Many students from Third World countries, who didn't fit in politically elsewhere, found a sympathetic home in the Socialist Club, an empty shell of an organization which we revived. Many were later to play significant roles in the fledgling years of independence from colonial rule. I'm thinking particularly of Sadiq al-Mahdi who became Prime Minister of Sudan; the Indian historian Partha Gupta; and the Kenyan Pan-Africanist and future trade unionist Tom Mboya. They contributed to the hothouse politicized atmosphere of the revived Socialist Club and formed our primary political constituency.

A charitable reading would suggest that during this period I was busy repairing my backward, lopsided political education by putting the untold history of radicalism, socialism and dissent back into the detoxified British history I had learned at school. I knew Oxford politics differed greatly from my pro-nationalist, anti-colonial instincts. But at the time I didn't feel that there was a necessary choice between them, though they had very different priorities and moved to a very different political rhythm. Nevertheless, my contrasting involvements helped set in play these contradictory pulls which, in subsequent years, became harder to reconcile.

I acquired a rudimentary knowledge of the world history of socialism. I learned about decolonization in parts of the world about which previously I had known nothing. I began for the first time to encounter domestic British politics at close quarters. I heard Tories declare that they planned to defeat the meddling social engineering of the Keynesian welfare state by unleashing deregulation – 'the bonfire of controls': a hint of political struggles to come. I witnessed Winston Churchill's decline and collapse as a political icon; he had been as revered in the colonies as he was in Britain during the war, notwithstanding his unrepentant dedication to colonial rule. It was a curious time for a colonial to be experiencing life in the metropole.

I started to understand the labyrinthine contours of that very English formation, Labourism. At first I couldn't really *see* the full significance of the constraints which the welfare state imposed on the freedom of movement of capital and, like other radicals with whom I mixed, at times it felt to me like a compromised mode of reformism. I should have known better. Even so, it was impossible to ignore the widespread effects of public welfare for the vast majority of people, the dreams and aspirations for a more equal and just society which it embodied, and the fierce class antagonisms that its very presence generated. Indeed, it wasn't long before I came to be convinced that the reforms of the 1940s undercut the facile distinction between reform and revolution. I began, too, to appreciate the political significance of the ideological splits in the Conservatives between diehards and reformers like Rab Butler, who were prepared to entertain some commitment to a redistributive social programme.

I found I was entering a political world composed of a heady stream of parties, factions and tendencies. Most conspicuous was the Labour Club, including its most prominent minority, the careerists. There existed also a significant, free-thinking intellectually distinguished group drawn to the Left of the Labour Party, who were frequently very far from Labour tribalism. There were a handful of Trotskyists, among whom was the charming Mike Kidron. The members of the formidably well-informed Communist Club boasted an ubiquitous presence. They were led by the intense and clever Raphael Samuel, who had come from a Communist family and whose political milieu he was to capture brilliantly in a later work. He was someone with whom everyone on the Left wanted to debate. But, because of the official Labour Party bans and proscriptions which the red scare had triggered, so long as he was still a Communist, Labour doors, officially at least, remained closed to him.

This phase of my political involvement was dominated by the debates, theories and histories of the Left. I became not just anti-colonial but self-consciously an independent socialist. I learned the distinctions between social democracy, socialism, Marxism, Leninism, Trotskyism and Maoist currents of thought. I read for the first time the work of figures like R. H. Tawney and G. H. D. Cole. We puzzled about the shape of the post-war world – global capitalism, a regressive Soviet Empire, poverty, underdevelopment and neo-imperialism. Across these issues, however, class remained the dominant theme, the working class the main agency of change. The future shape of the class struggle was uppermost in our political speculations.

For some time, like other Caribbean Marxists and radicals, I sought to think questions of race and decolonization as ultimately harnessed to the motor of class. It took some time before colonialism and racism, as distinct and relatively autonomous systems, began to destabilize this simplified conception. I was obliged to think again about the historical specificity of these social contradictions, their different origins, timescales and histories, as well as the means by which they were immediately experienced.

These contradictions could be, indeed were, *articulated* in ways we did not properly understand. Yet the very idea of articulation implies the forging of historically specific connections between phenomena which are significantly different. They do not necessarily hang together; nor are they harnessed in the same ways to capitalist exploitation. Class exploitation, racialized ideas of whiteness, the means by which genders and sexualities are inhabited, and plenty more in similar vein, do not all arise from the same cause. The fundamental relations of class, decisive as they were, couldn't tell us what politically we needed to know. Politics itself needed to be rethought. This was to prove a long lesson.

Between 1954 and 1958, when I finally left Oxford, I was deeply involved in debates about British politics, which was as much about how British culture was changing, as it was about politics narrowly conceived. Richard Hoggart's central question in *The Uses of Literacy* was whether mass culture was 'unbending the mainsprings of action' of the traditional working class. In similar vein, Hugh Gaitskell, the leader of the Labour Party, was of a mind that the Labour vote was being undermined by the new 'affluence', condensed in his idea of the 'telly', the fridge and the car. These were questions not only about mass production but about mass consumption, concerned with the degree to which British capitalism was moving in the direction of its US counterpart. Such questions led us into a burgeoning eclectic, new literature: C. Wright Mills's *White Collar* and *The Power Elite*; Paul Sweezy's *Theory of Capitalist Development*; J. K. Galbraith's *The Affluent Society*; David Riesman's *The Lonely Crowd* and William H. Whyte's *The Organization Man*.

The degree to which new cultural forms transfigured and expanded the ambit of politics itself was perhaps the dominating issue which possessed us. It was this that marked both the New Left and Cultural Studies. In this sense it's not wrong to suggest that Cultural Studies began here. It's salutary to go back to the opening editorials of the *ULR* and of its successor, the *NLR*. We were talking culturally about politics and politically about culture. At the same time we were endeavouring to get to grips with the new forms of class society and with the 'affluence' generated, selectively, by modern capitalism. This required us to think also about how these new relations of production and consumption demanded, in turn, a rethinking of inherited classical Marxism. It was in this milieu that my socio-political and theoretical interests developed, enlisting – but also transforming and, to a degree, supplanting – my earlier literary concerns.

At the same time events in the Caribbean were very close to me. The debates about Caribbean Federation were, in my early years in the diaspora, electric, galvanizing an entire political constituency. The problems Federation encountered, leading after its brief life to its destruction, undermined by inter-island rivalries, depressed me profoundly. These running failures contributed to my greater involvement in other arenas. I had always assumed that, once I had graduated, I would go back home. If Federation had eventually worked out, I reckon I would have returned to teach at the University of the West Indies and become involved in the Federal politics of the 1960s and 1970s. The thought that the Federation might collapse and these small islands be obliged to negotiate the shark-infested waters of post-Independence on their own, marked another turning point for me. Certainly it meant that there was no immediate urgency to return. What exactly would I be going back to, and for what? To a significant degree my energies became transferred to the political scene immediately in front of me.

ULR came out of the rich networks I've been describing, particularly within the milieu of the Socialist Club which acted as a magnet for these debates. As the Cold War began to thaw, off and on, so the political barriers between different tendencies diminished and a vigorous Left political culture started to develop across the conventional Cold War divides. This debate was intensely focused on the questions: 'How has the world changed?'; and 'Why was it so qualitatively different, both from what had prevailed before, and from what the political theories devised to explain historical change had predicted?' More particularly we came to be preoccupied with the question of 'What did culture – so long relegated to a subordinate sphere of interest – have to do with it?' This discussion had what I would call a necessarily 'critical' or 'post', even a 'deconstructive' edge to it, *avant la lettre*.

ULR represented an attempt to focus this debate, to give it a wider airing, to connect with similar developments in political thinking on the Left in other colleges and universities, as well as to reconnect with an earlier Left generation. Deciding to launch *ULR* was specifically triggered by the events of 1956, as significant to us as 1968 was to become to a later generation. The detonations set off by the twin events of the Suez Crisis and the return of Soviet tanks to the streets of Budapest, crushing the Hungarian Revolution in an exercise of pure Soviet colonialism, felt like the simultaneous operation of two colonialisms. The New Left was formed in the political space which opened up between those two opposing coordinates: between the military, aggressive authoritarianism of a nuclear-armed Soviet Empire, dramatizing the degeneration of the revolutionary ideals it had originally embodied; and the revived aggression of British imperialism, which many falsely imagined had already been put to rest by social democracy. These events signalled that the dream of Soviet Communism was dead; but so too was the illusion that Western imperialism was either finished or that it was benign.

Emerging into this space, personally and politically, was a formative moment for my whole political outlook. We couldn't claim that our immediate political objectives had been achieved, in terms of either the rejuvenation of a democratic Labour politics or of nuclear disarmament. Even so, I've stayed consistently identified with this political moment: if not with the actual positions adopted at the time, then with the set of predispositions and political sentiments that opened up. It is who I am politically.

ULR was launched as a student journal, but it expanded to include a wider, older, more politically experienced intellectual constituency, hence the awkward oxymoron of the title. It was, in retrospect, an extraordinary moment. The relationships between the two political generations continued – not without friction – until our merger with *The New Reasoner* and the launch of *NLR* in 1960.

The New Reasoner was the product of an older, Popular Front generation, many of whom had joined the Communist Party as part of the anti-fascist struggle and were active in political work throughout the war, when (eventually) Britain and the Soviet Union became allies. The revelations about the extent and depth of Stalinism made at the Twentieth Party Congress of the Communist Party of the Soviet Union in February of 1956 – although we only got to hear of it some time later – came as a grievous shock to the great majority of them. When the Soviet Union invaded Hungary to put down the popular uprising large numbers of these people left; for them the British Communist Party, although it survived, effectively went into liquidation. But before the final break, several dissidents, including Edward and Dorothy Thompson and John Saville, published – against Party rules – an internal bulletin called *The Reasoner* which was openly critical of the leadership; their expulsion became only a matter of time. Out of this collective experience came the journal *The New Reasoner*, which worked in an uneasy tandem with *ULR*.

Crucial in this respect was the Historians' Group of the Communist Party, which attracted a galaxy of young historians. It released some of the most gifted, sophisticated and creative Marxist historians, like Edward and Dorothy Thompson, from the Stalinist camp. It had cut an independent path for itself even during the days when the Party remained intact. Under the guidance of the enigmatic but significantly influential figure of Dona Torr, who taught the younger generation of Marxist intellectuals to read, among other things, *Capital* as a historical text, this new political generation now formed a powerful echelon in the internal opposition inside the Communist Party. It clustered around *The Reasoner*, breaking all the Party's protocols.

Perhaps the most immediate, felt distinction between *The New Reasoner* and the *ULR* wasn't to do with politics in a narrow institutional sense, but turned on popular culture or, to employ the more common idiom of the time, on mass culture. This was a matter profoundly shaped by political generation. The *ULR* group was much more prepared than the *New Reasoner* cadres to work with, rather than against, mass culture, for all the necessary difficulties involved. I think it's hard, today, to grasp the historical significance of this. In geopolitical matters we were of course neutralists, hostile to the politics emanating from the State Department in Washington; we followed the Bandung tendency in its search for a politics dependent on neither Washington nor Moscow; and we were unilateralists, believing that Britain could and should take a lead in nuclear disarmament. But culturally we were nonetheless attracted by the vitality of American popular life, indeed to the domain of mass culture itself. This complicated the political argument. Everywhere in the 1950s it was posed as the problem of Americanization. We were frightened by the military power of the United States, and by the consequent polarization of a heavily armed world. Through these years the US was notorious for its racial politics. And there existed also an anxiety about the stupendous power of the booming consumer capitalism of post-war America. We still inhabited, to some degree, the Leavisite slipstream, perhaps more than we acknowledged – although there was good reason to be concerned about the force of the commodification of daily life. Where the lines were to fall was always a matter of political debate, as it still is. But the vitality and raucousness of American culture certainly loosened England's tight-lipped, hierarchical class cultures and carried inside it the possibilities – or the collective dream? – for a better future, which we felt was a serious political loss to deny.

Thus a distinct, perhaps diverse group lay at the heart of the original *ULR* venture. It was decided, by quite informal means, in the Socialist Club circles that the four of us should be the appointed editors, reflecting the Club's principal balance of forces: two ex-Communists (Raphael and Gabriel), and two independents (Chuck and myself). The venture as a whole, by which the journal would work as an intellectual and political organizer, was supported by a wider, more politically heterogeneous group.

From the first, Raphael – whose initial idea it was – was the driving force. With his old, deeply internalized Communist habits in disarray, he remained a man of volcanic energies and high hopes. It was Raphael who induced the printers to deliver a second run before the first had been sold out (as it eventually was) without our possessing any actual or foreseeable financial collateral. He arranged for our taking out advertisements we couldn't pay for. It was he who contacted distinguished outside contributors, such as the grouping around *The New Reasoner*, as well as the formidable historian and biographer of Trotsky, Isaac Deutscher, whom few if any of us had ever met. The selection of authors to write for the first issue was broadly based, including Thompson himself; John Saville, the historian of labour; the *marxisante* Keynesian Joan Robinson; the art critic Michael Ayrton; the 'Free Cinema' film-makers Lindsay Anderson and Karel Reisz; Basil Davidson, the Africanist; and Eric Hobsbawm. The editors had to travel to Reading to be vetted by Deutscher before he'd let us print his essay 'Russia in Transition' which, contrary to every solemn undertaking, Raphael proceeded judiciously to emend.

Raphael was a remarkable figure. He poured out creative ideas in an unstoppable stream; yet in terms of practical organization he was a nightmare. Hearing a paper being delivered by Raphael – unfinished, handwritten in his heavy, black scrawl, with odd pages fluttering to the floor – was an amazing, if nerve-wracking, experience. Even so he was gifted and clever: an original social historian, with a massive accumulation of detailed knowledge at his command, very widely read, a fine teacher and a formidable inspirer of younger scholars. He was also a brilliant if erratic generator of political projects, the founding of *History Workshop Journal* being only one of many. Without his astonishing energy, perseverance and unswerving political commitment *ULR* would never have put its head above ground.

This was the *ULR*. Looking back, it's interesting for me to reflect on the shift (if that is what it was) from a literary sensibility, animated by a spontaneous anti-colonialism, to a more fully political viewpoint, in which my own metropolitan location assumed a sharper gravity. All I can say is that I was always interested in literature as part of a wider social and discursive field, which the term culture referenced. We should recall, too, the nature of the political debate at the time. The issues being discussed always went below the usual terrain of politics, in its traditional form, to the deeper cultural and social structural levels which provided the underlying historical conditions out of which politics, in the narrower sense – 'Who exercises power in the state?'; 'Who gets elected to government?' – always arises. The debates which spoke to me most forcefully were always those which addressed the connections between culture and politics, or, to put in more conceptually, about culture and power, including the vexed but critical issues of ideology.

Actually, there was a notion of hegemony operating there already, although the concept itself was foreign to us. In a practical sense we were edging towards a theory of hegemony, although none of us had yet read a word of Gramsci. The ideas, however, were beginning to take shape, and to coalesce: the notion that power is never exercised exclusively through political institutions and the state; that the state is always also 'educative'; the intricate relation between domination and consent; and the fact that the authority which enables power to accomplish some great historical task is always constituted on many different sites. We were never involved simply with an instrumental approach to state power or to its derivatives, which riveted others of our generation and which could be encapsulated in the question: 'Can Labour win?' That never seemed enough.

Allied to this were the practical skills of cultural reading, which I had formally learned through literary criticism and which, in the work of Richard Hoggart and Raymond Williams, were beginning to be applied, consciously and explicitly, to analysing society. Living in England as a migrant I found myself – unwilled – doing unending fieldwork in one's home village, as it were, as if my neighbours had suddenly been turned, by some strange alchemy, into native informants. The progression from a critical reading of literature to an expansive conception of politics proved not only increasingly persuasive intellectually, but also compelling.

As I've been explaining, migration posed the most pressing questions about identity and self-identification. These are matters which all Caribbean people confront, to some degree, in part because of the syncretic character of Caribbean culture and because of the violent fractures and brutal ruptures of its history. Identity has necessarily been a political issue for us all, both in the Caribbean and in Britain. Once I decided not to return immediately, questions of identity and belongingness assailed me with a special urgency. I felt required to confront my own past and to try to make sense of the Caribbean world, of the peculiar nature of its intimate subordinations, and how it had been shaped by, and in relation to, the colonial metropole. *My* unease, it slowly dawned on me, wasn't mine alone.

This was the moment when I decided to leave my own research aside for a while and studiously made my way to the Rhodes House Library in order to immerse myself in the history of slavery and the making of the New World. Central was the discussion of African 'survivals' in Melville Herskovits and others; early samizdat translations from the Portuguese of Roger Bastide on Afro-Brazilian cultures and of Jean Price-Mars from the French on Haiti; later Gilberto Freyre on Brazil; the incomparable Fernando Ortiz on Cuba and Afro-Caribbean 'religions of the oppressed' and folk customs. This is how, for me, culture moved definitively from Matthew Arnold's 'sweetness and light', or 'the best that has been thought and said' – or Leavis's 'mass civilization and minority culture' – to Williams's 'whole way of life' and (eventually, some while later) to 'signifying practices'. I can't emphasize too strongly the Caribbean, New World route through this journey.

I am in the middle of my discussion about politics and I'm having to explain my shifting relations to the concept of culture. I make no apology for this. This journey took me to an understanding of culture as the signifying dimension of human practice. In Althusser's terms, culture exists as one of the founding instances of every social formation, without which societies cannot exist as such.

This diversion in the Rhodes House Library, when everyone –

including me – was deep into the theoretical problematic of Hoggart and Williams, really marks for me the origins of Cultural Studies. In my lecture on 'Thinking the Diaspora', which I gave some years back in Salvador, in Brazil's Bahia – on my first, heart-stopping visit to Afro-Brazil – I called this earlier encounter with the black New World, when I knew so little and I learned so much, my Cultural Studies 'Bahian' moment.

This reminds me of how important in these years the discovery, or the rediscovery, of anthropology was to the makings of Anglophone Marxisant history. I still don't know how in British intellectual life this happened. Whenever Hobsbawm or Thompson were obliged to discuss it, they were curiously unrevealing. It just kind of happened. There's no denying, however, that happen it did. It's really when what we would now call 'culture' first registered as a distinct strand within a Marxist-inflected social history, as an analytically organizing principle. Primitive rebels and customs in common came to be the very stuff of historians for the coming generation.

And yet in the British historiography of the New World, racial dimensions were never prominent in the strands of anthropology that filtered back to the metropole. The work on the Caribbean that I was reading was mainly produced within French and New World anthropology. Mostly I was concerned with the literature on slavery, the degree of African 'survivals' in the Black Atlantic, creolization and what the inimitable Ortiz called, with reference to the Cuban case, 'transculturation'. Crucial for me was the impact of slavery in transforming the inherited African cultures into what I knew as a syncretic or creolized Jamaican folk culture. I also sought to understand more generally the impact of African and European cultures on the Caribbean and how an indigenous culture, related to but distinct from all its symbolic tributaries, had emerged as a result of the reciprocal but unequal processes of transculturation and the often brutal transactions between these different elements. I needed to understand, in other words, the cultural formation of the post-colonial nation. I felt this to be urgent, as I thought about the prospects for the new black diaspora in Britain. I wanted to find out, in other words, how the black British diaspora would have to construct its negotiated relationship to the colonizing culture *at home*, which had – by an unanticipated turn of fate – also become, literally, our new home.

As I was doing so – as I was immersed in Herskovits and Ortiz and the rest – I was also drawn to Raymond Williams. This may sound like an exemplification of double consciousness. That's because it's exactly what it was.

Williams was an extramural tutor in Hastings, which gave him a happily offbeat relation to the intellectual establishment. He was involved in adult education, in a quiet and provincial corner of southern England. But this also happened to be an outpost of the Oxford Delegacy of Extra-Mural Studies. This meant that he had often to be in Oxford. He used to come to F. W. (Freddie) Bateson's critical seminar in Jesus College. Bateson was a strange figure, even by Oxford standards. He founded and edited for many years *Essays in Criticism*, a sort of polite rival to *Scrutiny*. But also, following his war work for the government, he was preoccupied with the problem of agriculture and had edited a Fabian publication on the prospects for the socialization of agriculture. Which I suspect must have endeared him to Williams. Alan Hall and I met Raymond occasionally on these trips and we became friendly. He gave us two draft chapters of *Culture and Society* to read. That was very important to me.

Williams provided us with another way of reading the connections between the literary tradition, wider intellectual formations and ideas, social structures and the general culture. He did this partly by reinventing the culture and society tradition of English social criticism. He began exactly where my own interests lay, with the historical contexts of literature, but ended up somewhere distinctive and original: with a theory of culture. Part of the significance of Williams at this moment was that he was able to connect these debates, about literature and culture, to contemporary social events and to political argument, as he did in *The Long Revolution*, the paradigm-changing book which followed *Culture and Society*.

In this period, the wider political debate seemed to turn on what subsequently was to be called the thesis about the 'embourgeoisement' of the working class of the developed industrial world. This was partly a question about political agency. Where were the classic agents of social change, Marx's 'grave-diggers of capitalism'? What had happened to the emerging force – labour – whose onward march throughout the nineteenth and early twentieth century had transformed mass politics in the industrializing world? What had happened to the proletariat which was so dramatically *present* in the immediate aftermath of the First World War, seemingly poised to fulfil the prophecy of the socialist revolution: Petrograd in 1917; Rosa Luxemburg and the Spartacists in Germany in 1919; soviets in Hungary and Munich; the Turin factory occupations, which provided Gramsci with his earliest lessons in proletarian order; 'Red Clydeside'? What was happening, in our world in the 1950s, to this tradition of proletarian insurgency? As I came to understand these things, the classic proletarian moment was over. As a social force, the proletariat as the formal, choreographed antidote to capital was gone for ever. This marked another, powerful instance of my political revisionism.

Yet if this were so, where were the new 'relations of social force' to be located? More immediately the question was whether the collective politics which had underpinned the British compromise of the welfare state and social democracy were being – not just defeated by its enemies – but undermined by deeper economic, social and cultural trends. There were emerging new social configurations, driven by innovative consumer and managerial forms of capitalism, which – paradoxically – the dangers posed by the Depression and the war had conspired to bring into being. The transformation of the working class and of its cultural forms – in short, the Americanization of mass culture – had become an inescapable political issue.

This is the moment when the implicit politics of Richard Hoggart's *The Uses of Literacy*, published in 1957, and of Williams's *Culture and Society* (1958), which at first sight did not appear to have an immediately or overtly political relevance, came racing into view.

We were clearly stepping into a new political conjuncture. It's the moment too of that confusing and confused phenomenon, the Angry Young Men, the birth of the Royal Court Theatre in its new dispensation, rock and roll and of the Free Cinema movement of Lindsay Anderson and Karel Reisz.

The best way to recover this atmosphere may be this. In the summer of 1956 I was trying to write my chapter on *The Bostonians*. Alan Hall and I and two other friends – an Englishman, Peter Rhodes, and an American, Mario Lippa, who were painters studying at Ruskin College – went on holiday to Cornwall. Alan and I had planned to write a book about the fractures that were beginning to appear in British culture and politics, which were apparent even before the actual moments of Suez and Hungary. We felt an urgent need to re-evaluate the political past. These were some of the books we took away with us: the two draft chapters from *Culture and Society*; a sprinkling of Leavis; T. S. Eliot's *Notes Towards the Definition of Culture*; John Strachey's book on *End of Empire*; Tony Crosland's *The Future of Socialism*; C. Wright Mills's *White Collar*; Colin Wilson's bizarre, Anglicized existentialism, as set out in *The Outsider*, which had just been published; the autobiography of the very young (and now justifiably forgotten) George Scott, *Time and Place*; a collection of Orwell's essays; and various bits and pieces we'd compiled from the Free Cinema people. These were the raw materials out of which – somehow – we were going to conjure up our book that would explain how the changes which were rocking English culture were connected to the organization of advanced capitalism and to the reconfigurations underwriting British political life! We understood that these transformations were, in turn, connected in some manner to the end of empire, which was why Strachey was included in our reading; although in truth these colonial and post-colonial (though in 1956 the term would not have been ours) dimensions formed the outer horizon of our explorations.

It's instructive to think back to how we imagined the decolonizing perspective to be present. Undoubtedly labourism, the welfare state and domestic party politics were in the foreground. But these domestic preoccupations were inflected by my own involvement in

Caribbean debates, and of course by the Suez Crisis which that summer was visibly building up and in the press day by day. It would have been tricky, in the summer of '56, for Britain's imperial dimensions to have been absent (but not, in England, impossible). The unresolved question, however, was how these overseas determinations made themselves felt in the new metropolitan cultures which were *also* so visible and were also reverberating through, and undermining, the old order.

There was, in addition, another reason why these questions were important to me. The ethos of Oxford Labour politics was unremittingly white and English, in its deepest sensibilities. The Labour Party group, which had a restricted entourage closely geared to future parliamentary careers, I found peculiarly off-putting. I couldn't stand its combination of Puritanism, Fabian self-righteousness and a studied yet simultaneously unconscious commitment to the protocols of Oxford's England – especially first thing on a Sunday morning, which was when they met! One luminary of the Oxford Left in these years, Brain Walden, subsequently and all too predictably a Labour MP and political commentator (with a soft spot for Mrs Thatcher), once told me that the Labour Party was no place for the likes of me. I was grateful. I knew exactly what he meant!

The Socialist Club, and others on the independent Left, was constituted in opposition to all that, and gathered together a diverse assembly consisting of ex-Communists, Trotskyists and assorted socialists, as well as a variety of independently minded Labour supporters.

We were the last of the first New Left generation. But we were almost immediately replaced by a second, which included Perry Anderson and Mike Rustin. Mike and I did not actually overlap. He was one of the pioneers of the New Left second generation once he arrived in Oxford. He founded with Alan Shuttleworth and Robin Blackburn a successor journal to *ULR*, *New University*, with Perry Anderson present as well, which served to bring on figures such as Alexander Cockburn and Gareth Stedman Jones. It functioned organizationally, in other words, to create the second generation within the New Left, which ultimately came to dominate *NLR*. Mike was, and remains, a tireless, prolific generator of creative solutions to administrative and organizational problems, an active campaigner in a heady variety of causes, a gifted sociologist as well as a knowledgeable participant in the world of psychoanalysis. He has remained a person with an enormous enthusiasm for life in all its varieties. He has spent much of his time starting up, writing for and editing small political journals like *Views*, and now many years later, *Soundings*. Despite our different temperaments we have been close political colleagues as well as family members for most of my adult life.

The New Left, as it progressed from its initial stages, wasn't only *ULR*, or later *NLR*. It is easy to forget now that it was primarily a political movement. By the time of the founding of *NLR* in 1960 the journal was envisaged as the organizer for a broader movement, built up nationally on the New Left Clubs. Meetings were held in the renovated offices in Carlisle Street, Soho, where there was also a clubhouse, a library and a coffee bar.

In London, for a time, the *ULR* Club held large political meetings every Monday evening in hotels and whatever other places around central London we could afford and, on occasion, at 100 Oxford Street, more famous as a dance venue. The first was addressed by Isaac Deutscher. None of us could believe the size of the turnout. Maybe six or seven hundred people queued to get in. The political energies of the period are not easily recalled today. Tom Mboya, who was studying at Ruskin College, was another big draw. We held meetings on NATO and South Africa, and of course would entice as many of our adversaries in the Labour Party as would consent to come.

It's curious, looking back, to contemplate the exchanges between the young cadres of the New Left and the established leadership of the Labour Party. It's not that they liked what we said. But the lines of political and intellectual exchange held, at least for a while, which wouldn't happen now. We used the annual Labour conferences as opportunities to agitate; we organized an exhibition to expose the manipulations of the advertising industry which we mounted at one of the fringe meetings. We'd prepare daily cyclo-styled newssheets for the delegates. This was the time, not only of the deep splits within Labour over the nuclear deterrent, but over Clause Four as well: over 'the common ownership of the means of production, distribution and exchange'. During this period we debated with the heavyweights: with Hugh Gaitskell, Tony Crosland, Richard Crossman. We endeavoured to build bridges with *Tribune*, the *New Statesman* and with organizations such as the Movement for Colonial Freedom. A new generation of school teachers organized themselves under the banner of the New Left. Carlisle Street was the place from which the leafleting of London for the Aldermaston Marches by CND – 'Ban the Bomb!' – was organized, by folk such as Ernest Rodker, whose mother was a close friend of Doris Lessing's, who herself was active in the New Left.

The lead-up to the 1959 election triggered a massive Left–Right, orthodox–revisionist showdown in the Labour Party, into which we were all pulled. A furious, long-running debate developed among political commentators and within the Left about the future course and strategy of Labour and its chances of winning an election. A sense of the times can be gauged by looking at Mark Abrams and Richard Rose's polemic *Must Labour Lose?*, written with the help of the steely Rita Hinden and published by Penguin in 1960.

I'd left Oxford for London in 1958. By then our time in Oxford was coming to a natural end and for many of us London became the axis for New Left politics. Chuck Taylor went to Paris to work with Maurice Merleau-Ponty; Raphael Samuel moved to London, first to the London School of Economics and then to the Institute of Community Studies in Bethnal Green; Gabriel Pearson and Alan Hall both ended up teaching at Keele University. I went to London to play for time until I had made the big decision about going home.

I got a job as a supply teacher in a school in south London: Stockwell Secondary Modern School. The school was primarily composed of the white working class, with about a quarter made up of black boys from around Brixton and the Oval. These kids had been streamed by the 11-Plus and they had failed. They were at the very bottom of the educational pile. Many of the white fathers were in the newspaper trade and their sons were guaranteed work in 'the print', like hereditary peers destined for the House of Lords. They had very little attachment to formal education, although many of them were sharp as pins. They used to threaten to bring their elder brothers around to see to me when we fell out and it was all I could do to keep all thirty odd boys in their seats. On the way back to school from the swirling chaos of the swimming baths on a Friday afternoon, they'd simply peel off the end of the column when we passed their streets and quietly disappear. I'd pray that they would reappear safe and sound when we met again the following Monday morning.

I found somewhere to live in Clapham in the house of Jock and Millie Haston. Jock, a Glaswegian working-class seaman, had been a leading, extraordinarily energetic and thoughtful Trotskyist from the early 1930s to the late 1940s. I think that he had the distinction of recruiting Gerry Healy to Trotskyism, the long-time *jefe* of one of the more rectilinear *groupuscules* of the British Left. By the time I knew him Jock had broken with the sects and involved himself in trade-union education. Millie, his South African-born Jewish wife, worked as a kind of ideological entryist and was a mainstay of the local Labour Party. They were extremely kind people who mothered and fathered me during the difficult, lonely, transitional period in London.

I was, throughout this period, ferociously busy. During the days I taught class 1FX! Then in the afternoons I would head up to Soho to the *ULR* office to edit the journal with our only full-time employee, Janet Hase. Every Friday night I'd take the train to Bexleyheath to teach an extramural class on literature. On weekdays I usually left the office well after midnight and caught the night bus to Clapham to be up for school the following morning.

Soho was the site of the Partisan Café, which Raphael Samuel had managed to persuade his seriously reluctant fellow editors to support. As I recall the occasion, an all-night editorial meeting took place in Chuck Taylor's rooms – still in Oxford at this point – to discuss the founding of a café. The majority vote was against. But when did such formalities ever blunt Raphael's unstoppable organizing drive? He raised funds, partly from ex-Communist acquaintances who had abandoned the Party after the events of 1956. Raphael's preferred model was the Left cabaret culture of pre-war Berlin, transposed to Soho in time for the 1960s! Once it had opened, he actually bought the food himself in Berwick Street market for a time and supervised the Jewish/East European-influenced menu. One of the great causes of contention occurred over the question of coffee. Raphael was militantly opposed to the espresso revolution which had recently hit London. However, opposite the Partisan at the corner of Dean Street and Soho Square was the original Gaggia coffee bar, in whose window sat the first gleaming espresso coffee machine in London! How seductive was that? Renegades like me would steal over across the street from the Partisan, which only served filter coffee, in order to get our espresso fix.

Soho then was central, edgy and bohemian. It functioned as a kind of crossroads for a variety of social and political currents, especially after the *ULR* Club, which had its base there, became more closely involved in political activism. After *ULR* merged with *The New Reasoner* to create *NLR*, and New Left Clubs developed in centres across the country, many provincial connections evolved and people who didn't live in London would drop in when passing by. One uninvited guest who also popped in was the Special Branch operative who 'borrowed' the subscriber list from our office.

And yet, on my arrival in London I could feel the atmosphere of casual racism all around, although I was probably shielded from its full force by my middle-class background, my status as a student and my 'brown' colour. However, its palpable presence could not be ignored. The 1950s were, after all, a watershed period as far as overt expression of racist attitudes in public places was concerned. The local hostility and resentment at the formation of the early ghetto areas and the competition for jobs and housing; the discrimination on the doorstep; racketeering landlords who presided over the multi-occupation archipelago: all were sharpening at this time, culminating in the violence of Notting Hill.

I felt such racial simmerings in Oxford for a long while, and they surfaced in a very sharp way over Suez. But London was different. When I arrived, by way of the New Left networks I became active in anti-racist work in Notting Hill. This was to prove a decisive, diasporic reorientation in my political life. For the first time I saw what West Indian migrants had become. They were no longer newly arrived – as I'd first seen them, emerging from Paddington Station – searching for somewhere to stay. They had become embedded in the city. Their kids were already a presence in the schools. They were here to stay.

I was on the underground one afternoon on my way to the *ULR* office when a group of white pupils from my school got on. Since I knew they rarely left their 'manor' I asked them where they were going. They explained that they were on the way to Notting Hill because there were 'ructions' over there. This was the very moment that Notting Hill was on the point of erupting. The large, gracious but peeling residences of North Kensington, a decaying royal borough, had become an area of multiple occupation with a large number of Afro-Caribbean migrants rammed into grossly uninviting flats by rack-renting landlords. The fascist Mosleyites, who had seldom appeared in public politics since the end of the war, began to make their regular appearances each Saturday in the market, preaching their racism. These kids were going to Notting Hill to line the streets from the Tube station to the back-street areas of Powis Terrace, along which black men and women coming home from work were obliged to walk. As evening approached their sport commenced. The pubs opened. Black people started making their way home. Groups of white kids – later identified by the media as Teddy Boys – lined the pavements, screaming racial abuse and harassing the women, egged on by their elders. I asked my boys what on earth they thought they were doing. They gave me the stock racial line: 'The blackies are over here, with their big sporty cars, playing their loud music, taking our [*sic*] women, and stealing our [*sic*] jobs.' 'What are you talking about?', I asked. 'Do you mean people like me? Do you mean the black kids in your class?' They looked at me in astonishment. 'No, not YOU, Sirrr . . .', they replied, with heavy sarcasm. Some of my best friends, I thought . . . Our daughter, Becky, remembers me telling her about our accompanying black nurses home to make sure that they were safe.

The *ULR* Club was active in Notting Hill, working with local black activists and with the churches and Leftists in the local Labour Party – which was actually deeply split internally on the race issue – to put together local black and white tenants' defence associations. This was our first experience of local community politics. It continued for some time, inspired by community activists like George Clarke who led the *ULR* Club initiative.

One day Michael de Freitas walked into the *ULR* office. De Freitas was a mixed-race Trinidadian who subsequently became Michael X. He introduced himself modestly by announcing, 'I run Notting Hill'. What he meant was that he was part of Notting Hill's new, criminal underground and one of its emerging hard men. He probably had a hand in local prostitution and certainly admitted part-time involvement in evicting black tenants who couldn't pay their rent, decanting all their belongings onto the streets for the exploitative landlords. The gist of what he said was, 'I don't like it, but it's what I do to make a living. But I see you people around the area these days. What are you up to? Perhaps I could get involved?' We decided to try to help Michael to resolve his dilemmas, though it wasn't always clear who was helping whom. He introduced us into places in Notting Hill to which we'd previously had no access, and activists from the *ULR* Club went to stay with some of 'his' people, whom, we discovered, kept huge Alsatian dogs, although whether on duty as agents of protection or intimidation remained a mystery. It was through this work, and through the investigations by Club members such as Rachel Powell, that we first became aware of the role of the biggest rack-renting landlord of them all, Peter Rachman, who charged exorbitant rents for multi-occupation rooms with peeling walls, used an infrastructure of local black landlords and street thugs as intermediaries, and who in 1963 was to reappear in the background of the Christine Keeler/Mandy Rice-Davis/Profumo scandal.

This was a complex, volatile moment in the birth of new racial politics in Britain. Notting Hill was becoming one of the centres for shops, cafés, markets, music and drinking clubs catering mainly for a black clientele. Other urban areas in Britain developed similar locales at this time, such as Brixton in south London, Moss Side in Manchester, Toxteth in Liverpool, Handsworth in Birmingham, and St Paul's in Bristol – names which would come to be all too familiar to the news-reading English public during the black insurrections of 1980–1981. Notting Hill reconnected people to the Caribbean. It was also where an underground, diasporic cultural 'colony life' was beginning to flourish, around what Paul Gilroy was later to identify, in his powerful evocation of the moment, *There Ain't No Black in the Union Jack*, as a black expressive culture, especially among a younger generation. In the 1970s these locales were to become key sites for the consolidation of a popular anti-racist politics, not to say the seedbeds of a new black identity and of the multicultural city. Racial conflicts around clubs like The Mangrove in Notting Hill were the scene of major political confrontations between local blacks, white racists and the police.

This early contact with Notting Hill was significant for me and put me in touch with a wide variety of Caribbean migrants, signalling my first political lesson in black diasporic politics. Notting Hill in this period was a very different social and political milieu from that associated immediately after the war with the more respectable black residents, who were attempting to build a life for themselves and for their children, or black students, or indeed the West Indian writers around the BBC. This was another social layer altogether.

At the same time the transactions between blacks in Britain and the United States of Civil Rights and Black Power were close. Indeed a number of West Indians in Britain knew the US first-hand, and the West Indians in general acted as a bridgehead between black Britain and black America. West Indians were crucial, for example, in introducing Martin Luther King and Malcolm X to their British counterparts, and so too was Stokely Carmichael, although we shouldn't forget that he was Trinidadian by birth.

The fight for Civil Rights in the US, the Alabama bus boycott, voter registration in the South, school bussing, the birth of Black

Power, 'Black is Beautiful', and other manifestations of the struggle for African-Americans to secure a place in American life and history had an enormous impact on the development of black politics in Britain, and certainly transformed my life for ever. I spoke on a platform with Martin Luther King at a meeting organized by Canon Collins, the CND leader. After an early visit to London by Malcolm X there occurred the attempt to establish the first broad-based, black anti-racist organization in post-war Britain. And it was hearing Malcolm tell the story of his own conversion from street hustling to politics which inspired Michael De Freitas to rename himself Michael X, leading ultimately to the tragic events in Trinidad which culminated in Michael's execution for murder. Stokely Carmichael made a striking, memorable appearance at the *Dialectics of Liberation* conference much later, in the summer of 1967.

Notwithstanding the pace of decolonization in Africa, African politics didn't at this time possess me with the same intensity as the new race politics emerging from the US. Nor did it, really, until the politicized Africanization of the Caribbean during the Black Power years. Of course we were excited by the winning of independence by the African nations. The revival of older Pan-African traditions, particularly evident in the Independence of Ghana in 1957, was a moment of historic optimism. But we were only too aware of the extent of the problems unresolved across the continent, and unnerved by the resurgence of white ascendancy, both in apartheid South Africa and in the not-quite-apartheid Southern Rhodesia.

Through the later 1950s Kenya was certainly a burning issue. The extent to which Mau Mau were vilified, drawing from the entire lexicon of recidivist colonial stereotypes, was harsh to witness. Even Trevor Huddleston, a prominent, good-hearted figure active in the anti-colonial struggle, can be found in the press at this time condemning Mau Mau as barbaric. It's not that there was a silence, or lack of knowledge, about the systematic injustices inflicted by the British forces on the insurgents. One could read what was happening between the lines of the press reports, and there were campaigning Labour stalwarts who endeavoured to bring light to bear on the systematic mobilization of violence directed towards an entire population. Even Enoch Powell spoke out against the Hola killings, where the British military acted with a deliberate, orchestrated sadism. But the voices of the critics carried no public purchase. It was a powerful instance, within the context of British public opinion, of the workings of denial. It has taken four or five decades for the story of the mass imprisonment and torture of the Mau Mau fighters to emerge into the light of day in the metropole. It is only now that the extent and depth of the cover-up by the colonial and the metropolitan state is gradually being made known. Stacks and stacks of documents, many of them – we must assume – containing incriminating evidence, have disappeared in the bureaucratic *oubliette* of the state. Even so, thanks to the labours of intrepid researchers documents keep on resurfacing and the story is beginning, at last, to take shape.

We had to accommodate, simultaneously, the welcome we gave to colonial independence and our knowledge of the immediate travails which independence brought with it. In the Caribbean the fate of Cheddi Jagan pressed in close. The interconnections between decolonization and the emerging imperatives of neo-colonialism and of the murderous ethnic conflicts which broke out were deep and close. It soon became apparent that the anti-colonial struggle coexisted with the East-West polarization of the continuing Cold War, which was disastrously played out by proxy on the terrain of the new emerging nation states. Acts of military intervention threw into doubt the prospects for independence elsewhere. The Cold War necessarily supplied a new dimension to the politics of anti-colonialism which we had brought with us into the metropole. The flags were going down and the 'winds of change' had been announced. But the struggle was by no means over. As one new nation after another was engulfed by the overarching contest between two rival global systems and forced to move into line on one side or another, it became increasingly unclear when, how or indeed whether, the imperial afterlife would ever end. In 1957, the year of Ghana's independence, Richard Wright alighted upon the idea of what he called 'post-mortem terror'. This he defined as 'a state of mind of newly freed colonial peoples who feel that they will be resubjugated; that they are abandoned, that no new house of the heart is as yet made for them to enter'. This represents a brutal, but tragically judicious, insight.

These were all live matters for the London Left of my generation. We couldn't imagine our politics without these anti-colonial commitments, which animated our endless conversations about – less the fate of the world but, as we saw things, the fate of 'our' world, the world which we hoped to make ours. Night after night the discussions ran on. The full extent of the presence of the myriad of colonials in London, as the empire was coming to its end, hasn't yet been properly acknowledged.

From the vantage of today, for a different generation, our investments in *ULR* and then the founding of the *NLR* might seem parochial. But it didn't feel like that at the time. We laboured long and hard to seize the moment, as it were, and to recast the Left so that we weren't left behind by history. We endeavoured to keep our eyes on the prize.

This brings us to the *NLR* moment of 1960. *The New Reasoner* and the *ULR* represented the two political generations, although as I've already indicated political generations, as partly symbolic in formation, are never clearly demarcated and there were plenty of crossovers and hiatuses. The personnel attached to each of the two journals felt close to each other. After a while we started to have joint editorial board meetings and the connections became tighter. Pressing, though, was the financial issue. Both journals were struggling. It made sense to pool our resources. But there was more to it than that. Everyone was completely wiped out, exhausted. Since 1956 we'd all been on the run, with our everyday lives suspended. There's only so long one can continue like that. Edward and Dorothy Thompson had been working tirelessly, founding *The Reasoner* and then *The New Reasoner* and keeping each alive, agitating in the Yorkshire peace movement, and plenty more. I sometimes think of their house in Halifax. How they held everything together was a mystery.

The pressures mounted and we decided on the formal merger. We were then confronted by the question of who was going to be appointed editor. Edward declined, sure that his personal resources were depleted. Raphael's name was suggested, although I think that *The New Reasoner* cadres were certain that if this happened we'd be in serious financial difficulties! They weren't persuaded that he was the person who could ensure that copy was delivered on time. So they asked me and I stupidly said 'Yes'.

By then I knew the traditions of socialist politics in England. But I hadn't been *formed* in them, like Raymond Williams or Edward Thompson. I was a neophyte among them. Can anyone imagine what it must have been like being alongside these luminaries? Editorial boards were a nightmare for me. I'd indicate the possible contents of the next issue and then hold up my hands before the storm broke and the fathers spoke!

My salvation was the labour historian John Saville, who chaired the board. He protected me from the wrath that began to emanate from Halifax. The Thompsons, although they'd stepped back from the principal role, still had definite ideas about what they wanted *NLR* to be. Quite properly, they were sticklers for editorial procedures. They also nursed a deep suspicion of London and its ways: full of corruption and trendies. But John mediated as much as he could.

Edward was a powerful person, imaginative and romantic. He taught the Romantics and he was a romantic. He was a brilliant social historian. *The Making of the English Working Class* is a wonderful, wonderful book. It created a whole new intellectual field of work. I was proud to have read it in manuscript before it was published. Catherine and I used to go and visit Edward and Dorothy at their cottage in Wales. They were very kind to us, even though I found them a formidable couple.

But Edward also held a particular view of me which was not what I was. I can't pinpoint it exactly. He was committed to the cause of colonial liberation, but I didn't feel that he had a sense of what colonialism was and how it operated. He was very English in his imagination, in the fibre of his being. He didn't connect with my preoccupation about racial identity. Even while I was generously treated by them, I also felt misunderstood. Nor was I knowledgeable enough to get into scholarly debate with him about British history. Ours was always a tense relationship, in spite of our closeness, and it became more tense as time went on.

Later Thompson made it clear that he hated Cultural Studies. He couldn't see the point of *Policing the Crisis*, partly due to the analytical weight we gave to race. At the infamous History Workshop conference held at Ruskin College in Oxford in December 1979 he ripped us up and set out to destroy one of his greatest devotees, Richard Johnson. This was a savage, savage attack, and it represented a parting of the ways. We never really got it together again.

Raymond was different. He too was a wonderful thinker, with a huge range of things going on in his head. I still think his *The Country and the City* a magnificent book. The more excited Edward became the more animated he'd be, his hair getting increasingly wild, until he appeared to assume a prophetic figuration. The more excited Raymond became, the quieter he grew. He dropped into a sort of Welsh burr and you had to listen very carefully to hear what was being scrupulously formulated. Temperamentally they were opposites.

I found Raymond incredibly approachable and, because of his intellectual interests, much closer to my own formation than Edward ever had been.

They were my fathers. I was younger and more inexperienced than both of them, and hugely influenced by their ideas. It was a remarkable opportunity to have them as friends and mentors, although I never felt their equal.

I was editor of *NLR* for two years. The immediate issue which led to my resignation concerned the degree of editorial responsibility delegated to the New Left Clubs. This was a delicate, complex issue. It was all brought to a head at a meeting held at Wortley Hall in Leeds. When the divisions came out into the open I thought: 'You know what? This is not for me!' So I resigned.

This was followed by a rolling crisis, with various short-term, interim solutions to the question of who should be the editor. Gradually Perry Anderson emerged. Perry had arrived at Oxford just as the first generation of New Left figures was leaving. I think

I overlapped with him briefly, although I can't be sure. But he belonged to a new and distinct generation. He was obviously an incredibly intellectual, high-academic kind of man. He is the only person who still uses half a dozen words in his essays which I have never even seen before! If you have the kind of Eton education he did, you just know things that ordinary human beings don't know. He is very, very clever.

He was committed, though, to a very different conception of what *NLR* should become. The group he formed around the new editorship was not interested, practically, in British politics. His own commitments were to a highly theorized, scholarly, international manner of thought. One of the early intellectual salvos of the new *NLR* was its insistence that England had never undergone a proper bourgeois revolution. (Actually, my view is almost the opposite. I think it's the only real bourgeois revolution history has ever seen. Not like France; nor a textbook, Marxist bourgeois revolution. All over the place, undoubtedly, with the wrong actors in the wrong roles. But as I see it the only real thing.) Gradually the editorial board become restive with Perry's project, and the disaffection culminated when Edward wrote an inordinately long critique of the new tendency, which Perry refused to publish. As far as I know it still remains unpublished. At this point the original editors began to draw away.

But out of that came a high-powered journal which has lasted for many years, and also its publishing arm, New Left Books, which turned into Verso. In a serious initiative, *NLR* made available to an Anglophone readership the defining European traditions of Marxism. It was a great project. Not at all the aspiration of the previous New Left, but a great project nonetheless.

This closes a key, frenetic phase in my life. It gets us close to 1964, which kind of marks my destination for this volume. I stepped back from playing such an active role in politics. I was reconciled to making a life in England. Teaching, which I'd first imagined more than ten years earlier to be a possible vocation, became a reality. And Cultural Studies, and Birmingham, were just around the corner.

But also at this stage I'd met and married – or was about to marry – Catherine. This too forms part of the story of my moving out from my internal world of colonial subjugation. Catherine has kept on popping into these reminiscences, in part as the distinguished historian of the relations between colonial Jamaica and the metropole and, on occasion, as a participant in her own right. This occurred most memorably when she first travelled with me to Jamaica and encountered my mother.

She has also played a significant role in the making of this book as my initial, informal but constant interlocutor, allowing me to rehearse and refashion scores of the formulations which appear here. Even when we are not actually speaking, I am in perpetual conversation with her and have been for years. Much of Catherine is in this book.

My friend Mike Rustin had met Margaret – Catherine's older sister – at Oxford. Michael and Margaret have been together ever since and are our closest family friends. They introduced me to Catherine on the Aldermaston March in 1962. Afterwards we all went for a week's holiday in Wales. The following summer, In London, I met her again. And that was that.

I was black, significantly older and not in good emotional shape. The person with whom I had formed an attachment while teaching in Jamaica, and who was studying in Canada, had come to Oxford to stay with me. It was a disaster, for which I bear the blame. My mother had intervened from afar, telling her family in no uncertain terms how much she disapproved of the relationship. Her ghostly presence cast a dark shadow between us which we couldn't exorcize. When Catherine and I met it was after a series of unsatisfactory relationships and once again I was in any serious sense unattached. I was lonely, although politically very active, and still in the uncertain aftermath of my decision not to go home. I fell for Catherine at once, although she had only just finished A-Levels and was only seventeen. She was an enthusiastic member of Youth CND. But fourteen years younger than me, and just preparing to go to university.

However, it's not an exaggeration to say that among many other things – without I think quite knowing what she was doing – she rescued me, and saved my life. She must have understood something of me. Early in our courtship I kept her waiting for nearly two hours outside a West End cinema to see Antonioni's *L'Avventura* while I was at a CND committee meeting. When I finally arrived, she was still waiting.

When we started to date seriously the prospects must have looked to any concerned English family like a dicey proposition. However Catherine's parents, John and Gladys, treated me with great kindness and respect and – ultimately, after our marriage – with love and affection. They never once mentioned my colour, although it must have been in their minds. They never suggested that our racial difference, or the gap in our ages, or my lack of religious conviction might be a problem – which didn't mean that they never worried about these issues, for I am sure they did. One Sunday, when they had invited me to lunch and I had – rather unsatisfactorily for Gladys's tastes – washed up in too cavalier a fashion, John took me aside and asked whether, since I was seeing so much of Catherine and it seemed to be serious, perhaps I would tell him what my intentions were. When I did, he must have swallowed hard, but he raised no objections. He simply gave me a knowing, understanding and benevolent smile. Whatever their misgivings, they seemed prepared to entrust their younger daughter to this person who was so radically foreign to their own domestic, social, religious and professional lives. I recall Gladys seeing us off at Waterloo Station as we headed to Italy for our first summer holiday, together and unmarried. She issued no warnings or 'good advice', nor expressed any moral misgivings. Only a cheery wave and plenty of good wishes. Next stop: one room, a double bed and a collapsing wardrobe in the seedy Hotel Tre Re next to the Campo in Siena!

They were a good family. They'd lived for many years in Kettering and Leeds, and when I met Catherine they had only just retired to London. John, originally from a working-class background, was a person of great beneficence and gentleness, with a beatific smile. He was a Baptist minister on the liberal wing of the church and a revered figure of great distinction in the region he oversaw. Gladys came from a family of millers. She was a woman of formidable character, highly intelligent and knowledgeable about the world with strong, 'sensible', no-nonsense liberal opinions on things and an unbending moral backbone. She was quietly active throughout her adult life in good causes. In principle and practice, they were committed internationalists – although I believe that this was put to the test at the early appearance of a Trinidadian student as their older daughter's first boyfriend.

Gladys was the first person in her family to go to university. She and John first met in Oxford, where John was at theological college, and I'm sure at times she was disappointed that she had given up a promising career as a historian to be an active minister's wife and mother. They had three children and a long and rewarding marriage. In 1962 John was struck down by a severe stroke and was partially incapacitated. Gladys actively and selflessly looked after him for seventeen years and managed to construct a rich, sociable and varied life for them both. When John died she moved into her own flat in the house we bought together in Kilburn. Over time I became deeply attached to her. She was known in the family as

'G-Ma' and was a much-loved and forceful presence for us and for our children.

Notwithstanding my early and prolonged disenchantment with England, I actually met many kind and warm British people who showed no trace of racial prejudice and who were not only welcoming but generous to a fault. Many looked after me in the rough passages which accompanied my first years in England, as only families – even adopted ones – do. Among them I would number as special Paddy and Kay Whannel and their son Garry, with whom I spent countless weekends. When I finally moved to London I would spend Christmas with Graham and Mollie Martin and their family. Jock and Millie Haston I've mentioned earlier. When Catherine and I got married in 1964 – on 15 December, my mother's birthday! – on the eve of her transferring from Sussex to Birmingham University, and soon after I had gone to work with Richard Hoggart at the Birmingham Centre for Contemporary Cultural Studies, it was the Hastons who hosted our reception at their house. Graham and Paddy were Scots, and Mollie South African. Whether this made any difference I don't know. I was fortunate.

When Catherine and I first moved to Birmingham we were constantly anticipating the hostile reception we expected from people whose flats we were trying to rent. Men would shout abusive remarks in the street and on the buses, especially obscenities about mixed-race couples, whose polluting nature infuriated them. Passengers in railway compartments and on buses would voice openly racist things as if not noticing that I was present, although obviously intended for me to hear. I once had to endure a journey to London during which two white men complained about how the presence of 'the f***ing blackies' had driven down the value of their houses. I moved carriages. Catherine remembers the hostile looks and comments she received when, as a white mum, she took Becky, our mixed-race daughter, in the pram to the park; as did Becky, in her turn, twenty years later when she took her son, Noah, to the park.

Catherine and Becky and our son, Jess, open a new chapter in my life. Becky and Jess must look at the photos taken of me before they were born – or maybe even read these pages – and I'm sure can't help but wonder about the different world which made me what I am. As children do, inevitably, wonder about the unreachability of their parents' lives before their own existence.

I had to find a modus vivendi with the world I had entered and indeed with myself. Surprisingly, this turned out to be partly through politics. Establishing, as I had, a foothold in British radicalism and inhabiting a necessary distance from England and its values meant that I never came to be seduced by the old imperial metropole. It allowed me to maintain a space I felt I needed. I wanted to change British society, not adopt it. This commitment enabled me not to have to live my life as a disappointed suitor, or as a disgruntled stranger. I found an outlet for my energies, interests and commitments without giving my soul away. And I had found a new family.

Works Referenced in the Text

The titles referenced here include works directly referred to in the text; works which have been drawn on in particular sections; and a handful of others which are especially pertinent to various points in the narrative. The writings of Stuart Hall cited could have been multiplied many times over. Those included here serve only to help the reader follow up particular lines of argument which are aired in this book.

In most cases the dates given refer to first publication.

The most complete bibliography of Hall's writings, compiled by Nick Beech, will be published in a later collection of Hall's writings.

Works by Stuart Hall

'The New Conservatism and the Old', *Universities and Left Review* 1 (1957)

'A Sense of Classlessness', *Universities and Left Review* 5 (1958)

'The Habit of Violence', *Universities and Left Review* 5 (1958)

NATO and the Alliances. A CND London Regional Council Discussion Pamphlet (1960)

'Crossroads Nowhere', in Andrew Salkey (ed.), *West Indian Stories* (1960)

'End of the Grand Designs?', *War & Peace: The CND Quarterly* 1:2 (1963)

'The Social Eye of Picture Post', *Working Papers in Cultural Studies* 2 (1972)

'The Determination of News Photographs', *Working Papers in Cultural Studies* 3 (1972)

'Encoding and Decoding in the Media Discourse', *Centre for Contemporary Cultural Studies, Birmingham University: Stencilled Occasional Paper* 7 (1973)

'The "Structured Communication" of Events', in UNESCO, *Obstacles to Communication Symposium* (1973)

'Pluralism, Race and Class in Caribbean Society', in UNESCO, *Race and Class in Post-Colonial Society: A Study of Ethnic Group Relations in the English-speaking Caribbean, Bolivia, Chile and Mexico* (1977)

'Racism and Reaction', in Commission for Racial Equality, *Five Views of Multi-Racial Britain* (1978)

With Chas Critcher, Tony Jefferson, John Clarke and Brian Roberts, *Policing the Crisis: Mugging, the State, and Law and Order* (1978)

'Race, Articulation, and Societies Structured in Dominance', in UNESCO, *Sociological Theories: Race and Colonialism* (1980)

'The Williams Interviews', *Screen Education* 34 (1980)

'In Defence of Theory', in Raphael Samuel (ed.), *People's History and Socialist Theory* (1981)

'Reconstruction Work: Images of Post-War Black Settlement', *Ten.8* 16 (1984)

'The State in Question', in Stuart Hall, Gregor McLennan and David Held (eds), *The Idea of the Modern State* (1984)

'Migration from the English-Speaking Caribbean to the United Kingdom, 1950–1980', in Reginald T. Appleyard (ed.), *International Migration Today*, Vol. I, *Trends and Prospects* (1988)

'The "First" New Left: Life and Times', in Oxford University Socialist Discussion Group (ed.), *Out of Apathy. Voices of the New Left. Thirty Years On* (1989)

'Cultural Identity and Diaspora', in Jonathan Rutherford (ed.), *Identity* (1990)

'The DuBois Lectures', delivered at the Hutchins Center for African and African-American Research, Harvard University, 1994; forthcoming as Kobena Mercer (ed.), *The Fateful Triangle*, Harvard University Press, 2017.

'Obituary. Andrew Salkey', *Independent*, 16 May 1995

'Negotiating Caribbean Identities', *New Left Review* I.209 (1995)

'The Formation of a Diasporic Intellectual: An Interview with Stuart Hall by Kuan-Hsing Chen', in David Morley and Kuan-Hsing Chen (eds), *Stuart Hall: Critical Dialogues in Cultural Studies* (1996)

'New Ethnicities', in David Morley and Kuan-Hsing Chen (eds), *Stuart Hall: Critical Dialogues in Cultural Studies* (1996)

'Who Needs Identity?', in Stuart Hall and Paul du Gay (eds), *Questions of Cultural Identity* (1996)

'When Was the "Post-Colonial"? Thinking at the Limit', in Iain Chambers and Lidia Curti (eds), *The Post-Colonial Question: Common Skies, Divided Horizons* (1996)

'The *Windrush* Issue: Postscript', *Soundings* 10 (1998)

'Thinking the Diaspora: Home-Thoughts from Abroad', *Small Axe* 6 (1999)

'Conclusion: The Multicultural Question', in Barnor Hesse (ed.), *Un/Settled Multiculturalisms: Diasporas, Entanglements, Transruptions* (2000)

'Black Diaspora Artists in Britain: Three "Moments" in Post-War History', *History Workshop Journal* 61 (2006)

'Epilogue: Through The Prism of an Intellectual Life', in Brian Meeks (ed.) *Culture, Politics, Race and Diaspora: The Thought of Stuart Hall* (2007)

'The "West Indian" Front Room', in Michael McMillan (ed.), *The Front Room. Migrant Aesthetics in the Home* (2009)

'Introduction' to Dennis Morris, *Growing Up Black* (2012)

'Creolité and the Process of Creolization', in Encarnación Gutiérrez Rodríguez and Shirley Anne Tate (eds), *Creolizing Europe. Legacies and Transformations* (2015)

Other Writings Referenced

Mark Abrams and Richard Rose, with Rita Hinden, *Must Labour Lose?* (1960)

Chinua Achebe, *The Education of a British-Protected Child* (2009)

Louis Althusser, 'Ideology and Ideological State Apparatuses (Notes towards an Investigation)', in his *Lenin and Philosophy and Other Essays* (1970)

David M. Anderson, *Histories of the Hanged: Britain's Dirty War in Kenya at the End of Empire* (2005)

Anonymous, *The Seafarer* (date unknown)

Anonymous, *Sir Gawain and the Green Knight* (date unknown)

Anonymous, *The Wanderer* (date unknown)

Mordechai Arbell, *The Jewish Nation of the Caribbean: The Spanish-Portuguese Jewish Settlements in the Caribbean and the Guianas* (2002)

Aristotle, *Politics* (date unknown)

Matthew Arnold, *Culture and Anarchy* (1867–8)

Neal Ascherson, 'The Money's Still Out There', *London Review of Books*, 6 October 2011

Mikhail Bakhtin, *Rabelais and His World* (1965)

Mikhail Bakhtin, *The Dialogic Imagination* (1975)

James Baldwin, *Notes of a Native Son* (1955)

James Baldwin, *Nobody Knows My Name. More Notes of a Native Son* (1961)

James Baldwin, *Another Country* (1962)

Roland Barthes, 'Rhetoric of the Image', in his *Image Music Text* (1964)

F. W. Bateson, *Towards a Socialist Agriculture* (1946)

Harry Belafonte, *My Song: A Memoir of Arts, Race and Defiance* (2012)

Irwin M. Berg, 'The Jews of Jamaica – Then and Now', http://www.kulanu.org/jamaica/jews-of-jamaica.php (accessed 6 October 2015)

Homi Bhabha, *The Location of Culture* (1994)

Robin Blackburn, *The Overthrow of Colonial Slavery, 1776 to 1848* (1988)

Avtar Brah, *Cartographies of Diaspora: Contesting Identities* (1996)

Edward (Kamau) Brathwaite, *The Development of Creole Society in Jamaica, 1770–1920* (1971)

Edward (Kamau) Brathwaite, *The Arrivants* (1973)

Kamau (Edward) Brathwaite, *History of the Voice. The Development of Nation Language in Anglophone Caribbean Poetry* (1984)

Erna Brodber, *The Continent of Black Consciousness: On the History of the African Diaspora, from Slavery to the Present Day* (2003)

Judith Butler, *The Psychic Life of Power. Theories of Subjection* (1997)

Dipesh Chakrabarty, *Provincializing Europe. Postcolonial Thought and Historical Difference* (2000)

Aaron Cicourel, *Cognitive Sociology: Language and Meaning in Social Interaction* (1974)

T. J. Clark, *Farewell to an Idea. Episodes from the History of Modernism* (1999)

T. J. Clark, 'Grey Panic', *London Review of Books*, 17 November 2011

James Clifford, *Routes. Travel and Translation in the Late Twentieth Century* (1997)

Stan Cohen, *Folk Devils and Moral Panics. The Creation of the Mods and Rockers* (1972)

Michael Craton, *Testing the Chains: Resistance to Slavery in the West Indies* (1982)

Kimberlé Crenshaw, *On Intersectionality: Essential Writings of Kimberlé Crenshaw* (2012)

C. A. R. Crosland, *The Future of Socialism* (1959)

Stanley Crouch, *Considering Genius: Writings on Jazz* (2009)

Neville Dawes, *Fugue and Other Writings* (2012)

Jacques Derrida, *Writing and Difference* (1978)

Mary Douglas, *Purity and Danger. An Analysis of the Concepts of Pollution and Taboo* (1966)

Nicholas Draper, *The Price of Emancipation: Slave-Ownership, Compensation and British Society at the End of Slavery* (2013)

W. E. B. DuBois, *The Souls of Black Folk* (1903)

Brent Hayes Edwards, *The Practice of Diaspora: Literature, Translation, and the Rise of Black Internationalism* (2003)

T. S. Eliot, *The Waste Land* (1922)

T. S. Eliot, *Ash Wednesday* (1930)

T. S. Eliot, *Notes Towards the Definition of Culture* (1948)

Caroline Elkins, *Imperial Reckoning: The Untold Story of Britain's Gulag in Kenya* (2005)

Rotimi Fani-Kayode, 'Rage and Desire', *Ten.8* 28 (1988)

Frantz Fanon, *Black Skin, White Masks* (1952)

Frantz Fanon, *The Wretched of the Earth* (1961)

Moira Ferguson, *Subject to Others: British Women Writers and Colonial Slavery, 1670–1834* (1992)

Niall Ferguson, *Empire. How Britain Made the Modern World* (2011)

Michel Foucault, *Discipline and Punish. The Birth of the Prison* (1975)

Michel Foucault, *The History of Sexuality*, Vol. I, *The Will to Knowledge* (1976)

James Frazer, *The Golden Bough* (1890)

Sigmund Freud, *The Interpretation of Dreams* (1900)

Sigmund Freud, 'Family Romances', in *The Standard Edition of the Complete Psychological Works of Sigmund Freud*, Vol. IX (1909)

Sigmund Freud, *Civilization and Its Discontents* (1930)

Gilberto Freyre, *The Masters and the Slaves: A Study in the Development of Brazilian Civilization* (1933)

Peter Fryer, *Staying Power: The History of Black People in Britain* (1984)

Kevin Gaines, 'Exile and the Private Life: James Baldwin, George Lamming, and the First World Congress of Negro Writers and Artists', in Cora Kaplan and Bill Schwarz (eds), *James Baldwin: America and Beyond* (2011)

Works Referenced in the Text

J. K. Galbraith, *The Affluent Society* (1958)

Marcus Garvey, *The Marcus Garvey and Universal Negro Improvement Association Papers*, Vol. II, *August 1919–August 1920*, ed. Robert A. Hill (1983)

Marcus Garvey, *The Marcus Garvey and Universal Negro Improvement Association Papers*, Vol. III, *September 1920–August 1921*, ed. Robert A. Hill (1984)

Henry Louis Gates Jr, 'Editor's Introduction. "Race", Writing and the Difference it Makes', *Critical Inquiry* 12:1 (1985)

Henry Louis Gates Jr, *The Signifying Monkey: A Theory of Afro-American Literary Criticism* (1988)

Henry Louis Gates Jr, *Colored People: A Memoir* (1994)

Stuart Gilbert, *James Joyce's Ulysses. A Study* (1955)

Paul Gilroy, *There Ain't No Black in the Union Jack* (1987)

Paul Gilroy, *The Black Atlantic. Modernity and Double Consciousness* (1993)

Paul Gilroy, *Black Britain. A Photographic History* (2007)

Édouard Glissant, *Caribbean Discourse. Selected Essays* (1989)

Antonio Gramsci, *Selections from the Prison Notebooks* (1971)

Clement Greenberg, *Art and Culture* (1961)

Larry Grossberg, 'Does Cultural Studies Have a Future? Should It? (Or What's the Matter with New York?)', *Cultural Studies* 20:1 (2006)

Catherine Hall, *Civilising Subjects. Colony and Metropole in the English Imagination, 1830–1867* (2002)

Catherine Hall, *Macaulay and Son: Architects of Imperial Britain* (2013)

Catherine Hall, Nicholas Draper, Keith McClelland, Katie Donington and Rachel Lang, *Legacies of British Slave Ownership: Colonial Slavery and the Formation of Victorian Britain* (2014)

Alfred Harbage, *Shakespeare's Audience* (1941)

D. W. Harding, 'Regulated Hatred: An Aspect of the Work of Jane Austen', *Scrutiny* (March 1940)

Fernando Henriques, *Family and Colour in Jamaica* (1953)

Fernando Henriques, *Jamaica, Land of Wood and Water* (1964)

Philip Hensher, 'Why Paul Klee Was a Comic at Heart', *Guardian*, 5 October 2013

Melville Herskovits, *The Myth of the Negro Past* (1941)

Melville Herskovits and Frances Herskovits, *Trinidad Village* (1947)

Donald Hinds, *Journey to an Illusion. The West Indian in Britain* (1966)

E. J. Hobsbawm, *Primitive Rebels: Studies in Archaic Forms of Social Movement in the 19th and 20th Centuries* (1959)

E. J. Hobsbawm and Terence Ranger (eds), *The Invention of Tradition* (1983)

Richard Hoggart, *The Uses of Literacy. Aspects of Working-Class Life* (1957)

Christian Høgsbjerg, 'Remembering C. L. R. James, Forgetting C. L. R. James', *Historical Materialism* 17:3 (2009)

Christian Høgsbjerg, *C. L. R. James in Imperial Britain* (2014)

Thomas C. Holt, *The Problem of Race in the Twenty-First Century* (2002)

Homer, *The Odyssey* (date unknown)

Thomas Hughes, *Tom Brown's Schooldays* (1857)

C. L. R. James, *World Revolution, 1917–1936. The Rise and Fall of the Communist International* (1937)

C. L. R. James, *The Black Jacobins: Toussaint L'Ouverture and the San Domingo Revolution* (1938)

C. L. R. James, *Notes on Dialectics. Hegel, Marx and Lenin* (1948)

C. L. R. James, *Beyond a Boundary* (1963)

C. L. R. James, *American Civilisation* (1992)

C. L. R. James, Grace C. Lee [Grace Lee Boggs] and Pierre Chaulieu [Cornelius Castoriadis], *Facing Reality. The New Society: Where to Look for it and How to Bring it Closer* (1958)

Henry James, *The American* (1877)

Henry James, *Daisy Miller* (1878)

Henry James, *The Europeans* (1878)

Henry James, *Nathaniel Hawthorne* (1879)

Henry James, *The Portrait of a Lady* (1881)

Henry James, *The Wings of a Dove* (1902)

Henry James, *The Ambassadors* (1903)

Henry James, *The Golden Bowl* (1904)

Henry James, *The Ivory Tower* (1917)

Henry James, *The Sense of the Past* (1917)

Winton James, *Holding Aloft the Banner of Ethiopia: Caribbean Radicalism in Early Twentieth Century America* (1998)

Delia Jarrett-Macauley, *The Life of Una Marson. 1905–1965* (1998)

James Joyce, *A Portrait of the Artist as a Young Man* (1916)

James Joyce, *Ulysses* (1922)

James Joyce, *Finnegans Wake* (1939)

Isaac Julien, *Riot* (2013)

Victor Kiernan, *The Lords of Human Kind: European Attitudes to Other Cultures in the Imperial Age* (1968)

L. C. Knights, *Drama and Society in the Age of Jonson* (1937)

Jacques Lacan, *Feminine Sexuality. Jacques Lacan and the École Freudienne*, ed. Juliet Mitchell and Jaqueline Rose (1985)

Ernesto Laclau and Chantal Mouffe, *Hegemony and Socialist Strategy. Towards a Radical Democratic Politics* (1985)

R. D. Laing, *The Divided Self. An Existential Study in Sanity and Madness* (1960)

George Lamming, *In the Castle of My Skin* (1953)

George Lamming, *The Emigrants* (1954)

George Lamming, *The Pleasures of Exile* (1960)

William Langland, *Piers Plowman* (1370–90)

F. R. Leavis, *Education and the University. A Sketch for an 'English School'* (1943)

Q. D. Leavis, *Fiction and the Reading Public* (1932)

Legacies of British Slave-ownership (Catherine Hall, Nicholas Draper, Keith McClelland et al): www.ucl.ac.uk/lbs/

Claude Lévi-Strauss, 'The Structural Study of Myth', *Journal of American Folklore* 68:270 (1955)

Claude Lévi-Strauss, *The Scope of Anthropology* (1967)

Andrea Levy, *Small Island* (2004)

Gail Lewis, 'Birthing Social Difference', *Studies in the Maternal* 1:1 (2009)

John Locke, *Two Treatises of Government* (1689)

David Macey, 'Fanon, Phenomenology, Race', in Peter Osborne and Stella Sandford (eds), *Philosophies of Race and Ethnicity* (2003)

Sir William Macpherson, *The Stephen Lawrence Inquiry* (1999)

Karl Marx, *Economic and Philosophic Manuscripts* (1844)

Karl Marx, *Grundrisse* (1858)

Karl Marx and Friedrich Engels, *The Communist Manifesto* (1848)

Brian Meeks, *Narratives of Resistance: Jamaica, Trinidad, the Caribbean* (2000)

Brian Meeks, *Caribbean Revolutions and Revolutionary Theory: An Assessment of Cuba, Nicaragua and Grenada* (2002)

Kobena Mercer, 'Diasporic Culture and the Dialogical Imagination: The Aesthetics of Black Independent Film in Britain', in Mbye B. Cham and Claire Andrade-Watkins (eds), *Black Frames: Critical Perspectives on Independent Black Cinema* (1988)

C. Wright Mills, *White Collar* (1951)

C. Wright Mills, *The Power Elite* (1956)

Pankaj Mishra, 'Watch This Man. Niall Ferguson's Burden', *London Review of Books*, 3 November 2011

Pankaj Mishra, *From the Ruins of Empire. The Intellectuals Who Remade Asia* (2012)

V. S. Naipaul, *The Mystic Masseur* (1957)

V. S. Naipaul, *The Suffrage of Elvira* (1958)

V. S. Naipaul, *Miguel Street* (1959)

V. S. Naipaul, *A House for Mr Biswas* (1961)

V. S. Naipaul, *The Middle Passage* (1962)

V. S. Naipaul, *A Bend in The River* (1979)

V. S. Naipaul, *The Enigma of Arrival* (1987)

Ashis Nandy, *The Intimate Enemy: Loss and Recovery of Self under Colonialism* (1983)

Rex Nettleford, *Mirror, Mirror: Identity, Race and Protest in Jamaica* (1970)

Friedrich Nietzsche, *The Will to Power* (1910)

Mark Olden, *Murder in Notting Hill* (2011)

Fernando Ortiz, *Cuban Counterpoint: Tobacco and Sugar* (1940)

Diana Paton, *No Bond But the Law: Punishment, Race and Gender in Jamaican State Formation, 1780–1870* (2004)

Orlando Patterson, *Slavery and Social Death: A Comparative Study* (1982)

Orlando Patterson, 'The Paradox of Freedom. An Interview with David Scott', *Small Axe* 40 (2013)

Sheila Patterson, *Dark Strangers* (1963)

Michel Pêcheux, 'Ideology: Fortress or Paradoxical Space?', in Sakari Hanninen and Leena Paldan, *Rethinking Ideology: A Marxist Debate* (1983)

Mike Phillips and Trevor Phillips, *Windrush. The Irresistible Rise of Multicultural Britain* (1999)

Ken Post, *Arise Ye Starvelings: The Jamaican Labour Rebellion of 1938 and its Aftermath* (1978)

Ken Post, *Strike the Iron: A Colony at War, Jamaica, 1939–1945*, Vols I & II (1981)

Mary Louise Pratt, *Imperial Eyes. Travel Writing and Transculturation* (1992)

Herbert Read, *A Concise History of Modern Painting* (1959)

David Riesman, *The Lonely Crowd* (1950)

Jacqueline Rose, *Sexuality in the Field of Vision* (2005)

Sonya Rose, *Which People's War? National Identity and Citizenship in Britain, 1939–1945* (2003)

Runnymede Trust, *The Future of Multi-Ethnic Britain* (2000)

Salman Rushdie, *Imaginary Homelands: Essays and Criticism* (1991)

Edward Said, *Orientalism* (1978)

Edward Said, *Culture and Imperialism* (1993)

Edward Said, *Out of Place. A Memoir* (1999)

Andrew Salkey (ed.), *West Indian Stories* (1960)

Raphael Samuel, 'Class and Classlessness', *Universities and Left Review* 6 (1959)

Raphael Samuel, *The Lost World of British Communism* (2006)

Ferdinand de Saussure, *Course in General Linguistics* (1906/1911)

Bill Schwarz (ed.), *West Indian Intellectuals in Britain* (2004)

David Scott, 'Colonial Governmentality', *Social Text* 43 (1995)

David Scott, *Conscripts of Modernity: The Tragedy of Colonial Enlightenment* (2004)

George Scott, *Time and Place* (1956)

John Seeley, *The Expansion of England* (1883)

Sam Selvon, *The Lonely Londoners* (1956)

William Shakespeare, *Hamlet* (1603)

Georg Simmel, 'The Stranger', in *The Sociology of George Simmel* (1950)

Mrinalini Sinha, *Colonial Masculinity: The 'Manly Englishman' and the 'Effeminate Bengali' in the Late Nineteenth Century* (1995)

M. G. Smith, *The Plural Society in the British West Indies* (1965)

John Speirs, *Chaucer the Maker* (1951)

Michelle Stephens, 'Disarticulating Black Internationalisms: West Indian Radicals and *The Practice of Diaspora*', *Small Axe* 17 (2005)

John Strachey, *The End of Empire* (1959)

Paul Sweezy, *The Theory of Capitalist Development* (1946)

Charles Taylor, *Sources of the Self: The Making of Modern Identity* (1992)

Deborah A. Thomas, *Exceptional Violence. Embodied Citizenship in Transnational Jamaica* (2011)

J. J. Thomas, *The Theory and Practice of Creole Grammar* (1869)

Denys Thompson, *Voice of Civilisation: An Enquiry into Advertising* (1947)

E. P. Thompson, 'Commitment in Politics', *Universities and Left Review* 6 (1959)

E. P. Thompson, *The Making of the English Working Class* (1963)

E. P. Thompson, *The Poverty of Theory and Other Essays* (1978)

E. P. Thompson, *Customs in Common* (1993)

Colm Tóibín, 'Baldwin and "the American Confusion"', in Cora Kaplan and Bill Schwarz (eds), *James Baldwin: America and Beyond* (2011)

Universities and Left Review (1957–9): http://www.amielandmelburn.org.uk/collections/ulr/index_frame.htm

Françoise Vergès, *Monsters and Revolutionaries. Colonial Family Romance and Métissage* (1999)

Derek Walcott, *Omeros* (1990)

Derek Walcott, *What the Twilight Says. Essays* (1998)

Anne Walmsley, *The Caribbean Artists' Movement. A Literary and Cultural History* (1992)

Evelyn Waugh, *Brideshead Revisited* (1945)

William H. Whyte, *The Organization Man* (1956)

Eric Williams, *Capitalism and Slavery* (1944)

Raymond Williams, *Culture and Society* (1958)

Raymond Williams, *The Long Revolution* (1961)

Raymond Williams, *The Country and the City* (1975)

Colin Wilson, *The Outsider* (1956)

Patrick Wright, *Living in an Old Country. The National Past in Contemporary Britain* (1985)

Richard Wright, *White Man, Listen!* (1957)

Films

John Akomfrah, *The Unfinished Conversation* (2012)

John Akomfrah, *The Stuart Hall Project* (2013)

Mike Dibb, *Personally Speaking* (2009)

Isaac Julien, *Frantz Fanon. Black Skin, White Mask* (1996)

Horace Ové, *Baldwin's Nigger* (1969)

In 1991 BBC Television broadcast a seven-part history of the Caribbean, *Redemption Song*, scripted and presented by Stuart Hall.

Index

Index